United Keetoowah Band
Education Program

United Keetoowah Band
Education Program

THE COVERT WAR
AGAINST ROCK

THE COVERT WAR AGAINST ROCK

WHAT YOU DON'T KNOW ABOUT THE DEATHS OF
JIM MORRISON
TUPAC SHAKUR
MICHAEL HUTCHENCE
BRIAN JONES
JIMI HENDRIX
PHIL OCHS
BOB MARLEY
PETER TOSH
JOHN LENNON
THE NOTORIOUS B.I.G.

ALEX CONSTANTINE

FERAL HOUSE

The Covert War Against Rock © 2000 by Alex Constantine

ISBN 0-922915-61-X

Feral House
2554 Lincoln Blvd. #1059
Venice, California 90291

Design by Linda Hayashi

10 9 8 7 6 5 4 3 2 1

For the victims of
Operation CHAOS and COINTELPRO

COVERT

xi Acknowledgements

xii Foreword

1 — Prelude
**ASSASSINATION POLITICS OF THE VIETNAM WAR
PERIOD: FASCISM, AMERICAN-STYLE
AND THE RISE OF RICHARD NIXON**

9 — Chapter One
A [KILLING] FIELD DAY FOR THE HEAT

19 — Chapter Two
**TIME MACHINE: THE BIRTH OF TOP 40 RADIO
AND ALAN FREED'S NEAR-DEATH EXPERIENCE
(EARLY CIA AND MOB INFLUENCES ON THE
ROCK MUSIC INDUSTRY)**

24 — Chapter Three
PARAPOLITICAL STARS IN THE DOPE SHOW

35 — Chapter Four
**THE DEATH OF CASS ELLIOT AND
OTHER "RESTLESS YOUTH"**

42 — Chapter Five
**A MURDER IN THE HOUSE OF POOH:
BRIAN JONES**

53 — Chapter Six
**PORTRAITS IN CARNAGE:
THE END OF THE ROCK FESTIVALS**

CONTENTS

60 — Chapter Seven

**I Don't Live Today:
The Jimi Hendrix Political Harassment,
Kidnap and Murder Experience**

76 — Chapter Eight

**When You're a Stranger:
Fragrance dé CHAOS — Investigative
Findings on the Death of Jim Morrison**

87 — Chapter Nine

**Like Coffins in a Cage: The Baez Contras
and the Death of Phil Ochs**

100 — Chapter Ten

Who Killed the Kennedys? (and Sal Mineo?)

117 — Chapter Eleven

**"Project Walrus" and
Holden Caulfield's Warm Gun**

131 — Chapter Twelve

**What'cha Gonna Do? . . .
The Deaths of Bob Marley and Peter Tosh**

149 — Chapter Thirteen

**Gang War: Sons of CHAOS vs. Thugs
A Tupac Shakur and Notorious B.I.G.
Assassination Digest**

165 — Chapter Fourteen

**Dancing on the Jetty:
The Death of Michael Hutchence, et al**

THE COVERT WAR AGAINST ROCK

Acknowledgements

Operation CHAOS, a draft outline found among the papers of late political researcher Mae Brussell, provided the framework and inspiration for this study. The decision to write it was made ten years ago, and since that time the author has gathered pertinent material toward this end, often at the suggestion of friends who had a piece of the puzzle to contribute, including Will Robinson, Marilyn Colman and the Brussell Sprouts, David X, Patrick Fourmy, publisher of *Prevailing Winds*, Al Marcelliene, John Judge, Lee Lew-Lee, Cynthia Ford, Lynn Moss-Sharman, Adam Parfrey, Bennett Theissen, Matty, DasGoat, Virginia McCullough, Dick Farley, "Cynthia Richards," the late Sharon White, Andrew and David, MIHRA, Linda Minor and CTRL's researchers, Vicky Flores-Guerra, Michael Putini, S.M., Melissa Darpino and the patient librarians at UCLA's Research Library and Los Angeles municipal library system. The author also wishes to thank Elliot Mintz, spokesman for Bob Dylan and Yoko Ono, reggae archivist Roger Steffans and *Realist* editor Paul Krassner for the admirable roles they have played in opposing some of the ignoble acts described in this volume.

FOREWORD

The corporate media harbors hundreds of CIA propagandists and fawning loyalists who find revelations concerning domestic political assassinations inconvenient and stroll by with little comment. The central revelation of this volume is the fact that the Agency and Organized Crime have, for over over thirty years, engaged in a program to silence popular musicians whose influence subverts the cynical thought control tactics of American government and media. There exists within both worlds a rigidly "conservative" infrastructure that has little regard for human rights. This infrastructure has contributed to the rise of every fascist regime in the Third World. It has overthrown many a democratically-elected leader and favors death squad rule. It thrives on war, propaganda and social control. It takes a dim view of critics in the music industry, particularly young "communards" who advocate demilitarization, dread-locked musicians standing up for their rights, or street Thugs who condemn police violence and suggest shooting back.

The untimely deaths of John Lennon, Bob Marley, Tupac Shakur, and other rock musicians who lashed out at the established order were followed by widespread suspicion of foul play. The murder of Lennon led Fenton Bressler, an English barrister, to descend reluctantly into the hidden labyrinth of CIA mind control operations, and the result of his investigation, *Who Killed John Lennon?* (1989), raised provocative questions regarding the deep history of Mark David Chapman. But Bressler was an exception. Hard questions concerning the deaths of most musicians in this book have never been asked. On the contrary, many reporters and biographers are inclined to dismiss, with varying degrees of condescension, evidence of murder as grist for exotic conspiracy theories (though these, of course, do tend to run rampant when fascism, which is inherently conspiratorial, dominates the intelligence community). This unwillingness to dissect covert operations renders reporters with integrity incapable of evaluating the evidence and arriving at an objective judgment. An attempt is made here to correct this imbalance, to treat the evidence with the seriousness it deserves.

A sobering example: ten years ago, the statement that Brian Jones, founding member of the Rolling Stones, was murdered would have been met with ridicule. Everyone *knew* that Jones died in 1969 by accidental drowning. The "rational" view held that Jones was a fiercely talented but precocious, drug-crazed rogue with an irrepressible death wish. But the subsequent confession of his killer, and the testimony of several witnesses intimidated into silence, has since dispelled the status quo belief (though the press remains largely indifferent). Brian Jones was murdered. Journalists should take care not to let it happen again, but this is not a profession that readily learns from its mistakes. Reporters will transcribe the official verdict on the next "accidental drowning," pride themselves on their "objectivity" for refusing to be lured by bothersome details into contradicting the official record. A politically indifferent public will accept all this and the hypocritical distortions of the propagandists.

Anyone with a penchant to research the subject is advised that there are patterns to look for to distinguish a political hit from the apolitical variety and accidental or natural causes. Nearly all celebrity subjects of this volume knew extreme "paranoia" before their deaths. John Lennon and Jim Morrison were both driven to desperation by constant FBI harassment. Jones was made a nervous wreck by police raids and the intimidations of a circle of killers who infiltrated his household. Jimi Hendrix feared Michael Jeffrey, his manager, a self-avowed intelligence agent with Mafia ties, who stole from him, then arranged for his kidnapping and probable murder. Bob Marley received a death threat from the CIA, and sang about his "War" with the Agency. Tupac Shakur lived in defiance of a COINTELPRO-type operation waged, he realized, to destroy his career and silence him.

Another recurring theme is the posthumous publication of books libelling the deceased and misleading the reader on the circumstances of death. Bob Woodward, Danny Sugarman and the late Albert Goldman worked this genre and profited handsomely from it. In the "mainstream" media, discrediting tactics are also common, and the death is almost always blamed on the victim. Cass Elliott, according to one fraudulent medical expert and a flurry of erroneous press reports, was claimed by "gluttony." Jones was a victim of vague "misadventure," and drugs were said to have contributed—despite the fact that he had been off them for a month before he died. It was widely reported falsely that Jimi Hendrix overdosed on heroin, and it is universally held that he "choked on his own vomit," though the true circumstances are complex and have driven many of his friends to demand an investigation. Michael Hutchence was supposedly done in by auto-erotic sex, but a broken hand, split lip and contusions on his body have not been explained. In each case, cruel exaggeration and blatant falsehood parade as fact.

The victim often leaves behind witnesses whose testimony is wildly at variance. Sometimes they even contradict themselves on the essential facts. It's tempting to walk away from a case like this in a fit of frustration—until considering the chill that death threats put on eyewitness testimony. A coerced witness makes false statements to police and the press. Three or four witnesses, knowing that the killers mean business, will fabricate details to fill in the gaps of information they are forced to withhold under threat of retaliation. When seen in this light, blaring contradictions in a murder case should be interpreted as possible duress.

And this brings us to another recurring theme: the cover-up proves the crime. And in each case examined, the perpetrators and their accomplices have altered history by concealing crucial evidence. This book is an attempt to return that evidence to the historical record.

Alex Constantine

PRELUDE
Assassination Politics of the Vietnam War Period: Fascism, American-Style and the Rise of Richard Nixon

I'M NOT SCREAMING, I'M NOT SCREAMING, TELL ME I'M NOT SCREAMING. **PHIL OCHS**

In 1980 Danish journalist Henrik Krüger collected scraps of suppressed information on the Nixon wing of Republican politics, then observed in *The Great Heroin Coup*: "Assassination became a modus operandi under Richard Nixon."[1] Political murder, an unplumbed scandal in the bulging file of criminal acts collectively known as Watergate, went unexplored while investigative committees and reporters taking dictation concentrated on milk funds, Nixon's possible knowledge of a routine bugging and the cover-up.

As a result, the dankest political horrors—including the assassination of celebrities on the left and Nixon's rivals for the White House—have never been ventilated by the corporate media. Beneath the surface of Watergate ran a spring of excesses far more scandalous than any exposed by the *Washington Post*, and these never did see the light of day—for the simple reason that everything known about the Nixon administration was planted in the *Post* by ranking intelligence officers.[2] The leading candidates for the identity of "Deep Throat," the professed source of Woodward and Bernstein's most significant Watergate leads:

+ Washington attorney Robert Bennett, then director of Mullen and Associates, the firm that founded the Free Cuba Committee, a front that once claimed Lee Harvey Oswald as a member, employer of White House Plumber E. Howard Hunt in his glory days.
+ Former CIA official Richard Ober, director of Operation CHAOS, the most expansive domestic surveillance and covert operations network in American history, the intelligence sector's response to the anti-war and civil rights movements. (Bennett and Ober both ran covert assassination programs, as will be seen.)
+ General Alex Haig, who gave up the Pentagon but "not to shuffle papers." Formerly a staffer under General Douglas MacArthur in Korea and scion of the National Security Council, he was chief of staff at the White House under Nixon, nosing out some 245 generals for the appointment.

Whoever the skulking insider may have been, "Deep Throat" proved to be a shallow well of revelations after all. The depths of CIA corruption under Nixon, particularly political murder, went unreported by the celebrated authors of the *Post*'s Watergate coverage because one of them, Bob Woodward, was himself a cut-out for distant "conservative" forces in the intelligence and military establishment.[3] This was a "journalist" who could be counted on to contain the Watergate story, steer it away from the most serious acts of corruption.

Bob Woodward has taken a walk around the block repeatedly when asked about his military intelligence bona fidés: On June 13, 1965, three days after his graduation from Yale, young Woodward was declared a Navy ensign in a 20-minute ceremony conducted by Senator George Smathers in a school auditorium. (As it happens, the Democratic senator from Florida was a partner in the real estate holdings of the Lansky Family,[4] a branch of the Mafia closely aligned with the CIA.) One Naval intelligence officer on the USS Wright recalls that Woodward held "top secret 'crypto' clearance, which allowed him access to nearly any declassified [government] document." Reporter Adrian Havill notes that, at the hub of the nation's defense networks, Woodward "had plenty of time to ingratiate himself with the nation's military leadership inside the Pentagon, across the Potomac River from the nation's capital."[5]

The Nixon administration rose on a foundation of political murder, a fact obscured by Woodward and the *Post*, and it continued to be a useful policy in the Watergate period, according to Edward Jay Epstein in *Agency of Fear* (1990): "E. Howard Hunt, after forging a State Department telegram implicating President Kennedy in the murder of Diem, showed the forged document to [Lucien] Conein, who then appeared on an NBC documentary and divulged its contents. (Hunt also briefed the producer of the program, Fred Freed, on the 'secret telegram,' which shaped the program in such a way as to imply Kennedy's complicity in the murder.) However, in an interview with the *Washington Post* on June 13, 1976, Conein acknowledged that he had been brought to the Bureau of Narcotics and Dangerous Drugs to superintend a special unit which would have the capacity to assassinate selected targets in the narcotics business."[6]

Assassination was all the rage among Nixon's inner-circle. One of them, "Eduardo" Hunt, mustered a pair of professional hit-men to kill syndicated columnist Jack Anderson—G. Gordon Liddy, subsequently of Watergate and talk radio fame, and Dr. Edward Gunn, a toxin specialist and director of the CIA's Medical Services Division. Liddy's deposition concerning his recruitment to the murder plot was submitted to the court in a 1980 suit filed by Hunt against reporter

A.J. Weberman:

Q: Did Hunt ever discuss any assassination plots?

Liddy: Well, there came a time in 1972, I think it was around February, when Mr. Hunt came to me concerning the journalist Jack Anderson. . . . Mr. Hunt came to me, and he said, "Anderson has now gone too far. He has just identified and caused the death or imminent death under torture of one of our human assets abroad." And he, Hunt, had been charged by his principals, meaning his superiors at the White House, with conferring with me and someone from the CIA who was represented as retired, namely Dr. Gunn, as to how best to prevent Mr. Anderson from repeating his behavior.

This meeting was held in the then existing downstairs luncheon room of the Hay Adams Hotel, now no longer in existence. And Mr. Hunt brought up that LSD business again. Dr. Gunn rejected it on technical grounds. I suggested that the only way to effectively stop Mr. Anderson, was to kill him. Mr. Hunt and Dr. Gunn agreed. The remainder of the conversation consisted of how we ought to do it best. The conclusion was that the Cuban assets were to stage a mugging in Washington which would be fatal to Anderson.

Q: All right. Now if Mr. Hunt had said he had merely discussed with you and Dr. Gunn nothing more than a discreditation of Mr. Anderson, would that be correct or incorrect?

Liddy : That would be absolutely incorrect.

Q: The story reflecting this situation occurred in The *Washington Post* under an article by Woodward and Bernstein. Are you aware of that article, and were you surprised to see that that had come to light?

Liddy : I was in prison at the time. The article was made available to me. I read it at the time. And I was surprised to see that it was incorrect in that it did not narrate the incident as I have just narrated it to you, which is what actually happened.[7]

In July, 1984, Liddy testified in another lawsuit, this one filed by E. Howard Hunt against the ultra-conservative *Spotlight* press, an arm of the Liberty Lobby, proclaiming that several approaches to disposing of the columnist were considered—killing methods with the stamp of the CIA. The Agency assigned Hunt the task of killing Anderson, employing methods found routinely in foreign political plots: "We discussed with Mr. Gunn aspirin roulette in which one takes a single tablet of deadly poison, packs it in a Bayer aspirin jar, we place it in the man's medicine chest, and one day he gets the tablet and that's that. Hunt referred to aspirin roulette . . . " Hunt at this time was employed by the aforementioned CIA front, Mullen and Associates, then run by Washington attorney Robert Bennett. "We discussed Dr. Gunn's suggestion of the use of an automobile to hit Mr. Anderson's automobile when it was in a turn in the circle, up near Chevy Chase. There is a way . . . known by the CIA that if you hit a car at just the right speed and angle, it will . . . burn and kill the occupant. . . . But what I suggested is we just kill him. And they both agreed that would be the way to go about it, and the task would be assigned to Cuban assets."[8]

Hunt's employer, the Mullen agency, had a long history of participation in political killings. *Rolling Stone* reported on May 20, 1976: "The Bay of Pigs and the Kennedy assassination are motifs that run through the Watergate affair. Howard Hunt, the chief Watergate burglar, helped establish a CIA front group for the Bay of Pigs, and Robert Bennett, as head of the Mullen Agency, played a decisive role in the undoing of Richard Nixon."[9]

Liddy's deposition in the Hunt suit exposed a death squad in the executive branch: "We had perhaps a dozen men who were willing to come on board in this connection. And Mr. Hunt, to impress upon me the high caliber of these individuals, stated that they had accounted among them for a substantial number of deaths [22], including two who had hanged someone from a beam in a garage."[10]

Were these the same "high caliber individuals" who killed gossip columnist Dorothy Kilgallen, the only reporter to interview Jack Ruby and the author of an open letter to Lyndon Johnson that appeared in her syndicated column on December 21, 1964: "MEM-ORANDUM TO PRESIDENT JOHNSON; Please check with the State Department . . . the leaders of our Armed Forces or our chief scientists, to discover what, if anything, we are doing to explore the ramifications of [electromagnetic] thought control . . . could change the history of the world."

Kilgallen, one of the very few reporters in the country to question the Warren Commission's findings, told friends in the entertainment industry that she was going to "bust the Kennedy assassination wide open." But she never had the opportunity. She abruptly died of acute barbiturate and alcohol poisoning—the New York medical examiner could not say whether Kilgallen died accidentally or was murdered—on November 8, 1965. Mary Branum, one of Kilgallen's editors, received a telephone call several hours prior to the discovery of the body. The anonymous caller informed Branum that the columnist had been "murdered."[11]

Indisputably, she had. This was the conclusion of a forensic chemist who reported to Dr. Charles Umberger at the New York City Medical Examiner's office—and was told to keep the chemical analysis under wraps—in 1978. The chemist ran an analysis of the glass Kilgallen had been drinking from when she died, using forensic techniques that did not exist in 1965. The tests turned up traces of Nembutol on the glass . . . but Nembutol was not found in her blood. The blood analysis revealed a lethal cocktail of drugs, three from the fastest-acting groups of barbiturates: secobarbitol, amobarbital and phentobarbital.[12] None of these drugs were detected on the glass.

The CIA had assembled a thick concordia of lethal methods. On April 2, 1979, the *Washington Post* reported that the Agency had experimented with exotic poisons that left the subject in a condition that would indicate natural causes to an unsuspecting coroner. The project began with an anonymous, undated memo on assassination by "natural causes." "Knock off key people," the heavily censored document specified, "how [to] knock off key guys . . . natural causes . . ."

And then there's a declassified memo from a CIA consultant to an official of the agency discussing clandestine methods for killing us softly:

1. bodies left with no hope if the cause of death being determined by the most complete autopsy and chemical examinations.
2. bodies left in such circumstances as to simulate accidental death.
3. bodies left in such circumstances as to simulate suicidal death.
4. bodies left with residue that simulate those caused by natural diseases.[13]

Kilgallen was not the only whistle-blower dispatched in the aftermath of the Kennedy assassination. In January, 1968, *Ramparts* magazine reported on the death of Gerrett Underhill, a staffer at the Army's Military Intelligence Service and advisor to the Agency: "Immediately after the [John Kennedy] assassination, a distraught Underhill told friends that a semi-autonomous CIA clique which had been profiting in narcotics and gun-running was implicated." A few months later, "Underhill was found dead of a bullet wound in the head."

Some of the same "high-caliber individuals" behind the murders of Kilgallen and Underhill may have turned up yet again in the shooting of George Wallace, the fiercely segregationist Democratic governor of Alabama who vied with Richard Nixon for the presidency in 1972.

Wallace was campaigning at a shopping center in Laurel, Maryland, an appearance that drew a crowd of some 2,000 supporters. Two critical primaries were a couple of days off and the polls predicted that Wallace would take Michigan and Maryland by a landslide. If he survived the primaries, there was every chance that he could walk away with a sizable share of conservative votes that otherwise would have gone to Nixon. Wallace was therefore perceived as a threat. "Remember one thing," Wallace exhorted all in his last campaign speech, "there's not a dime's difference between Nixon and McGovern, or Nixon and Humphrey. It's up to you to send them a message in Washington, a message they won't forget!"

But it was Wallace who received the message when, after stepping down from the podium, a short, plump, smiling 21-year old man in sunglasses pushed through the crowd. "Hey, George. Over here!" Governor Wallace turned toward the voice of a grinning Arthur Bremer, an unemployed busboy from Milwaukee, who produced a snub-nosed .38 caliber revolver and fired four rounds into the candidate from Alabama. Three of the governor's entourage were also wounded before the gun was pried from Bremer's hand.

Wallace survived but spent the remainder of his life in a wheelchair, his legs paralyzed. He took potent anti-depressants for years after the shooting. Bremer was summarily convicted on four counts of assault with intent to kill and was led away to serve a 53-year prison sentence. It was quickly determined that he had acted alone. Subsequent events suggest otherwise:

A few minutes after the shots were fired, Nixon aide Charles Colson directed E. Howard Hunt to fly to Milwaukee, break into Bremer's apartment and recover all "embarrassing evidence," according to Woodward and Bernstein in *All the President's Men*. Gore Vidal, novelist and literary critic, opined that Hunt actually penned Bremer's diaries. Wallace himself stated openly, "my attempted assassination was part of a conspiracy."

All told, the four victims suffered 18 bullet wounds—but Bremer's gun was a five-shooter. Arthur told his brother that he had accomplices who had paid him handsomely to shoot George Wallace. Bremer was out of work, so who picked up the tab for his repeated stays at the opulent Waldorf-Astoria in New York?

Milwaukee police files on Bremer portrayed him as a "subversive" with ties to Students for a Democratic Society (SDS). These were seized after the shooting and classified secret by the ATF acting "under the highest authority."

Tim Heinan, a Marquette University student who moonlighted as an undercover agent for the Milwaukee Police Department's Special Assignment Squad, learned that Arthur Bremer had ties to a CIA operative named Dennis Salvatore Cossini, a federal "counter-terrorist" who specialized in the infiltration and control of radical organizations including the local SDS chapter the gunman had joined. The agent was fired after Heinan confessed his links to Bremer. Cossini headed for Toronto and was next seen dead, slouching in a parked car with an overdose of heroin in his veins. One of the police investigating the death mused: "Somebody gave him a hot shot."[14]

Heroin "overdoses" would recur in the coming hit parade, and the Nixonites would dance on the graves of the casualties in a covert war that ultimately altered the political course of the country.

NOTES

1. Heinrik Krüger, *The Great Heroin Coup: Drugs, Intelligence & International Fascism*, Boston: South End Press, 1980, p. 164. Krüger and others have documented assassination and extermination campaigns in Vietnam, Guatemala, Argentina and Brazil—represented in Latin America by local death squads. "The White House appears to have sponsored a secret assassination program under cover of drug enforcement. It was continued by the DEA, which seemingly overlapped with the CIA in political rather than drug enforcement. Until 1974 the training of torturers [and] Latin American death squads came under the auspices of the CIA and USAID's Office of Public Safety."

2. Henry Kissinger, an old CIA hand, was untouched by the scandal. He lied repeatedly to Congress concerning illicit wiretaps placed by his office on the telephones of newspaper reporters and National Security Council staff, yet gracefully escaped leaving the administration in disgrace with Richard Nixon (See, John Marks, "The Case Against Kissinger," *Rolling Stone*, no. 166, August 1, 1974, pp. 10–14). Throughout the Watergate exposures, the media sustained a hands-off policy toward Kissinger, despite the revelation of his threat to "destroy" anyone who leaked information on the secret bombing of Cambodia. He was portrayed by the press not as a perjurer or wire-tapper, but at all times as an eminent statesman and moral bulwark against Communist tyranny.

3. Adrian Havill, *Deep Truth: The Lives of Bob Woodward and Carl Bernstein*, New York: Birch Lane, 1993, p. 43.

4. Krüger, p. 155. Senator Smathers was a controlling shareholder in the Major Realty Co. with Lansky subordinates Ben Siegelbaum and Max Orovitz.

5. Admiral Moorer, Woodward's superior officer, was the stereotypical hard-bitten Pentagon hawk, a close friend to two of the most powerful Nixon appointees, Henry Kissinger and John Mitchell. He was an enigma to most employees at the Pentagon, best known for his temper tantrums. The Admiral, a ferocious anti-communist, pushed for open warfare with the Soviet Union and denounced as a "dirty bastard" and "unshaven peacenik" anyone who disagreed with him on this score or any other. He was the most feared official in Navy history. Mark Perry, a *Nation* correspondent, found that Moorer's "apparent lack of intelligence was his most important quality." Thus the Nixon administration's

"secret plan to end the war" echoed Moorer's sentiments. The "plan": the US should step up the Vietnam war to pressure North Vietnam to concede. Nixon considered Moorer to be a model "loyalist," a figure he could respect. The Admiral won a reappointment to chairman of the Joint Chiefs in 1972, and continued to urge Nixon on to more devastating levels of military violence in Vietnam.

Under the watch of Admiral Thomas Moorer, Bob Woodward held authority over all communications to the Naval wing of the Pentagon, including the Secretary of the Navy's office. The Admiral and former Secretary of Defense Melvin Laird both stated on tape in 1989 interviews that Woodward's duties included briefing Alex Haig at the Nixon White House. "Later," Havill found, "Moorer attempted to back away from his recorded statement."

The Admiral back-stroked, made "contradictory statements and [sounded] befuddled. Laird said he was 'aware that Haig was being briefed by Woodward.'"

6. Edward J. Epstein, *Agency of Fear: Opiates and Political Power in America*, Verso Books, 1990. First published in 1977 by Putnam.
7. Liddy Deposition, September 30, 1980. *Hunt v. Weberman*.
8. Hunt's testimony, July 11, 1984. *Hunt v. Spotlight*, USDC Miami, Florida.
9. Howard Kohn, "The Hughes-Nixon-Lansky Connection: The Secret Alliances of the CIA from World War II to Watergate," *Rolling Stone*, May 20, 1976.
10. *Hunt v. Weberman*.
11. Lincoln Lawrence, *Mind Control, Oswald & JFK: Were We Controlled?* Kenn Thomas, ed., Kempton, IL.: Adventures Unlimited, 1997, pp. 162–63.
12. Lee Israel, *Kilgallen*, New York: Delacourte, 1979, p. 441.
13. Jim Marrs, *Crossfire: The Plot that Killed Kennedy*, New York: Carroll & Graf, 1989, p. 557. A significant CIA leak confirms that the Agency has a keen interest in the lethal arts. Barry Rothman, a CIA assassination methods specialist, was interviewed by *Playboy* in January, 1977, and explained that he'd been enlisted by an unidentified spy with "an encyclopedic knowledge of guns, particularly Nazi weaponry." The recruiter was "a fascist, basically. He had a deep-seated, violent prejudice against anything that wasn't Aryan." Rothman was recruited in 1952 and graduated from the development of certain explosives to sophisticated biochemical warfare toxins. Not an agency to let talent go to waste, the CIA requested that he write a handbook on improvised weapons systems. He surveyed plant poisons. "Common things you can walk out and find right now in your backyard can, if treated properly, yield very deadly poisons that are not easily detectable. I think I included about forty plants and instructions on how to use them. The Agency was very pleased with it." He moved on to biological agents that "can be made without too much grief. There are a fair number of those." But there was "one peculiar thing" about the CIA assignment that disturbed him: "I was specifically instructed to orient [the handbook] toward domestically available materials and plants. Plants that grow in the U.S. and materials that are sold in the US. What that means, I don't know, but it makes you wonder."
14. Eric Norden, "The Shooting of George Wallace—Who Really Wanted Him Dead," April 1984, pp. 21ff.

CHAPTER ONE
A [Killing] Field Day for the Heat

TIME MACHINE: THE SWING KIDS

SWING KIDS INVOLVES A VERY SMALL FOOTNOTE TO A VERY LARGE HISTORICAL
EVENT. IN NAZI GERMANY IN 1939, WE LEARN, WHILE HITLER WAS ROUNDING UP
JEWS AND LAUNCHING WORLD WAR II, A SMALL GROUP OF KIDS WORE THEIR HAIR
LONG AND DANCED TO THE SWING MUSIC OF SUCH BANNED MUSICIANS AS BENNY
GOODMAN AND COUNT BASIE. OCCASIONALLY THEY GOT INTO FIGHTS WITH THE
BROWNSHIRTS OF THE HITLER YOUTH BRIGADES.

IF THE SWING KIDS HAD EVOLVED INTO AN UNDERGROUND MOVEMENT DEDICATED
TO THE OVERTHROW OF NAZISM, WE MIGHT BE ONTO SOMETHING HERE. BUT NO. A
TITLE CARD AT THE END OF THE FILM INFORMS US THAT SOME OF THE KIDS DIED AT
THE HANDS OF THE NAZIS, AND OTHERS WERE FORCED INTO THE GERMAN ARMY AND
KILLED IN BATTLE . . . .[1] ROGER EBERT, FILM REVIEW, MARCH 5, 1993

In 1967, an increasingly sub-
versive form of music melded with politics in San
Francisco. Still eclipsed by federal classification are the tactics
of the intelligence sector in the destabilization of the lives of politi-
cally-tuned musicians on the fringe of the anti-war movement, as
revealed before the Senate Intelligence Committee in a leaked intelligence memorandum submitted for the record on April 26, 1976:

> Show them as scurrilous and depraved. Call attention to their habits
> and living conditions, explore every possible embarrassment. Send in
> women and sex, break up marriages. Have members arrested on mar-
> ijuana charges. Investigate personal conflicts or animosities between
> them. Send articles to the newspapers showing their depravity. Use
> narcotics and free sex to entrap. Use misinformation to confuse and
> disrupt. Get records of their bank accounts. Obtain specimens of
> handwriting. Provoke target groups into rivalries that may result in
> death. ["Intelligence Activities and Rights of Americans," Book. II,
> April 26 1976, Senate Committee with Respect to Intelligence
> Report]

For the first time since its creation, the warfare state meticulously
erected by the Dulles brothers, J. Edgar Hoover, Dean Acheson,
General Douglas MacArthur, Henry Kissinger, Richard Nixon and an

army of anti-Communist cold warriors was threatened by an increasingly militant segment of the population. "Fascists" and "Pigs" burned in effigy on campus from sea to psychedelic sea.

The Federal Bureau of Investigation rose to the challenge. Many rock musicians of the day struggled for a place in the American pantheon of stardom only to experience ferocious political repression. "That's what killed us," recollects Roger McGuinn, lead guitarist for the Byrds. "We got blackballed after drug allegations in 'Eight Miles High,'" and Hoover's spies never seemed far away. "They'd been chasing after us because somebody left some hashish in the airplane coming back from England. So they came down on us in a recording studio and said, 'Whose is this?' Of course nobody claimed it." On one occasion, on tour in Iowa, David Crosby, lounging on the balcony of a Holiday Inn, whiled away the time before a concert firing .22 caliber blanks with a slingshot at a brick wall about thirty feet down. A group of "Rednecks" staying at the Motel played poker at the ground level, and riled by the tiny explosions, "started climbing over the balcony, fuming, 'Guys died in Iwo Jima for punks like you,'" McGuinn recalls. "They were pounding on Crosby, when suddenly the FBI appeared. You know, 'FBI, son. Break it up!' They took these guys out and sent them off to their room. I don't know if it was just a coincidence, but what were [the FBI] doing in the middle of Iowa? From then on I used to be looking over my shoulder, thinking the government was after me." [2]

The deaths of Byrds' guitarists Clarence White in July, 1973, and Gram Parsons two months later, have long been grist for speculation. Clarence White and his brothers were packing the car after a show in Palmdale, California—the home of Lockheed (military contractor and CIA haunt)—when Clarence was struck by a drunk driver named Yoko Ito. Alan Munde, a banjo player for the White Brothers when they toured England and Sweden in the spring of 1973, recalled in an interview taped at the Tennessee Banjo Institute that White then lived "near Lancaster, California, where his mother and dad had lived. . . . But that's where Edwards Air Force Base was, and that's where there was a lot of aircraft industry up there, and Roland [White's dad] worked there . . . and then Clarence bought a house . . . and [performed] at a club, you know, that Clarence had played many many times before he was with the Byrds, to pick, and was just comin' out loadin' up the stuff, and had put the stuff in the trunk and walked around to get into the car, and the lady came by and side-swiped the car and hit him, and knocked him on down the road, and Roland had just walked around to the front . . . and he was—you know, they don't know that, but he was hit also and knocked over the hood of the car, by the lady . . . and you know, Clarence was, you know, 150 feet down the road."[3]

"The driver of the car, Yoko Ito," according to a brief in *Nashville Babylon* (1988) by Randall Riese, "was booked on suspicion of felony drunk driving and manslaughter." The glassy-eyed Ms. Ito was reportedly pregnant, yet had gone on an alcoholic binge, picked a fight in a bar and capped off the evening by running over a popular musician and dragging him down the road, completely unaware of the fatality. Clarence White came tumbling over the hood of her car, and yet she didn't know that she'd even struck a pedestrian.

White's close friend Gram Parsons, a sometime Byrd with his own band, the Flying Burrito Brothers, was laid low at the Joshua Tree Inn shortly after midnight, September 19, 1973 (one day before singer Jim Croce was killed in an airplane crash, resulting, according to press reports, in the filing of a $2.5-million lawsuit against the FAA by the singer's widow—the tree that killed him was not indicated in the map of the airport runway prepared for Croce). "The circumstances of Gram's death were shrouded in mystery," writes *Rolling Stone* correspondent Ben Fong-Torres.[4] Initially, the press reported that Parsons died of "heart failure," like Jim Morrison before him, "due to natural causes." His death certificate, however, signed by Dr. Irving Root, states that Parsons was claimed by drug toxicity over a period of weeks. Traces of cocaine and amphetamine were detected in his urine, and a high concentration of morphine. The latter was found in his bile and liver. Convincing on the surface—until it is considered that morphine toxicity requires that the drug be found in the blood. It wasn't. Forensic tests did detect alcohol, but no drugs were found in his bloodstream, so the cause of death was not an overdose, as many have since claimed, and drug toxicity is still possible but highly unlikely.

Dr. Root noted that Parsons had reached "toxic levels of drug intake" and sustained them for weeks. (The source of supply has never been publicly identified. A rumor has it that Gram had been buying drugs from a woman, now deceased.) Dr. Margaret Greenwald, a San Francisco coroner, told Fong-Torres that narcotics accumulate over time in the liver and urine. The morphine and trace deposits indicate not that they

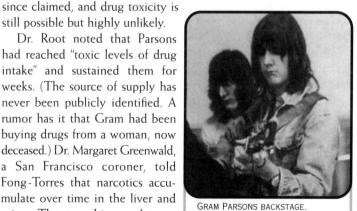

GRAM PARSONS BACKSTAGE.
PHOTO: JOHN LOMAX III

killed him, but that "he'd been using [those drugs] for a long period of time," she explained.[5] So the exact cause of death remains a mystery and there is no hope of exhumation to resolve critical inconsistencies because Parson's cadaver was stolen at the Los Angeles International Airport in transit to New Orleans for burial and burned at Joshua Tree.

The coffin heist was perpetrated by Phil Kaufman, road manager for the Flying Burrito Brothers. Kaufman was a fledgling Hollywood actor before he met Parsons. In the meantime, he'd been arrested on drug charges and sentenced to Terminal Island Correctional Institute in San Pedro, California. It was here that Kaufman met Charles Manson, then an aspiring rock musician. Kaufman wrote about his first contact with Manson in an autobiography, "there was a guy playing guitar in the yard one day at Terminal Island. And it was Charlie, singing his ass off." When Manson was released, Kaufman, from prison, put him in touch with contacts in the Los Angeles music industry. Kaufman was released from prison in 1968. He moved in with Manson and lived with him for a couple of months, met and befriended the Rolling Stones that summer, and in August was introduced to Parsons.[6] Gram Parsons was one of many unexplained casualties on the periphery of Manson's cult.

Many musicians of note shared McGuinn's suspicion that Big Brother was stalking them. Evidence that they were not suffering from paranoid delusions was deposited in the 1980s at the FBI's reading room in Washington, D.C., scores of declassified files. This collection included seven pages of notes on Jimi Hendrix, 89 on Jim Morrison, and, oddly, 663 documents about Elvis Presley. (Presley's file opens early in his career, when "concerned" conservatives petitioned J. Edgar Hoover to "do something" about this swivel-hipped, slack-jawed, decadent despoiler of American adolescents. A former spy ripped off a letter to the FBI in 1956 to complain that Presley had masturbated on stage with his microphone to "arouse the sexual passions of teenage youth." The complainant confessed: "I feel an obligation to pass on to you my conviction that Presley is a definite danger to the security of the United States."[7])

But the attentions of Hoover's agents were lavished not only on Top 40 pop idols. Even a celebrated conductor of Leonard Bernstein's caliber could be stalked by the Feds—the FBI monitored his *every move* for more than thirty years.

On July 30, 1994, the *London Times* reported: "Intelligence files on [Leonard Bernstein] reveal that the bureau spent countless hours examining his links with associations deemed either Communist or subversive." Bernstein swore under oath in 1953 that he was not affiliated with the Communist Party in any way, and three decades of unrelenting spying by the Bureau, beginning in the mid-'40s, failed to produce a scrap of evidence to the contrary. "It also observed his support for the civil rights and anti-war movements, in particular the Black Panthers. . . . Bernstein, however, was known by both his friends and family as a man who espoused liberal causes in a totally arbitrary manner."[8] Bernstein was a liberal with an audience that respected his beliefs, and Hoover's secret police watched him as closely as they would any anarchistic, dope-addled rock idol.

One agent provocateur on the FBI payroll, Sarah Jane Moore, the would-be assassin of President Gerald Ford, observed the Bureau's counter-revolution from the inside. She described an atmosphere of cynical acrimony in a note to reporters curious about her motive in the assassination attempt:

"The FBI directed me to people and organizations seriously working for radical change. . . .

"There was no coordination not even any communication between these groups. The whole left as a matter of fact seemed disorganized, strife-ridden and weak. And I realized the reason for this was the FBI whose tool I was who clearly and correctly saw the strength and power of the idea of socialism, realized it represented a very real danger to our profit-motivated corporate state and who had declared total covert war against not only denim-clad revolutionaries but also against all progressive forces, even those working for the most acceptable 'American' reforms." She explained:

I listened with horror once to a bright young agent as he bragged about his abilities in the area of anonymous letter writing and other forms of character assassination, not of big important leaders, but of little people as soon as they showed any leadership potential. The Bureau's tactic is to cut them down or burn them out before they realize their potential.

I remember Worthington (my Bureau control) saying: "You don't seem to realize that this is war!" He thought the next two or three years would be the most crucial in our nation's history. His greatest fear at that time was that the left would rediscover the documents and ideas from the first and second American revolutions and use them to spark a new revolution.

He said that these words are as powerful today as ever and that properly used (actually he said "cleverly" used) the people could be aroused by these ideas and would fight again to achieve them. . . .

That explains my political beliefs. It does not explain why in the name of a dream whose essence is a deep love for people and a belief in the essential beauty and worth of each individual I picked up a gun intending to kill another human being.

When I was getting ready to go public regarding my spying activities, a journalist attempting to verify some facts was told by the FBI that if the story appeared I would be in danger.

This warning was repeated to me by the FBI with the additional suggestion that I should leave town. Charles Bates told me that of course they couldn't stop me from talking but that I was placing myself in danger if the story appeared. He stated that at any rate he was not going to allow the FBI to be embarrassed. If there was anything they didn't like in the story they would simply see that it was edited out, that they had done that before, that he had "friends" on that particular paper somewhat higher up than the reporter level.

I had already had a phone call saying I was next that was just after the murder of a friend. Now friends and foes alike vied with each other to warn me, each claiming to have heard from sources they refused to name that I was to be "offed" or at the very least beaten.

Beyond a certain point pressure and threats are counter-productive. When one is threatened to a point where one is convinced; that is, when I finally accepted the fact that I was not going to be able to get away—that I wasn't willing to pay the price—the realization I would probable be killed ceased to frighten—it brought instead a sense of freedom.[9]

Conservatives, blind to the slag-pile of political corruption within their own ranks, suspected a Soviet conspiracy in the rising challenge to authority and organized against the storm.

In 1970, three weeks after Nixon invaded Cambodia, Edwin Meese III—the godfather of the far-right political school christened by the *Washington Post* (on January 26, 1984) the "Alameda Mafia," then Governor Ronald Reagan's legal affairs secretary—observed in a McCarthyesque lecture delivered at a state law enforcement conference, "The challenge is clear. The enemies of society who are here in California are willing to sacrifice a generation of youth to obtain their objectives. They are not only willing but desirous of losing an international conflict. They will not stop at endangering life and indeed they have killed several and injured thousands." The solution: "Maximum photography, maximum evidence gathering by officers who are not involved in the actual [political demonstration] control activity"—maximum spying, maximum keeping of secret files on private citizens.[10]

At the federal level, the CIA was already pursuing similar objectives under the aegis of an illegal domestic operation code-named CHAOS. Among the political targets of CHAOS, count Black

Panther Geronimo Pratt, framed for the murder of two radicals on a tennis court in Santa Monica, California. Pratt was subsequently released from prison in June 1997, 27 years after his sentencing, because it was proven that a witness had lied on the stand.[11] The International Secretariat of Amnesty International issued a press release the following year citing the court's "failure to disclose crucial information about a key prosecution witness in the trial of Geronimo ji Jaga [Pratt]—a former leader of the Black Panther Party released last year." This stonewall, insisted AI, "should result in the reversal of his conviction and finally put an end to 27 years of injustice."[12] Pratt is generally considered a target of COINTELPRO, the FBI's notorious counter-surveillance program, but Pratt is aware since requesting his files under FOIA that CHAOS agents hitched horses with the Bureau to drag the Panther into an erroneous conviction.

Politically active hippies were also fair game. One victim of the onslaught was the underground press, according to Donna Demac, an instructor in interactive telecommunications at NYU, "that diverse assortment of publications that . . . empowered many of the social movements of the 1960s." The CIA and FBI "collected information on each paper's publisher, its sources of funds and its staff members. Many underground newspapers were put out of business when they were abandoned by advertisers who had been pressured by the FBI. The Bureau also created obstacles to distribution, fomented staff feuds and spread false information to create suspicion and confusion."[13]

The Central Intelligence Agency and its military counterparts, covert templars of the ruling caste, watched the dissent movement's rise with growing anxiety; the Operation was the Agency's response to civil unrest and cultural upheaval. If nothing else, the word CHAOS implied that officials of The Firm were aware of the social upheaval they were about to unleash upon an unsuspecting proletariat.

Freedom of Information Act requests for the most sensitive files are consistently denied.

"During six years [1967–1972], the Operation compiled some 13,000 different files, including files on 7,200 American citizens," concluded the Rockefeller Commission, which failed to pursue leads to settle critical allegations. The files inspected by the CIA's in-house committee concerned some 300,000 individuals and political organizations, and the CIA's Directorate of Operations created an index of some seven million names.[14]

Leaks were handled at the top. In April 1972, an article by Victor Marchetti, an ex-CIA officer, "CIA: The President's Loyal Tool," appeared in *The Nation*, charging the Agency with deceiving and manipulating the media, and co-opting the youth movement, cultural organizations and labor. William Colby, then the CIA's executive director, recruited John Warner, a deputy general counsel, to halt the publication of a book that Marchetti planned to publish on the criminalization of the CIA. Warner turned to White House aides John Ehrlichman, the head Plumber, and David Young, a right-wing extremist from Young Americans for Freedom, a Nazi front for "conservative" agents emigrating to the US from Munich. Together, they obtained approval from President Nixon to drag Marchetti into court where US District Court Judge Albert V. Bryan, Jr. ordered him to submit the book to the Agency for redaction.[15]

Operation CHAOS was the inevitable mutation of covert domestic ops conceived during the Eisenhower administration and its directive to monitor émigré political groups on domestic soil. A reformed insider, Vern Lyon, former CIA undercover operative and current director of the Des Moines Hispanic Ministry, writes that the directive led the CIA to establish a network of proprietary companies and covers for its domestic operations. So widespread did the network become that in 1964 President Johnson allowed CIA Director John McCone to conceive "a new super-secret branch called the Domestic Operations Division (DOD), the very title of which mocked the explicit intent of Congress to prohibit CIA operations inside the US."

The classified charter of the DOD mandated the exercise of "centralized responsibility for the direction, support, and coordination of clandestine operational activities within the United States." This would include break-ins of foreign diplomatic sites at the request of the National Security Agency (NSA). Lyons: "The CIA also expanded the role of its 'quasi-legal' Domestic Contact Service (DCS), an operation designed to brief and debrief selected American citizens who had traveled abroad in sensitive areas." The DCS also helped with travel control by monitoring the arrivals and departures of US nationals and foreigners. In addition, the CIA reached out to former agents, officers, contacts and friends to help it run its many fronts, covers and phony corporations. This "old boy network" provided the CIA with trusted personnel to conduct its illicit domestic activities.[16]

A massive destabilizing effort was waged against the peace and civil rights movements. The Army's Counter-Intelligence Analysis Branch collected personality profiles, mug shots and compiled "blacklists" of anti-war activists, stored them on computer-files and microfilm reels. The Pentagon's intelligence operatives, disguised as reporters, gathered information at peace demonstrations—the "Midwest Audiovisual News," an Army intelligence front, interviewed Abbie Hoffman at the 1968 police riot in Chicago.[17]

The military program came complete with "operations centers," direct lines to local police, teletype machines to field intelligence units, street maps, closed-circuit video, and secure communications channels. A 180-man "command center" appeared in 1968 following the riots in Detroit. By 1969, the center was housed in a $2.7-million war room in the cellar of the Pentagon.[18]

This was the year Richard Helms prepared a CIA research paper on the antiwar movement entitled "Restless Youth" for Henry Kissinger. The cover letter explained, "in an effort to round out our discussion of this subject, we have included a section on American students. This is an area not within the charter of this agency, so I need not emphasize how extremely sensitive this makes the paper. Should anyone learn of its existence it would prove most embarrassing for all concerned." But a small group at the CIA's Office of Security was already monitoring student organizations in the Washington, D.C. area. Helms expanded the domestic spying operation with the creation of the Special Operations Group (SOG), directed by Richard Ober, one of the "Deep Throat" candidates, to conduct "counterintelligence." This was the direct precursor of CHAOS. SOG operatives provided the CIA Office of Current Intelligence with scuttlebutt on the peace movement. Within a couple of years, domestic operations swelled to meet the perceived threat to military-industrial rule, even paralleling the growth of antiwar protest.[19] But invisibly, in the shadows of the resistance.

In 1974, investigative journalist Seymour Hersh exposed CHAOS in the *New York Times*. Hersh reported that the CIA had conducted a massive spying and covert operations program on domestic soil. The story inspired the Church and Pike hearings of 1975. These investigations verified Hersh's allegations. But the media, especially the leading newspapers and news weeklies, ridiculed and reviled Hersh. *The Washington Post*, *Newsweek* and editorial pages across the country actually questioned his sanity and dismissed the story as a whimsical "conspiracy theory." *Time* rushed to the Agency's defense: "Many observers in Washington who are far from naive about the CIA nevertheless consider its past chiefs and most of its officials highly educated, sensitive and dedicated public servants who would scarcely let themselves get involved in the kind of massive scheme described."[20]

NOTES

1. Peter Wicke, a music historian at Hummboldt University in Berlin, emphasizes that the Nazi suppression of jazz and swing was motivated largely by economics: "January 30, 1933 marked a deep cut for some forms of popular music under the fascist dictatorship in Germany. The

new ruling powers left no doubt about their role in the arts with the renewal of Germany. A once flowering European center of music expired into the Agony." Propaganda expenditures directed against the emergent musical movements "targeted the economic competition of the American music industry," and, oddly enough, "the Jewish population—who had less to do with jazz than the other subpopulations of Germany." American recordings were banned, but Telefunken Studios artists Peter Kreuder's Orchestra, Heinz Wehner's Swing Band and Kurt Widmann were promoted in Nazi Germany, and the business of jazz recording continued after the prohibition was enacted against imports, "not undisputedly, but evenly, without closer inspection, minus the annoying competition from overseas." The corporate influence on Nazi policies concerning jazz and swing music contributed to "a beautiful banknote of private feeling" in Germany. See Peter Wicke, "Populäre Musik im Faschistischen Deutschland," http://www2.huberlin.de/inside/fpm/ wicke2.htm.

2. Bruce Pollock, *When the Music Mattered: The Musicians Who Made it Happen Tell How it Happened*, New York: Holt, Rinehart & Winston, 1983, p. 86.
3. Randal Morton, "Alan Munde's Interview," *Clarence White Chronicles*, no. 14, September 13, 1998.
4. Ben Fong-Torres, *Hickory Wind: The Life and Times of Gram Parsons*, New York: St. Martin's, 1991, p. 228.
5. Fong-Torres, pp. 200–201.
6. Fong-Torres, pp. 116–17.
7. "Rock Heroes on the FBI Record," *Correspondent* (UK), October 1, 1989.
8. Tom Rhodes, "Files show FBI tried to settle score with the maestro of radical chic," *London Times*, July 30, 1994, p. 11.
9. Sarah Jane Moore, correspondence with Linda-Marie, Internet posting, http://www.playink.com/sjmore.htm.
10. Edwin Meese, executive secretary to Governor Reagan, untitled lecture typescript, 1970, released under FOIA request.
11. Geronimo Pratt interviewed by former Black Panther Lee Lew-Lee, 1997. Angus Meredith, in *Secrets: The CIA's War at Home* (Berkeley: University of California Press, 1999): "The FBI's COINTELPRO [was] run in collaboration with CHAOS" (p. 69).
12. "USA: Crucial information 27 years too late for Black Panther leader," Amnesty International press release, AI INDEX: AMR 51/41/98, 1 July 1998.
13. Donna A, Demac, *Liberty Denied: The Current Rise of Censorship in America*, New Brunswick: Rutgers University Press, 1990, p. 77.
14. *Rockefeller Report to the President by the Commission on CIA Activities Within the United States*, June 1975, New York: Manor Books, pp. 23, 41.
15. Angus Mackenzie, *Secrets: The CIA's War at Home*, Berkeley: University of California Press, 1999, pp. 43–44.
16. Verne Lyon, "Domestic Surveillance: The History of Operation CHAOS," *Covert Action Information Bulletin*, Summer 1990.
17. Blanche Wiesen Cook, "Surveillance and Mind Control," Howard Frazier, ed., *Uncloaking the CIA*, New York: The Free Press, 1978, p. 178.
18. Daniel Brandt, "The 1960s and COINTELPRO: In Defense of Paranoia," *NameBase NewsLine*, no. 10, July/September 1995.
19. Thomas Powers, *The Man Who Kept the Secrets: Richard Helms and the CIA*, New York: Pocket Books, 1979, pp. 314–15.
20. Kathryn Olmsted, "Watchdogs or Lap Dogs?" *Albuquerque Weekly Alibi*, July 21, 1997.

CHAPTER TWO
Time Machine:
The Birth of Top 40 Radio and
Alan Freed's Near-Death Experience

(Early CIA and Mob Influences on the Rock Music Industry)

The Mafia was to be enlisted for the covert war against the counterculture, an incarnation of Operation Underworld (the WWII-era alliance between the military and the Mob to sabotage the Italians under Mussolini) on the domestic front, a natural since gangsters already dominated much of the popular music industry. "The music business," Albert Goldman acknowledged in 1989, "has always been a dirty business with strong ties to organized crime and a long tradition of corrupting the media. One of the dangers that researchers in this field run is that they will stumble across something that will alarm the crooks, who are paranoid from the jump." Goldman reported that the lesson was driven home when Linda Kuehl, a friend writing a book on the life of Billie Holiday, was killed in Washington, DC by a plummet from the terrace of her hotel room. Goldman phoned police and learned that they had ruled suicide out as the motive (she'd been cleaning her face with cold cream when she fell). He also "learned that she had been running scared because she was getting calls from strangers who kept admonishing her, 'Why don't you just write about the music?'" [1]

In the mid-'60s, CHAOS officials and the Mob both eyed the rising tide of political rock music askance. Each had an incentive for exercising control over the industry. The CIA was in the business of decimating the New Left and popular music had, in the wink of a half-note, been transformed into a viper pit of long-haired "communards" screaming for revolution and an end to the war in Vietnam. The Mafia, of course, wanted more constrictive financial control over the recording industry, the artists it signed, everything from production to distribution.

It's not as though these two powerful entities, the CIA and organized crime, were unknown to the industry. Top 40, the reigning broadcast format in America, owes its very existence to the NSC-CIA-Mafia combination.

In the beginning there was Morris Levy. Morris began his career as an appendage of the Genovese Family and rapidly rose through the ranks. He was enlisted by the Mob as a juke box promoter in the 1940s. His brother was gunned down by business rivals who mistook him for Morris—who lived to become one of the most feared men in the business. He was the owner of the famous Birdland jazz club in New York City, and a partner, with George Goldner, a seedy record promoter, for the Rama label (home of R&B doo-wop group The Crows) and a subsidiary, Gee Records (Frankie Lymon & the Teenagers, The Regents).[2] These labels and further subsidiaries (Roulette, End) pumped out apolitical bubblegum (Tommy James, Little Anthony, The Shangri-Las) through the 1960s.

Gee Records was founded by Levy and Goldner specifically to draw in Alan Freed, then a rising R&B concert promoter in Cleveland (he oversold one concert and thereby incited the first rock 'n' roll riot), to New York. Freed was hired at Gee in the Fall of 1954 to work his promotional genius, and from the gun he and Goldner were close allies. Levy did not entirely trust his new partner, however, and schemed to bring him under control, eventually arranging a meeting in which Alan Freed—drunk at the time—was convinced to sell his share of the label to Levy. The Mafioso now had a controlling interest in the company, one of the first to enter the rock 'n' roll market.

John Elroy McCaw, another early kingpin in the genre, was also instrumental in bringing Alan Freed to New York. McCaw was a veteran of the Office of Strategic Services (OSS), the predecessor of the CIA.[3] After the war, McCaw bought a New York radio station, WINS at Seven Central Park West, and geared the station's programming to hockey and basketball games. But by the early 1950s, the station pioneered the very first disk jock format, twenty-five minutes of Tony Bennett, Perry Como, Steve Lawrence and other popular crooners of the day, followed by five minutes of news. It soon became clear to the programming directors at WINS that the jock was the radio personality of the future. When Freed arrived in New York, he found himself in the historically unprecedented position of shaping not only the music youth would dance to (under Mafia control), but the medium that delivered it, as well (at a station run by a veteran intelligence agent).

Freed, at a starting salary of $75,000, was expected to boost the ratings, and toward this end he had no use for Perry Como. Rick Sklar, then an apprentice copywriter and producer, reports that when Freed arrived in New York, along with him "came hundreds of 45-RPM singles that he piled helter-skelter in an old five-shelf supply cabinet in our office. That chaotic, uncatalogued collection would become the most influential record library in commercial radio, imitated by stations everywhere. It would change the sound of popular music in America and the world for generations."

The WINS jocks couldn't know that in ten years time the invention of rock radio would inspire a subculture of anti-war activists and flag-burning bohemians to "tune in." Dissent inevitably died with a drugged whimper. Drugs would enter the equation of music plus youth with the politics of heroin and LSD. Hallucinogens fragged organized resistance to the war, but they were only one of many dubious contributions the Agency has made to American culture. Strains of drugged hedonism found their way to Top 40 radio with tambourine men peddling magic swirling trips, pink-eyed adolescents wringing their hands at mother's little helpers. The surf wave of Top 40 radio was transformed into a spawning ground of countercultural self-medication, and with the escalation of the Vietnam War, quasi-Marxist politics infused with strains of mystical idealism.

Ironically, "Top 40," the pied piper of rebellion, owes its very existence to McCaw, Alan Freed's boss, the entrepreneurial brains behind "big beat" radio and an old covert warrior at ease in the closed chambers of Washington's national security "elite": "Elroy's government contacts were extensive," writes Sklar. "He had maintained many of his OSS connections after the war and was quite probably still engaged in government intelligence work during the time that he owned WINS. McCaw associates tell of saying good-bye to him in New York, with plans to meet him in Chicago the next day, only to have McCaw call from Cairo and cancel the meeting. . . . He was a member of the Advisory Council of the National Security Council, placed there, along with other key industry figures, by his old boss, Air Force General Hap Arnold."[4] Elroy McCaw was the "unauthorized civilian" whose inadvertent admission to an NSC meeting at the White House, chaired by John F. Kennedy—who

JOHN ELROY MCCAW, A SCION OF THE NATIONAL SECURITY COUNCIL DURING THE EISENHOWER REGIME AND THE PROPRIETOR OF WINS IN NEW YORK, THE ORIGINATOR OF THE 'HIT PARADE' FORMAT. MCCAW TOOK OVER THE STATION WITH A MEAGER DOWN PAYMENT, PAID A TOTAL OF $450,000 FOR IT, AND THE NEXT DECADE SOLD WINS FOR $10 MILLION, THEN A RECORD BUY-OUT FOR A RADIO STATION.

had never met the man and thought him an intruder—caused a press furor in 1961. (The NSC and General Henry H. "Hap" Arnold, commanding general of US Army Air Forces during WWII, both played significant roles in seeding the prevailing Cold War culture. The NSC was patterned after Hitler's security council, and its jurisdiction was to oversee the CIA by dictate of the National Security Act of 1947.[5] McCaw was therefore instrumental in determining CIA policy.)

The yawping, warbling, mind-numbing repetitions of Top 40 radio were given trial runs first in Omaha, Kansas City and New Orleans. The format was fine-tuned at WINS under McCaw, and the radio industry would never be the same: "WINS hit the air in September of 1957," Sklar recalls, "with sharp jingles, screaming contests and promotions, and Top 40 music. The city had never heard anything like it." The jocks had personalities, an unprecedented development. "News was introduced with ear-splitting sensationalist effects. . . . A different sound was played each hour. One newscast would be introduced by a woman screaming, another by a fire engine siren, and still another by the sound of machine guns."[6]

The station lured more listeners than any other radio station in New York within a month of breaking out the hit parade format. But corruption thrived behind the DJ's mindless bluster, whistles and the latest "Pick Hit of the Week."

Alan Freed, the godfather of hit radio, was scapegoated by Orrin Hatch's House Legislative Oversight subcommittee probe of payola in 1959. He was also very nearly a target of assassination the year before. In 1958, McCaw called Freed into the WINS owner's office and announced his intention to fire him. The DJ was so shocked that he canceled a concert and spent the entire day pleading for his job. Freed was still in McCaw's office when a rock promoter, enraged by the sudden cancellation, exploded through the rear entrance to the radio station, gun in hand, searching for Freed. Sklar's pregnant wife, Sydelle, and Inga Freed were standing at the Coca-Cola machine. They immediately bolted into the record library and locked the door behind them. The gunman was unable to find Freed, who was still pleading with McCaw in the latter's office, and stomped out of the station in a cloud of disgust.[7]

NOTES

1. Albert Goldman, "Rock's Greatest Hitman," *Penthouse*, September 1989, p. 222.
2. Marc Eliot, *Rockonomics: The Money Behind the Music*, New York: Citadel, 1989, pp. 47–48.
3. Rick Sklar, *Rocking America: How the All-Hit Radio Stations Took Over*, New York: St. Martin's, 1984, pp. 11, 17 and 19.
4. Sklar, p. 54. John E. McCaw died in 1969. He sired four sons, including Craig McCaw, who has been as influential in the molding of media and culture as his spook father. McCaw, Jr. entered the cable industry early. A Craig McCaw timeline: 1973: Craig takes over the daily operation of a small cable television operation in Centralia owned by him and his three brothers. 1974: The company enters the radio common carrier (paging) industry. 1982: The company is granted spectrum licenses made available by the FCC. 1986: The company buys out MCI's cellular and paging operations. 1987: Deciding to invest heavily in the emerging wireless industry, the company sells its cable holdings. 1990: McCaw Cellular purchases 52 percent of LIN Broadcasting stock—LIN owned interests in five of the top ten cellular markets. 1991: McCaw initiates an upgrade of its systems from analog to digital. 1992: The Wireless Data Division contracts with UPS to track packages throughout the U.S. 1994: McCaw merges with AT&T (Source: 1995 AT&T press release).

   The latest Forbes Four Hundred report notes that in 1994, the McCaw family "agreed to invest up to $1.1 billion in Nextel Communications." All four brothers are exceedingly wealthy. Bruce R. McCaw, *Forbes* reports, is worth $800 million; Keith W. McCaw, $775 million; John Elroy McCaw, Jr., $750 million.
5. Mae Brussell, "Why is the Senate Watergate Committee Functioning as Part of the Cover-Up," *Realist*, August 1971, p. 22. After WWII, a Nazi base was established in the Caribbean. The NSC, "patterned from German intelligence, provided the espionage framework inside the White House for our political assassinations as well as the Watergate 'Plumbers' and election manipulations."
6. Sklar, p. 28.
7. Sklar, p. 46.

CHAPTER THREE
Parapolitical Stars in the Dope Show

BOOKS WERE BANNED, BOOK SHOPS CLOSED DOWN. OFFICES AND SOCIAL CENTRES
WERE BROKEN INTO AND THEIR FILES WERE REMOVED, DOUBTLESS TO BE FED INTO
THE POLICE COMPUTERS. UNDERGROUND PAPERS AND MAGAZINES COLLAPSED
UNDER THE WEIGHT OF OFFICIAL PRESSURE, GALLERIES AND CINEMAS HAD WHOLE
SHOWS CONFISCATED. ARTISTS, WRITERS, MUSICIANS AND COUNTLESS UNIDENTIFIED
HIPPIES GOT DRAGGED THROUGH THE COURTS TO ANSWER TRUMPED-UP CHARGES OF
CORRUPTION, OBSCENITY, DRUG-ABUSE, ANYTHING THAT MIGHT SILENCE THEIR
VOICES. **PENNY RIMBAUD, CRASS (ANARCHIST UK PUNK BAND)**

The nation entered a mode
of heightened security after the appearance of alien
youth that grew its hair long and balked at the idea of hurling
itself into the Asian inferno. This was the summer of the Denver Pop
Festival at Mile High Stadium, featuring Jimi Hendrix, Joe Cocker,
the Mothers of Invention and Credence Clearwater Revival, among
other emerging acts. The festival was marred by slugfests between
club-swinging cops, gatecrashers, and—foreshadowing the hellish
landscape of Altamont—bikers hired to maintain security.
Thousands in the stadium were forced onto the field when tear gas
wafted through the stands, a police response to bottle-throwing
gate-crashers. The next day, the police arrived armed to the molars.
Some 300 cops with police dogs assembled at the foot of a hill where
a group of non-paying long-hairs sat listening to "free music." The
police brought along a weapon called the "Pepper Fog," a device that
pumped plumes of tear gas and scalding mace. They were also armed
with high-caliber rifles loaded with bird shot.

The mood of the crowd was idyllic. Nevertheless, the authorities
cranked up the Pepper Fog machine, and its loud motor attracted the
attention of some concert-goers who wandered down the hill to
investigate. A single watermelon rind flung by a young rocker or
provocateur arced into the platoon of cops. Immediately, the rind toss
was addressed by a huge cloud of choking and blistering Pepper Fog.
Everyone on the hill swallowed the gas.

Police clubbed anyone caught scaling the fence to crash the
concert, even women, into a sorry state of submission. To force a
mass confrontation, the men in blue marched into the stadium with
their rifles raised—but there was no show of resistance from the

crowd. After the event, the Denver police chief mislaid blame for the violence on the American Liberation Front, a group of anti-war activists who had recently held a "live-in" at City Park to demonstrate that "revolution through music is possible."[1]

A clandestine counter revolt was waged by the intelligence agencies and their allies in the corporate sector. Former FBI agent Paul Rothermeil told reporter Peter Noyes that he had been asked by Texas Millionaire Nelson Bunker Hunt (his father, bombastic ultra-conservative H.L. Hunt, was a suspect in the killing of John Kennedy; Nelson himself was at one time among the world's wealthiest men, the sole title-holder to all of the oil reserves in Libya) to form a "killer force" in Southern California to prey on liberal organizations and peace activists. Hunt's death squads would recruit from the John Birch Society (a fascist front that received generous financial support from the Texan) and train in the desert. The killers were to be armed with exotic "gas guns" manufactured in Europe. These beauties induced heart attacks that deceived any coroner. Rothermeil refused the offer, and shortly thereafter discovered that his telephone had been tapped by the millionaire's private security force.[2]

LSD appeared on the streets as if on cue to destabilize student dissent. More potent drugs used in federally-sponsored behavior modification studies also found their way to society at large. STP, a hallucinogen developed by the Dow Chemical Company in 1964, was considered an "incapacitating agent" by scientists on the CIA payroll. Research subjects were rendered semi-comatose for several days after dropping the hallucinogen. In 1967, Lee and Shlain report in *Acid Dreams*, "for some inexplicable reason, the formula for STP was released to the scientific community at large."

Five thousand tablets of STP were distributed in Haight-Ashbury as the "Summer of Love" embarked: "Few had heard of the drug, but that didn't matter to the crowd of eager pill poppers. They gobbled the gift as if it were an after-dinner mint." Some of the attendees were still tripping three days later. Emergency wards in San Francisco were choked with freaking bohemians.

Phencyclidine, or PCP, an animal tranquilizer sold by Parke-Davis, made its first appearance in San Francisco's bohemian underground, one of many mind-blistering drugs that spilled from the CIA's medicine cabinet into the streets of San Francisco.[6]

The marketing possibilities were not lost on La Cosa Nostra, of course. The Mob revived its Prohibition role, opened mass production labs and a meticulously organized a network of traffickers to move black market hallucinogens.[7]

Lee and Shlain ask, "And what was the CIA up to?":

According to a former CIA contract employee, Agency personnel helped underground chemists set up LSD laboratories in the Bay Area during the Summer of Love to "Monitor" events in the acid ghetto. But why, if this assertion is true, would the CIA be interested in keeping tabs on the hippie population? Law enforcement is not a plausible explanation, for there were already enough narcs operating in the Haight. Then what was the motive? A CIA agent who claims to have infiltrated the covert LSD network provided a clue when he referred to Haight-Ashbury as a "human guinea pig farm."

A dozen years earlier in the same city, George Hunter White and his CIA colleagues had set up a safe house and begun testing hallucinogenic drugs on unwitting citizens. White's activities were phased out in the mid-1960s when the grassroots acid scene exploded in the Bay Area. Suddenly there was a neighborhood packed full of young people who were ready and willing to gobble experimental chemicals—chemicals that had already been tested in the lab but seldom under actual field conditions.[8]

Charles Manson and Timothy Leary arrived in San Francisco at roughly the same time. Both had a keen interest in mind control. In the labyrinth of *Helter Skelter*, Vincent Bugliosi observes: "Somewhere along the line—I wasn't sure how or where or when—Manson developed a control over his followers so all-encompassing that he would ask them to violate the ultimate taboo—say 'kill' and they would do it."

In 1993, a book appeared in Germany offering up a partial solution to the Manson mind control mystery, an intimate glimpse of the CIA's activities in the Haight district: *Murder's Test-Tube: The Box of Charles Manson*, by Carol Greene. A French review found the book's other characters "far more frightening than Manson himself." There was Dr. Wayne O. Evans, director of the Military Stress Laboratory of the US Army Institute of Environmental Medicine in Natick, Massachusetts in the 1960s. Evans took part in the Study Group for the Effects of Psychotropic Drugs on Normal Humans, a conference held in Puerto Rico in 1967, and issued a report, *Psychotropic Drugs in the Year* 2000:

In considering the present volume, it is our hope that the reader will not believe this to be an exercise in science fiction. It is well known that the world of 15 years hence presently exists in the research laboratory of today.

When we consider the effects of these advances in pharmacology we must ask:

A. TO WHOM DO THE YOUTH LISTEN?

B. WHAT ARE THEIR SOCIAL AND PERSONAL WORTH?

Evans glimpsed shimmering vistas of mass mind control on the horizon. The average citizen might consider military psychopharmacology a morbid subject: "If we accept the position that human mood, motivation, and emotion are reflections of a neurochemical state of the brain, then drugs can provide a simple, rapid expedient means to produce any desired neurochemical state that we wish. The sooner that we cease to confuse scientific and moral statements about drug use, the sooner we can rationally consider the types of neurochemical states that we wish to provide for people." The unstated provider of said "neurochemical states" would, of course, be agents of the federal government.

Consider Charles Manson's contacts in Haight-Ashbury:

Dr. David E. Smith [currently an associate clinical professor of occupational medicine and toxicology at the University of California, San Francisco, and a visiting associate professor of behavioral pharmacology in the department of psychiatry, University of Nevada Medical School] and his colleague Roger Smith (no relation), both of whom were associated with the famous Haight-Ashbury Clinic in San Francisco. They shared an interest in the concept of "behavioral sinks"; believed that rats, in response to overcrowding, were naturally inclined to violence, criminality, and mass murder; and believed that the percentage of rats who would engage in such behavior could be increased by the influence of drugs. Dr. David Smith . . . added a new dimension by injecting the rats with amphetamines. Author Greene presents and defends the thesis that for both Smiths, Haight-Ashbury represented an opportunity to test these theories [on humans]. David Smith referred to Haight-Ashbury as the national center for habitual drug abuse, and the first slum for teenagers in America. Both Smiths were personally acquainted with Manson, and Roger Smith was Manson's parole officer when Manson first came to Haight-Ashbury, direct from prison.[9]

"No doubt about it," Lee and Shlain conclude, "LSD was a devastating weapon."[10]

And that's exactly how officials of the CIA saw it. Allen Dulles wrote in a memo to the Secretary of Defense in 1955 that Langley took an interest in hallucinogens in the first place due to "the enthusiasm and foresight" of Dr. L. Wilson Greene, technical director of the chemical and radiological labs at the Army Chemical Center. Greene was the author of a 1949 paper, *Psychochemical Warfare: A New Concept of War*, a bit of Orwellian inspiration for CIA and Army officials who have cited the report as their inspiration in the study of drugs as military ordnance.

Dulles reported in his memo that the Agency was testing hallucinogens on "groups of people" or "individuals engaged in group activities."[11]

The list of groups susceptible to drugging did not exclude the Nixon administration. UCLA's Sidney Gottlieb testified in September, 1977 that once, when Nixon visited a foreign country, his traveling party was secretly drugged by the CIA.[12] ABC News later reported that the incident took place during Nixon's sojourn to the Soviet Union in May, 1972.[13]

At the dawn of the counter culture, CIA personnel mingled with drug dealers in San Francisco's swelling hippie district. Scientists with Agency credentials moved to the Haight and set up "monitoring" stations, among them Louis J. West of UCLA, formerly Jack Ruby's psychiatrist. (Dr. West testified that Ruby had an epileptic fit and accidentally shot Lee Harvey Oswald as a result of his involuntary twitchings.) West also went on to the chair of UCLA's Neuropsychiatric Institute and oversaw the illicit mind control experiments of Drs. José Delgado, author of *Physical Control of the Mind* (1969), and Ross Adey, a veteran of Operation Paperclip. Dr. Margaret Singer, currently an advisory board member of the CIA-anchored "False Memory Syndrome Foundation," also participated in the study of LSD as a politically-destabilizing weapon.

Pete Townshend, guitar thrasher for The Who, was one of the few popular musicians who shunned the drug, found it politically and spiritually useless. He let that particular bandwagon roll by. "When you trip, you love yourself. You don't realize you were better off as you were," he said. "The trips are just a side street, and before you know it you're back where you were. Each trip is more disturbing than the one that follows until eventually the side street becomes a dead end. Not only spiritually, which is the most important, but it can actually stop you thinking." Townsend tried a hit of LSD given to him by Berkeley chemist Owsley Stanley III at the Monterey Pop Festival in June, 1967. It would be 18 years before he gave the drug another try. "It was incredibly powerful," Townshend recalled. "Owsley must have had the most extraordinary liver."[14] By the time he got to Woodstock, Townshend was completely put off by the CIA's mind control drug. As a "cynical" English culturatum, he "walked through it all and felt like spitting at the lot of them and shaking them, trying to make them realize nothing had changed and nothing was going to change." The alternative society that blossomed in the mid-1960s was already rapidly disintegrating. Townshend blamed Woodstock, "a field full of six-foot-deep mud laced with LSD. If that was the world they wanted to live in, then fuck the lot of them."[15]

Rock historian Charles Kaiser also considers LSD a weapon, and not a tool of spiritual revelation as the guinea pigs were led to believe: "One CIA memo called the drug a 'potential new agent for unconventional warfare.'" Potential? "That was certainly what many people hoped it would be for the swarms of hippies who descended on the Haight in the summer of 1967. Vastly more powerful than marijuana or hash, LSD was the drug that took you, instead of the other way around. In 1966 Leary had founded the League for Spiritual Discovery, explaining, 'Like every great religion of the past, we seek to find the divinity within and to express this revelation in a life of glorification and worship of God'. . . . But to the disappointment of the left, there never was any direct correlation between drug use (or promiscuity) and politics. This was one aspect of the deeper dichotomy between recreations of the sixties and their political content. Worshiping under the banner of sex, drug, and rock 'n' roll, millions of young Americans smoked marijuana, tripped on acid, sped through the decade on superfluous amphetamines, dressed wildly, danced violently, and seduced one another assiduously. Then in roughly the same proportion as their parents, they continued to vote Republican."[16]

"Dropping out," ditching the corporate warfare state, was postulated by the emerging leadership of the anti-war subculture. And the philosophical direction of the swelling drop-out class was influenced by metaphysical, counter-cultural spokesmen with CIA support, each talking a blue streak about self, transcendence, consciousness expansion and equally high-minded, apolitical flights of mental expatriation.

On the East Coast, Ira Einhorn, an eclectic new-age quack, and his friend Andrija Puharich, inventor of the tooth implant and a CIA-Army mind control researcher, lectured the counter-culture on drug reveling and "alien" visitations. Among the business sponsors of Ira Einhorn (currently a fugitive living in France, wanted for the alleged murder of his girlfriend Holly Maddox): the Bronfman family of Seagram's fame; Russell Byers, a HUD director; John Haas, president of Rohm and Haas chemical conglomerate; Bill Cashel, Jr., a former Marine and president of Bell Pennsylvania. Einhorn wrote a chapter for a book edited by Humphrey Osmond, the infamous LSD chemist, Tim Leary and Alan Watts. His attorney was Arlen "Magic Bullet" Spector.[17]

Whole Earth Catalog editor Stewart Brand was the prototypical drop-out . . . or was he? Brand was born in 1938, a native of Rockford, Illinois. He attended elite Phillips Exeter Academy, graduated with a degree in biology from Stanford University in 1960. Between 1960 and 1962, Brand was assigned to active duty as a US Army officer. He qualified for Airborne, taught basic infantry and worked as a Pentagon photojournalist. In 1968 he founded the original *Whole Earth Catalog*, a compendium of tools for alternative living.

"Brand organized one of the key events of the LSD era," writes Benjamin Woolley in *Virtual Worlds* (1992)—the 1966 'Trips Festival' in San Francisco: It was to be the grand finalé of Ken Kesey's Acid Tests, a blissful "state of collective psychic intimacy that caused individual minds to melt into one single, seamless consciousness." Stewart Brand saw in the Acid Test a glitzy public gathering to rival a rock concert for spectacle: "Hard though it may now be to believe, [he] set about attracting business sponsors. Brand's commercial pragmatism and boy scout enthusiasm resulted in a sort of huge village fête, one that attracted an estimated 10,000 people and perhaps, though this goes unrecorded, a profit. It was so successful that a New York promoter reportedly wanted to book the acid test for Madison Square Garden."

In September 1967, precisely as CHAOS was launched by the CIA and the White House, Dr. Timothy Leary, tossed out of the Army for erratic behavior, abandoned experimenting with LSD on prisoners for the CIA in upstate New York, dropped a reading of the *Tibetan Book of the Dead* and donned the robes of designated LSD media prelate.

"In addition to this long mainstream tradition of far-out Sufi gnostic experimentation," Leary told religious historian Rick Fields in 1983, "there was another branch of drug research."[18] While still at Harvard, Leary was approached by Henry Murray, chief of psychological operations for William Donovan's Office of Strategic Services during WWII (and after the war a mind control researcher at Harvard who enlisted as a subject of experimentation one Ted Kaczynski, the Unabomber[19]). At the 1950 spy trial of Alger Hiss, Murray openly testified: "The whole nature of the functions of OSS were particularly inviting to psychopathic characters; it involved sensation, intrigue, the idea of being a mysterious man with secret knowledge."[20] And so Leary was fascinated with psychedelic compounds, "like most intelligence men," he added, and volunteered early on for the psilocybin trials, surreptitiously sponsored by the Company.

Kesey and Allen Ginsburg, among many others, first tasted LSD by signing onto Agency-funded research programs.

"Hundreds of Harvard students had been tripped out by answering ads in the *Crimson*," Leary explained to Smith. "So when I got here, I must tell you, I was the square on the block. We shared these drugs as novices, as amateurs, hesitantly moving into a field that had no signposts or guidelines. There was simply no language in western psychology to describe altered states of consciousness or ecstasies or visions or terrors. The psychiatrists said these were 'psychomimetic' experiences."

Dr. Leary's CIA resumé has roots in 1954, with his promotion to director of clinical research and psychology at the Kaiser Foundation Hospital in Oakland, California. At Kaiser, Dr. Leary developed a personality test, "The Leary"—administered to Leary himself in 1970, in prison[21]—adopted by the Agency to test applicants.

Dr. Leary was the bosom ally of Frank Barron, a former grad school classmate and CIA acid head.[22] Barron was employed by the Berkeley Institute for Personality Assessment and Research—Leary later admitted that the Institute was "staffed by OSS-CIA psychologists." In 1966, Barron founded the Harvard Psychedelic Drug Research Center. Mark Riebling, a Leary biographer, writes: "Leary follows Barron to Harvard and becomes a lecturer in psychology. After Barron administers to him some CIA psilocybin and LSD, Leary begins tripping regularly. He also studies the effects of psychedelics on others in controlled experiments. He later admits to knowing, at the time, that 'some powerful people in Washington have sponsored all this drug research.' In addition to Barron, Leary's associates and assistants during this period include former OSS chief psychologist Murray, who had monitored military experiments on truth-drug brainwashing and interrogation, and Dr. Martin Orne, a researcher receiving funds from CIA."[23] (Orne, with the late Dr. West and Dr. Singer, was a guiding light of the False Memory Syndrome Foundation, an organization that specializes in discrediting ritually-abused, mind-controlled children and their therapists.)

Leary swapped hallucinatory epiphanies with Aldous Huxley, a visiting professor at Harvard University. Huxley convinced Leary to form a "secret society," writes Riebling, "to launch and lead a psychedelic conspiracy to brainwash influential people for the purposes of human betterment. 'That's how everything of culture and beauty and philosophic freedom has been passed on.'" Huxley suggested that he initiated "artists, writers, poets, jazz musicians, elegant courtesans. And they'll educate the intelligent rich."

In 1962, Mary Pinchot Meyer (gunned down on a Potomac towpath, October 12, 1964), divorced from Cord Meyer, her CIA official husband visited Leary at Harvard: "Leary will later recall her as 'amused, arrogant, aristocratic.'" Meyer informs Leary that the government is "studying ways to use drugs for warfare, for espionage, for brainwashing." She asks that he "teach us how to run [LSD] sessions, use drugs to do good. Leary agrees. He provides her with drug samples and 'session' reports, and is in touch with her every few weeks, advising her on how to be a 'brainwasher.' She swears him to secrecy." One day after the assassination of John Kennedy, she phoned him, Leary recalled, and she was overcome with fear and grief. "They couldn't control [Kennedy] anymore," she told Leary. "He was *learning* too much. . . . They'll cover everything up."[24]

Leary was a magnet for espionage agents. He was constantly surrounded by operatives of the intelligence agencies. In the end, he paired up with G. Gordon Liddy in a traveling radio road show. Liddy was a CHAOS veteran.[25]

On September 12, 1970, Tim Leary escaped from prison, aided, according to Benjamin Woolly, "by the Weather Underground . . . apparently funded by [CIA runamuck] Ronald Stark and the Brotherhood of Eternal Love." Leary's famed flight to Switzerland was facilitated by CIA contractees: "May 1971," writes Riebling, "Leary and his wife escape to Switzerland with the assistance, according to Leary, of an 'Algerian bureaucrat named Ali,' who 'made no bones about his connection to the CIA' . . . and [Leary says] 'that's the best mafia you can deal with in the twentieth century.'"

The prison escape was financed by the Brotherhood of Eternal Love, and the LSD distributed by the Brotherhood was provided by convicted CIA terrorist Ron Stark. Profits from the sale of the LSD were deposited in Castle Bank, a CIA hot money cooler legally represented by Paul Helliwell, a business promoter for Meyer Lansky and the CIA's chief launderer of heroin proceeds.[26]

NOTES

1. Jim Fouratt, "Denver Festival: Mace with Music," *Rolling Stone*, no. 38, July 26, 1969, pp. 6–8.
2. Jim Hougan, *Spooks: The Haunting of America—The Private Use of Secret Agents*, New York, William Morrow, 1978, pp. 20, 74–75.

3. Dick Russell, *The Man Who Knew Too Much*, New York: Carroll & Graf/Richard Gallen, 1992, pp. 191, 321.
4. Thomas Powers, *The Man Who Kept the Secrets: Richard Helms and the CIA*, New York: Pocket Books, 1979, pp. 319–20.
5. E. Howard Hunt, *Undercover: Memoirs of an American Secret Agent*, Berkeley, 1974, pp. 211–12.
6. Martin A. Lee & Bruce Shlain, *Acid Dreams: The Complete Social History of LSD: The CIA, the Sixties, and Beyond*, New York, Grove Weidenfeld, 1992, p. 187.
7. Ibid, p. 188. "Hard core Cosa Nostra-type criminal figures [run] an extremely well-organized traffic in hallucinogenic drugs"—James Finlator, FDA official.
8. Ibid., pp. 188–89.20.
9. David E. Smith, MD biography, Haight-Ashbury Free Clinic publicity release. Manson was released from prison in March 1967. Dr. David Smith, according to Vincent Bugliosi in *Helter Skelter*, "got to know the [Manson] group through his work in the Haight-Ashbury Free Clinic" (p. 222). Before opening the clinic, Smith had lived in the Haight-Ashbury district for 32 years. He was a student at the University of California at San Francisco medical school, specializing in psychopharmacology, the study of the effects of drugs on the mind.

    Smith is a past president of the American Society of Addiction Medicine (ASAM), in Chevy Chase, Maryland. He was succeeded as president of ASAM in 1995 by Dr. G. Douglas Talbott, MD, who served three years in the Korean War as an Air Force captain. He was Chief of Medicine at the 275th Hospital, Wright Patterson Air Force Base, a medical aide to both the Secretary and the Chief of Staff of the Air Force. Upon his discharge in 1956, he returned to his hometown of Dayton, Ohio, where he entered private practice. He worked closely with NASA in its nascent Nazi-overrun days, and was a civilian consultant in charge of crew selection for Project Mercury, among other responsibilities.

    The military-industrial connections of Smith and Talbott are among many indications that ASAM is an intelligence front.
10. Lee and Shlain, p. 190.
11. Alan W. Scheflin and Edward M. Opton, Jr., *The Mind Manipulators*, New York: Paddington Press, 1978, p. 159.
12. Ibid., p. 158.
13. Ibid., p. 499.
14. Geoffrey Giuliano, *Behind Blue Eyes: The Life of Pete Townshend*, New York: Plume Books, 1996, p. 77.
15. Giuliano, p. 91.
16. Charles Kaiser, *1968 in America: Music, Politics, Chaos, Counterculture, and the Shaping of a Generation*, New York: Weidenfeld & Nicholson, 1988, pp. 205–06.
17. See Steven Levy, *The Unicorn's Secret: Murder in the Age of Aquarius*, New York: Prentice Hall, 1988.
18. Rick Fields, "Flashback & Fast Forward: Psychedelics in the '80s," *New Age*, July 1983, p. 41.
19. Alexander Cockburn, "We're Reaping Tragic Legacy from Drugs," *Los Angeles Times*, July 6, 1999, p. B-5. Murray was chairman of Harvard's Department of Social Relations, and, Cockburn notes, "zealously

prosecuted the CIA's efforts to carry forward experiments in mind control conducted by Nazi doctors in the concentration camps. . . . Just as Harvard students were fed doses of LSD, psilocybin and other potions, so too were prisoners and many unwitting guinea pigs."

20. R. Harris Smith, *OSS: The Secret History of America's First Central Intelligence Agency*, Berkeley: University of California Press, 1972, p. 7.

21. Lee and Shlain, p. 260.

22. Frank Barron, born in 1922, a psychologist and presumably a philosopher, earned his Ph.D at Berkeley in 1950. Early in his career, Barron's publications in the field of creativity attracted the interest of the Agency. He was employed for over thirty years at the Berkeley Institute for Personality Assessment and Research, an organization funded and staffed by former OSS-CIA psychologists. On two occasions, Barron rejected offers to become director of psychological personnel for the CIA. Frank Barron biography, Council of Spiritual Practice home page, www.csp.org.

23. Mark Riebling, "Tinker, Tailor, Stoner, Spy," Osprey Productions/Grand Royal web page, 1994.

24. Russell, p. 461.

25. A Nazi link to G. Gordon Liddy foreshadowing his escapades in the Nixon White House: In 1961, Interpol—a world police force reorganized and Nazified by Heinrich Himmler and J. Edgar Hoover in 1937, with Nazi General Kurt Daluege holding the reins—was charged by the World Jewish Congress with providing "an unexpected sense of safety" to Nazis in hiding. Vaughn Young, in "The Men from Interpol," describes the events preceding the appearance of G. Gordon Liddy in the Nixon White House: "By 1968, the Nazi issue had quieted sufficiently to allow the election of Paul Dickopf as president. Besides working in Heydrich's SD, where Interpol was located during the war, Dickopf had assisted in rebuilding the police infrastructure in postwar Germany, achieving a senior position for himself in the *Bundeskriminalamt*. During his four-year reign, the organization achieved a momentary state of financial affluence. . . . " At the White House, in 1969, events were transpiring that would reach across the ocean five years later. The image of fair and efficient law enforcement, carefully nurtured since Heydrich, was about to fall away. Eugene Rossides, as Interpol's boss in the Treasury Department, moved up the international ladder to follow in Hoover's footsteps. Elected to serve with Dickopf as a vice-president, Rossides was also busy in the US Treasury giving a job to a young man by the name of G. Gordon Liddy."

Leary's tie to a disgraced agent of the FBI is consistent enough—after his extradition from Switzerland, according to his file, the LSD advocate agreed to inform on the counter-culture for the bureau.

26. See Penny Lernoux, *In Banks We Trust*, New York: Penguin, 1984. Helliwell, the smack-infested CIA attorney, also snatched up 27,000 acres of prime real estate in Florida on behalf of Walt Disney, the site of Disney World.

CHAPTER FOUR
The Death of Cass Elliot
and Other "Restless Youth"

(The late) Mae Brussell, a
mercurial encyclopedia of political research in Carmel,
California, reached some startling conclusions in an unpublished
manuscript entitled "Operation CHAOS":

> By August, 1967, Special Operations Group went after the youth. By
> July, 1968, Operation CHAOS, identical to Chilean "Chaos," went
> after the "restless youth." This wasn't a study. It was an attack.
>
> Mid-summer of 1969, one month before the Manson Family mas-
> sacres, Operation CHAOS went into the most tight security [mode].
> . . . They had perfected enough LSD to cause every violent act or
> symptom associated with the violence in Los Angeles or at Altamont.
>
> It was identical to giving poison candy at Halloween. LSD was the
> moving force, the cause for the Sharon Tate-La Bianca slaughters. It
> was fed at the Spahn Ranch for a steady diet.
>
> July, 1968, explicit orders went out to proceed, accompanied with
> instructions to neutralize segments of our society, including those
> restless youth. By 1969, the SSS, Special Services Staff of the FBI,
> combined with the Justice Department, and with CIA's Operation
> CHAOS.
>
> August, 1969 was the Sharon Tate-La Bianca slaughter.[1]

What Manson called home was a relic of Hollywood's past. The
Spahn Ranch was the backdrop for movies made by Tom Mix, William
S. Hart and John Mack Brown. Parts of Howard Hughes's *The Outlaw*
were shot there. But the ranch had one more claim to historical significance. Next to George Spahn's property stretched the Krupp Ranch,
owned by one of the wealthiest families in Nazi Germany, a ranking
sponsor of Hitler's aggression and its accompanying atrocities. The
chief US prosecutor at the International Court determined that "both
Krupps, Gustav von Bohlen as well as Alfried, are directly responsible.
They led German industry, violating international agreements and
international law. They employed forced labor, dragged and forced
into Germany from almost all countries occupied by Germany. . . .
These workers in Krupp's care and in Krupp's service were under-
nourished and overworked, misused and inhumanely treated." Thousands
in the Krupp-owned concentration camps were worked to death.[2]

The Krupp Ranch has since been transformed into a blooming commercial Bavarian beer garden. Howard Hughes purchased some 500 acres of Krupp-owned land in Nevada after his move to Las Vegas.[3]

Much has been made of Manson's interactions with the Process Church of the Final Judgment in Los Angeles, a religious organization that worshipped a buffet of Jehovah, Lucifer and Satan. "Release the fiend that lies dormant within you" was one Process teaching. "Learn to love fear" was another.

A Process newsletter from London, written by "Soror H" shortly after the Tate-LaBianca murders, celebrated Manson and claimed him as a fellow Process Satanist:

> Manson went astray where others in the PROCESS have succeeded. He was sucked into the whirlpool of Fame and Fortune and when he didn't cut it, he decided to cut it up. . . . He testifies to those areas many of us deny exist. Perhaps the fascination is that he carried out his ideas in action, and showed many of us what it's like to actually commit the crime we'd like to commit. . . .
>
> Manson was clever in his choice of beliefs: the whole Beatles Helter Skelter thing was, of course, a model to instill the PROCESS into his followers, who were more likely to respond to such "turned-on" symbols than the more traditional ones. The whole thing was a scam; a guru trick, but Manson's intention was to open up the occult centres of perception by a unique, pop-based outlook influenced primarily by the PROCESS.[4]

Manson, the aspiring rock artist, and his family of tripping satyrs socialized with established recording artists in Los Angeles. He lived for a year with Beach Boy Dennis Wilson, who would drown in twelve feet of water in 1983. Bobby Beausoleil, convicted for the torture-murder of Gary Hinman, was a devotee of Manson's. The rock group Love, founded by Beausoleil's musical companion Arthur Lee (of the signature multicolored glasses), was not a band of laughing survivors. Since the Manson episode, a curse has dogged their heels. Guitarist Bryan MacLean and bass-player Ken Forssi are dead. Tjay Cantrelli, born John Barberis, a sax player and flutist, is also presumed dead, at least this is the most probable conjecture. Johnny Echols has disappeared and is also thought to be deceased. Michael Stuart, drummer, changed his name to conceal his identity and his whereabouts are unknown. Arthur Lee, convicted in 1995 to 12 years at the Pleasant Valley State Prison in Coalinga, California, for firing a handgun into the air, is fiercely reluctant to discuss the group's past, and so are survivors of Love's many incarnations. But the prison sentence is unreasonably harsh—considering that a fan visiting Lee at his home on Mulholland Drive confessed to firing the pistol himself, and that the fan suffered such remorse over the conviction that he developed a bipolar disorder and was hospitalized. William Cenego, the fan, insists that the forensic test for gun-powder residue on Lee's hand was negative. "I think Arthur had an incredibly unfair trial," Cenego laments. "It's almost not accurate to describe it as a trial."[5]

The death of Dennis Wilson was questioned by Mae Brussell in her weekly "Worldwatcher's International" broadcast on KAZU-FM, Monterey, California, on January 16, 1984:

> There's [an] article in the *San Francisco Chronicle* . . . that said: 'Dennis Wilson was responsible for one of the group's darkest secrets. 'Me and Charlie, we started the Family.'" He said he'd founded the Manson Family. He made a record with Charles Manson. On the 20/20 album, Dennis Wilson is credited as author . . . .
>
> Bill Oster was the fellow who allegedly owned the yacht where he drowned. [Oster:] "He appeared to be clowning [Wilson] when he dove into 12 feet of water. He did not surface after the dive. He poked his hand above and waved. I saw the body slip. I thought he was clowning. I knew he had to come up for air."
>
> The *Los Angeles Herald* said that "His wife called at the boat at 4:30." That would be the exact time he was going under. A woman answered and she was "kind of rude."' She said: "We've got some trouble here" and slammed down the phone. That would be the exact time that he was bubbling and waving and nobody jumped in for him. And at 5:30, one hour later, according to another account, he was picked up.

Two days before the drowning, Wilson had signed into St. John's Hospital to "be clean of alcohol and drugs." A man and a woman visited him. Wilson became agitated and signed out of the unit. He was taken immediately to the boat.

Medical examiners found a gash on the drummer's forehead:

> The coroner said [the gash] "didn't contribute" to his death. He died as a result of "drowning." . . . He has a hit on the head and drowns in 12 feet of water.
>
> Wilson's friends check him out and supplied him with alcohol, and he has a hit on the head and drowns in 12 feet of water. He was buried at sea. This assures that there will be no autopsy after that bang on the head. He's fed to the sharks . . . that's the old Grenada trip they're using. . . . And there's no way now to ever know what caused that bang on his head, or how deep it was. . . .

In Sharon Tate's home there were video movies of military VIPs. I know there were, but who was on those tapes? They belonged to the LAPD. Would Dennis Wilson know who was on those tapes? He was close to that scene.

Ed Sanders notes that Manson met Abigail Folger, the wealthy coffee heiress found dead among the carnage on Cielo Drive, at the home of Mama Cass Elliot.[6]

"Gibby," Maury Terry learned, "had more money than she knew what to do with. She was into finding herself and new directions, and she was always investing in things." She doled out cash to Manson on occasion. Then stopped. "Manson turned against her when she refused to lay out any more bucks for him."

When Manson lived in San Francisco, Folger loaned $10,000 to the Straight Theater at Haight and Cole Streets. Manson then lived on Cole Street, on the same block as the Process Church. On September 21, 1967, the Magick Powerhouse of Oz performed at the Straight in celebration of the "Equinox of the Gods." Bobby Beausoleil was the lead guitarist at this august function.

Folger also funded Timothy Leary, filmmaker Kenneth Anger, and the Process Church of the Final Judgment in the establishment of the "Himalayan Academy," not far from the Esalen Institute. The Leary Lab was chock-a-block with pricey brain-scanning gear, oscilloscopes, and advanced bioelectronic hardware. Manson was a hanger-on at the Himalayan Foundation. In fact, he first encountered the Process there, joined the openly Satanic sect, according to Terry, "and later convened with the group in Mill Valley and at a dwelling in San Anselmo occupied by a well-known personage aligned with the LSD scene. Both cities are in the Bay area."[7]

Folger, a financier of a covert CIA lab, knew another regular of Mama Cass's entourage, Bill Mentzer, currently serving a life term for the murder of fledgling Hollywood producer Roy Radin, a partner in *The Cotton Club*. He never lived to see the movie—Robert Evans, a partner with the deceased in the film and a friend of Henry Kissinger, did.

Mama Cass

The nucleus of this pathological parade, Cass Eliot, nee Ellen Naomi Cohen, born in 1941 and raised in Washington, D.C., was a German baronness by marriage. Her second husband, Baron Donald von Weidenman, a German nobleman, is currently an artist living in New York.

Cass was one of a famed quartet, The Mamas and The Papas, sometimes described as America's first hippies. The quartet formed in New York City in 1963 around songwriter John Phillips. Holly Michelle Gillian Phillips, born in Long Beach, California on June 4, 1945, gave up a modeling career to sing with Phillips and married him in 1962. The Journeymen, as they were then known, also included Scott McKenzie, who would join the surviving Mamas and Papas in 1985.

Cass moved with the group from the East Coast to Los Angeles in 1964, and they were signed by Lou Alder's Dunhill label. The Mamas and Papas split up in 1968. Michelle Phillips set out on a successful acting career, appearing in *Dillinger* and *Valentino*. She was a regular on *Knots Landing*. Michelle married actor Dennis Hopper for eight days in 1970. John Phillips and Dennis Doherty, the Papas, also went solo with mixed success. Cass Elliot, however, launched a highly successful career. She produced seven albums and several singles before her death in 1974.

Cass' beau at the time of her fatal heart attack was Pic Dawson, then under investigation by Scotland Yard for international drug smuggling, and the son of a State Department official under Henry Kissinger.

Cass had recently finished two weeks at the London Palladium. The coroner's report was not conclusive. She "probably choked to death," but there was also "a possibility of heart attack."

In his career biography of Cass Elliot, Jon Johnson published twelve photocopies from her FBI file, released after an FOIA request. The pages are almost entirely obscured by black ink (?). Hoover's Bureau surveilled Cass at the request of Alexander P. Butterfield, a retired Air Force commando and Nixon's chief security advisor.

"She reportedly has associated with drug addicts," the FBI report mentions, "and individuals opposed to the President's Vietnam policy."

One report marked "urgent" and "confidential" states that Cass Elliot attended a fund-raiser in Hollywood attended by Jack Nicholson and Ryan O'Neal, among other celebrities. The event was hosted by the Entertainment Industry for Peace and Justice Committee (EIPJ). The FBI file gossips that "between dates with Henry Kissinger, Marlo Thomas also attended the EIPJ meet with Barry Diller." Tuesday Weld, Burt Lancaster and Jane Fonda, among others, also attended the fund-raiser.

Cass had political ambitions. "I think that I would like to be a senator or something in twenty years," she told Mike Douglas. She attended a variety of Democratic Party functions, participated in a

Madison Square Garden rally sponsored by Rose Kennedy. "I saw in the Democratic Convention in Chicago that there were more people interested in what I was interested in than I believed possible. It made me want to work . . . there would be room in an organized movement of politics for me to voice myself" (Johnson).

Paul Krassner, editor of *The Realist*, a fixture of the "underground" press, suspects Cass was the target of political foul play. "Cass Elliot was a friend," he says. "I believe she may have been killed. She knew an awful lot about the incredible criminal links between Hollywood and Washington and Las Vegas. . . . She was also a friend of Sharon Tate's. On the night Bobby Kennedy was killed, [Cass] had dinner with Sharon and Roman Polanski at the home of film director John Frankenheimer in Malibu Beach."[8]

Pathologists in London refused to specify the cause of death at a public hearing. They did, however, mutter fatuously that she may have "choked" to death. The most-ludicrous-explanation award went to Dr. Keith Simpson, whose autopsy detected a "left-sided heart failure. She plainly had a heart attack." He claimed, to cries of outrage from the medical community, that a section of Elliot's heart muscle had actually "turned to fat." The coronary lapse was attributed to "stress." Johnson:

> The conclusion was termed "improper" by a Vanderbilt University heart specialist immediately after it was made public. "It is true that obesity is related to high blood pressure and stroke, but there's no correlation with a heart attack," disputed Dr. George V. Mann. "He's stating an old-fashioned dogma, a Victorian concept of fatty degeneration that has gone out in modern times. Old time pathologists tend to look at deposits of adipose tissue around the surface of the heart and associate it with a heart attack, but a heart attack is due to limitation of blood supply to the heart muscle with the result that some of the muscle dies."
>
> Whatever the underlying cause, the verdict remained unchanged. She died of a massive heart attack.[9]

Blood tests detected no drugs or alcohol in her system—but then this is the same report that arrived at ersatz "Victorian" conclusions. She took to her grave knowledge of drug trafficking by Pic Dawson, a State Department official's son, and any information that Manson and Mentzer may have shared with her—exactly as Abigail Folger was silenced on Cielo Drive, taking with her any knowledge she may have had of the Himalayan Institute and related federally-sponsored "human guinea-pig farms."

NOTES

1. Mae Brussell: "Operation CHAOS: The CIA's War Against the Sixties Counter-Culture," unpublished ms.
2. State Archives Administration of the German Democratic Republic, *Brown Book: War and Nazi Criminals in West Germany*, East Germany: Verlag Zeit im Bild, 1965, pp. 41–2.
3. Brussell.
4. Soror H., undated *Process* newsletter, London, vol. 2, no. 1, 1970.
5. Sara Scribner, "Love Hurts," *New Times* (Los Angeles weekly), March 11, 1999, pp. 15–21.
6. Maury Terry, *The Ultimate Evil: An Investigation into America's Most Dangerous Satanic Cult*, New York: Dolphin, 1987, pp. 494–95.
7. Ibid., pp. 495–96.
8. Paul Krassner in: Craig Karpel, "The Power of Positive Paranoia," *Oui*, May 1975, p. 111.
9. Jon Johnson, *Make Your Own Kind of Music: A Career Retrospective of Cass Elliot*, Hollywood: Music Archives Press, 1987, pp. 71–72.

CHAPTER FIVE
A Murder in the House of Pooh: Brian Jones

"Merry Old England" is a stubborn non sequitur. The UK is one of the gloomiest places on earth. In the late 1960s the shadow of Big Brother fell on British youth and civil rights activists as ominously as it did in the States. The National Union of Students and the National Council for Civil Liberties, based in London, collected a dossier on police agents who'd approached students to spy on their fellow academics. One of these cases concerned John Bell, former chairman of the Durham University Conservative Association. Bell reported that he'd been visited by a detective who attempted to recruit him to inform on student leftists. Bell rejected the offer and told the leader of a campus Socialist organization about the incident.[1] Another student, Bill Clinton, was also courted by the CIA, while attending Oxford University, and enlisted—by Operation CHAOS, the most sweeping covert program in the history of the Agency—for the same purpose.[2]

Counterintelligence operations in the UK kept pace with those in the States. Robert Lashbrook, a representative of the Human Ecology Fund—the notorious CIA front at Cornell that quietly disbursed grants for mind control experimentation, with or without the consent of the human subjects—was then assigned to the London station. Agents under Lashbrook's supervision slipped LSD to English rock groups before performing without their prior knowledge to "study the drug's effects on their musical abilities."

Before long, some of the most popular rock acts in Britain were scoring the mind control drug directly from Lashbrook's CIA colleagues.[3]

David Schneidermann, the Rolling Stones' LSD supplier for one night, certainly exhibited that air of cloak-and-dagger. Schneidermann, Mick Jagger recalls, was a "sinister" Yank hailing from California, but "he had so many passports no one was certain of his origin." Schneidermannn brought to Keith Richards' hotel room "a suitcase [that] contained every herb and chemical to stab or stroke the mind . . . along with choice LSD from San Francisco. Schneidermann had let believe he was bending the law all over the world. He was on a James Bond thing, the CIA or something."[4]

Singer Marianne Faithfull recalls Schneidermann as "a fantastic" drug peddler. "He was a Californian who dressed in proper suit-and-tie and carried a leather attaché case in which he had almost every kind of drug you could think of, including several types of LSD."[5]

Schneidermann nearly destroyed the Stones with one stroke. On February 11, 1967, the band whiled away the evening recording a four-track rough cut tentatively titled "Blues One." Afterwards, Keith Richards drove to the Mayfair Hotel in a chauffeur-driven Bentley. The remaining Stones and their entourage followed Jagger in a Mini-Cooper "S" to West Sussex, a convoy that included photographer Michael Cooper, Marianne Fathfull, King's Road jet-setter Nick Cramer, and "Acid King" David Schneidermannn. They were met at Keith's hotel room by George and Pattie Harrison.[6]

Bob Dylan and the Who blared on the stereo. "While the party was in full swing," bassist Bill Wyman wrote in his autobiography, "an informant, who had earlier telephoned the *News of the World*, arrived at the newspaper's offices. In that first phone call at about 10 PM, he told a reporter that he had some information about a party some of the Rolling Stones were holding. The informant rejected the paper's suggestion that he should go to the police, saying, 'I want to remain anonymous, but I think the police should know what's going on.'" The informant, Wyman realized, was an insider. "Who else would know that only 'some' of the Stones would be there?"

The newspaper's editor, finding the "insider" credible, phoned police and was referred to the West Sussex narcotics squad.[7]

Marianne Faithfull told historian A.E. Hotchner that the next morning, "Schneidermannn came to our rooms and distributed Sunshine [LSD] to all of us. . . . By afternoon we all began to emerge from our rooms, floating on LSD trips."[8]

THE ROLLING STONES IN 1963.

Wyman wrote that Schneidermann woke the guests "with cups of tea and offered some of them 'white lightning,' a hallucinogenic drug that had the effect of LSD but was slightly less powerful."[10] As Richards recalls it, "we had all taken acid and were in a completely freaked-out state when the police arrived." The television was on with the sound off and the stereo blasting. Keith answered the door, and said, 'Oh, look, there's lots of little ladies and gentlemen outside.'"

Another drug peddler arrived, a mystery man Richards had never met. "He'd come with some other people and was sitting there with a big bag of hash," said Richards. "They even let him go, out of the country." He wasn't what they were looking for.[11]

This was a peculiar enough squad of drug police. For one thing, they weren't in the least concerned with drugs. In fact, the Stones were wanted for their political sympathies and all that anti-establishment wriggling, prancing, sneering and taunting. One of them, guitarist Brian Jones, had gone so far as to publicly criticize establishment war policies: "Nothing destroys culture, art or the simple privilege of having time to think quicker than a war."

"The whole raid was a set-up," Marianne Faithfull insists to the present day. Keith Richards and others who witnessed the bust likewise came to the conclusion that Schneidermann had arranged it: "We also believed information was supplied by the fink, Schneidermannn, who, despite having an attaché case chock-a-block with drugs, was not searched. When a cop asked to see the contents of his case, Schneidermann said it was full of exposed film and couldn't be opened, and the cop let it go at that. Also, Schneidermann mysteriously disappeared that very evening, never to be seen again."

The police got satisfaction from the raid—until it dawned on them that none of the suspects present at Richard's flat actually had drugs on them. Schneidermann was released and boarded a plane for California, taking the evidence with him. "When it came down to it, they couldn't pin anything on us at all," said Richards. "All they could pin on me was allowing people to smoke on my premises. It wasn't my shit. All they could pin on Mick was these four amphetamine tablets [benzedrine, legally prescribed and obtained] that he'd bought in Italy across the counter. It really backfired on them because they didn't get enough on us."[12]

But the arrests of Jagger and Richards did land them before the bench. They were both found guilty and sentenced to prison. A third defendant, art gallery owner Robert Frazier, was also convicted. (It was Frazier, an occultist on the Aleister Crowley path, who introduced Jagger to film-maker Kenneth Anger, an early recruit of Anton LaVey's Church of Satan. Anger received generous grants from the Ford and Rockefeller Foundations to fund his movies. He relocated to England after living for a spell in San Francisco's Haight-Ashbury district, where he co-habitated with convicted murderer Bobby Beausoleil.[13]) When the verdicts were read, Jagger turned pale. He nearly fainted, wept openly in the courtroom. Protests of the sentencings broke out on Fleet Street and at the *News of the World* editorial offices.

Under questioning by Mr. Morris, the Crown's prosecutor, Keith Richards openly discussed the conspiracy. He assumed under questioning that the *News of the World* had arranged the bust, but Schneidermannn was no journalist, and the coordination of phone taps and a full-blown intelligence operation is beyond most newspapers. The busting of Jagger and Richards was an act of political harassment, a coordinated attempt to discredit the Stones. They were spied upon. Richards testified that one night when he stayed with Brian Jones, he noted "a brown furniture van with white side-panels. There was no name on the van. The same night I saw it outside Mick's house. In the same week, I was followed by a green florist's van, which had the same white panels."[14] (After his move to the United States, John Lennon also complained that he was constantly tailed by parties unknown who drove him to a state of "paranoia."[15])

Faithfull recalls hearing "peculiar noises" on Jagger's telephone. She and Jagger also noticed "a blue and white van permanently parked near our house, so we figured we were both being watched and listened in on."

Keith Richards was mystified and annoyed the night he fell asleep and woke up to find that someone had slipped through a newly-installed and very costly security system.[16]

The fusion of music and politics made the Stones enemies of the state. Mick Jagger had watched the anti-war protests at the London Embassy and followed the youth rallies in Paris. While awaiting trial, he told the *Daily Mirror*, "I see a great deal of danger in the air." The fans "are not screaming over pop music anymore, they're screaming for much deeper reasons. We are only serving as a means of giving them an outlet. Teenagers the world over are weary of being pushed around by half-witted politicians who attempt to dominate their way of thinking and set a code for their living. This is a protest against the system. And I see a lot of trouble coming in the dawn."[17] Jagger openly sassed the wigs: "War stems from power-mad politicians and patriots. Some new master plan would end all these mindless men from seats of power and replace them with real people, people of compassion."[18]

The "half-wits" and "mindless men," of course, were not numb to Jagger's venom and replacement was not on their desk calendars.

Ultimately, the convictions of Jagger and Richards were overturned on appeal. The judge declared in each case that "no proper evidence" had been presented by the prosecution to prove possession or even indulgence in drugs.

But Marianne Faithfull looks back at "all that *persecution*, the fact that every time any of us were in a car we were stopped and searched." One evening, "one of many, many busts, the cops very obviously planted something during their search. Mick set the guy up—the detective, whoever he was—to pay him off, and filmed the payoff with a hidden camera." All charges were immediately dropped.[19]

The police had Jagger and Richards, and, Bill Wyman observes, "wanted to bust another one and dispatch the Stones for good." On May 10, the very same evening of the arrests in West Sussex, the doorbell chimed at the Brian Jones home. About a dozen bobbies entered and conducted a 45-minute search of the premises. The detectives turned up one planted vial of "pathetic grass," according to Wyman, a bit of low-grade marijuana to justify an arrest. They also found a small quantity of marijuana resin, and Jones, who confessed to smoking pot in the past, was charged. Like Jagger and Richards, he was convicted the first time around. But within a month of the arrest, his emotional state wavered under the pressure. The possibility of going to prison terrified him and continual police harassment aggravated his fears. Prince Stanislaus Klossowski de Rola, a close friend with Jones on the day of the arrest, explained why the guitarist's behavior was erratic toward the end: "An artist can be hounded into a state in which his mental health will deteriorate and that's what happened to Brian."[20]

But Brian's legal problems were not the entire cause of his decline and fall. A hostile clique, a very odd construction crew hired to restore Brian's home, originally A.A. Milne's cottage, muscled their way into his private life at Cotchford Farm. Brian's friend Nicholas Fitzgerald ran into the rhythm guitarist and founder of the Stones at a pub before he was found at the bottom of his swimming pool. Jones was in a snit over "a bunch hanging out at the farm." For a lark, they'd hidden his motorcycle. When on the phone, the line would sometimes suddenly go dead. "Then when I get the engineers in, they say there's nothing wrong. They're always leaping up to answer the phone and then they tell me it was a wrong number. I just can't trust anybody. I know you think I'm paranoid. Maybe I am, but not about this. I know they're up to something."[21]

Bassist Bill Wyman found the crew "a horrible group of people," and it was largely due to their intimidations that Jones decayed "physically, mentally and musically." [22]

Richards recalled the bullying by Jones' house "guests" after the murder: "Some very weird things happened the night Brian died. We had these [people] working for us, and we tried to find out. Some of them had a weird hold over Brian. I got straight into it and wanted to know who was there and couldn't find out. The only cat I could ask was the one I think who got rid of everybody, and did a whole disappearing thing so that when the cops arrived, it was just an accident. Maybe it was. I don't know. I don't even know who was there that night, and finding out is impossible. It's the same feeling with who killed Kennedy. You can't get to the bottom of it." [23]

Not, that is, until the killer confessed on his death bed. In April, 1994, the UK's *Independent* reported:

MURDER CLAIMS RAISE DOUBT OVER ROLLING STONE'S DEATH
Police are to consider reopening the investigation into the death of former Rolling Stone Brian Jones 25 years ago, after claims in two new books that he was murdered.

The books, to be published this month, conclude that the 27-year-old guitarist was deliberately drowned in the swimming pool of his country mansion by one of his aides. Both name a builder, Frank Thorogood, who died last year, as the man responsible for the killing at the star's home in Cotchford Farm, Sussex, on 2 July 1969.

An inquest recorded a verdict of death by misadventure, assuming that Jones—who was notorious for his rock-star excesses—had drowned because of the drink and drugs he had been consuming in the weeks after he was sacked from the Rolling Stones. . . .

Paint It Black by Geoffrey Guiliano and Terry Rawling's *Who Killed Christopher Robin?* claim to have unearthed fresh evidence about Jones' final hours which proves he was deliberately killed. Mr. Guiliano's book quotes an unnamed associate of Mr. Thorogood's, described as "a husky Cockney," who admits helping him hold Jones's head under the water. [24]

Witnesses have elaborated on Thorogood's death-bed confession, and the story that has emerged completely contradicts press accounts. Nick Fitzgerald now acknowledges that he arrived at the Jones estate shortly after the drowning, walked past the summer house behind the mansion and "saw the full glare of the lights over the pool and in the windows of the house. We had a clear view of the pool." Fitzgerald approached to find three men dressed in sweaters and blue jeans, probably workmen, but the spotlights "blotted out their features and made their faces look like white blobs. At the very moment I became aware of them, the middle one dropped to his knees, reached into the water and pushed down on the top of a head that looked white." Two others, a man and a woman, watched passively. "The kneeling man was pushing down on the head," Fitzgerald told Hotchner, "keeping it under. The man to the right of the kneeling man said something. It sounded like a command." One of the men leaped into the pool and "landed on the back of the struggling swimmer." A third man was "commanded" into the pool to hold Jones down.

From the bushes near Fitzgerald, a "burly man wearing glasses" rushed him. The man pushed Richard Cadbury, a companion, out of the way and grabbed Fitzgerald by the shoulder. He stuck a fist in Fitzgerald's face. "Get the hell out of here, Fitzgerald," the man spat, "or you'll be next."

"He meant it," Fitzgerald reported decades after the fact. He had never seen the Cockney before, yet somehow the brute knew his name. Shaking, he stumbled to his car and Richard floored it away from the murder scene. They were too terrified to go to the police. "Brian was dead. I couldn't rectify that and I might be putting my own life in danger. So I let it pass, but that scene hasn't passed from my mind and even to this day it troubles me very much."[25]

Who authorized the clean-up after the murder? Fitzgerald attempted to contact Cadbury the day after Jones died. He was told that Cadbury had picked up and moved, leaving no forwarding address. A pair of other witnesses, Anna Wohlin and Linda Lawrence, received instructions to leave the country immediately.[26]

Wohlin was visiting Cotchford Farms at the time of death and was instructed to alter her testimony. She writes in *The Murder of Brian Jones* (1999) that Frank warned her: "Just think about what you say to the police. The only thing you need to tell them is that Brian had been drinking and that his drowning was an accident. You don't have to tell them anything else. 'I left Brian to go to the kitchen and light a cigarette and I don't know any more than you.' But there's no need for you to tell the police that you saw me in the kitchen. Just tell them we pulled Brian out of the pool together." Wohlin recalls, "Frank was worried, and I knew he had every reason to be. But I was scared, too. I didn't want to end up like Brian, so I did what Frank had told me to do. I didn't dare challenge fate. Frank lied during the interview. Janet's recollections seemed confused. And I concealed the truth. . . . I know I let Brian down. I'm still ashamed of withholding information, but I was scared of reprisals."

The coroner ruled that Jones was felled by "misadventure." In Merry Old England legalese, this means "accidental death not due to crime or negligence," a spurious judgment at best. The word "murder" did not appear in the report, and he laid blame on the victim with emphasis on liver deterioration brought on by chronic narcotics and alcohol abuse.

The death of Brian Jones has since been universally laughed off, attributed to drug use, when in fact he was completely off drugs, with the exception of ale and wine, for several weeks prior to his drowning. It is evident that he was drugged the evening of his murder, suggesting premeditation, planning. Eyewitnesses reported that he drank a couple of brandies before taking a swim. But Jones biographer Laura Jackson was shocked to discover in the bio-chemist's analysis "far and away the most disturbing truth relating to Brian's death": Jones was "subjected to thin-layer chromotography, a technique designed minutely to separate and analyse the body's components, and which failed to reveal the presence of any amphetamine, methedrine, morphine, methadone, or isoprenaline. What it did reveal, however, is far more alarming: two dense spots, one yellow-orange in color and one purple which were not able to be identified. Brian's urine revealed an amphetamine-like—not amphetamine, and the distinction is important—substance 1720 mgs per cent, nearly nine times the normal level."

The tell-tale signs of a cover-up by authorities are unmistakable. The bottle of brandy that Jones drank from was confiscated by PC Albert Evans "for analysis," and was never seen again. No lab report on the wine appeared in court papers.[27] Any probes into the drowning of Brian Jones were relegated to the Sussex Criminal Investigations Division (CID). The CID had the option of referring the case to the Director of Public Prosecutions—instead, the division chose to monopolize the investigation, in the end claiming there was "no evidence" to warrant prosecution, although at least one senior investigator protested this decision. East Sussex coroner David Wadman suggested falsely that the Home Office and police had thoroughly investigated the drowning. "I am bound to say that I think it is extremely unlikely that you'll obtain any further information," he insisted. But a Home Office spokesman subsequently rejected the claim that an investigation had been conducted at all, admitting flatly, "We do not have any information touching Mr. Jones' death."[28]

A.E. Hotchner found that the death is still, some thirty years later, a sensitive subject in some quarters. While living in London, Electra May, his editorial assistant, scheduled an interview with Justin de

Villeneuve, the mentor of Twiggy, the doe-eyed celebrity model of the 1960s. Two days before the de Villeneuve (his real name was Nigel Davies) interview, Hotchner took a train to Eastbourne to meet with the coroner, Mr. E.N. Grace, "who kindly provided me with all the police and medical reports relative to Brian's death, and a transcript of the inquest. A few days later, Electra phoned de Villeneuve to confirm the interview for that day. 'There is no interview,' de Villeneuve's assistant said." Electra asked why he had chosen to cancel. "Because Hotchner has been to see the coroner, hasn't he? We didn't know he was opening that can of worms. That's why." Hotchner's secretary was unnerved by this response, he notes, since "she thought she was the only person who knew about my meeting with Coroner Grace." [29]

Who sent the lorries to the estate to cart off Brian's possessions, the same sort of looting that followed the death of Jimi Hendrix, Bob Marley, and other star-crossed musicians? After the funeral at St. Mary's Church, the workmen who killed Jones repaired directly to his mansion, girlfriends in tow. An estate worker said, "They drank, laughed and joked crudely and cavorted about. They even took their women to Brian's bed. It really turned me over. I was out in the grounds and they hadn't even bothered to close the curtains. You just couldn't help but see them in there, in Brian's bed. It was utterly appalling." Jones' belongings, with the exception of a couple of his most valued musical instruments, were systematically loaded into vans lined up in front of the house. Shortly thereafter, a bonfire was set in the garden. "A group of men were burning an enormous amount of stuff. I know, because I had a very nice little Bible and they'd flung that on, too," said a gardener. "They were burning Brian's things—his clothes, shirts and what have you. I don't know on whose sayso, but they cleared no end of stuff out of his house and burned the lot." [30]

Jones was buried at Cheltenham Cemetary two days after the murder. In 1980, *Rolling Stone* staked an epitaph to the life of Lewis Brian Hopkin-Jones: "Jones played rhythm guitar for the group since its inception in 1962, but his contribution was more spiritual than musical. His flamboyant appearance and notorious lifestyle—which included fathering two illegitimate children by the time he was sixteen—set the tone for the band's image." Rock critic Greil Marcus likewise found the essence of the band in him: "What the Stones as a group sang about . . . Jones did." [31]

But the account of his death left by police and the media industry is a fiction, because he was off drugs completely at the time. His death was not an accident caused by a life of abuse. He was murdered.

NOTES

1. "Random Notes," *Rolling Stone*, no. 38, July 26, 1969, p. 4.
2. Ambrose Evans-Pritchard, "Student Bill Clinton 'Spied' on Americans abroad for CIA," *London Telegraph*, June 3, 1996. Also see, Roger Morris in *Partners in Power* (1996). Among the first to publicly note the relationship of Clinton with the CIA was Gene Wheaton, formerly an NSC con-tractee and a Christic Institute investigator, in radio interviews following the first Clinton inaugural. On June 10 1996, the *Telegraph* reported, "in the late 1960s, Mr Clinton worked as a source for the Central Intelligence Agency. . . . He was certainly no dangerous radical. 'No attack by his reactionary opponents would be more undeserved than the charge that young Bill Clinton was 'radical,' concludes [Roger] Morris. . . . The bearded, disheveled Rhodes scholar was recruited by the CIA while at Oxford—along with several other young Americans with political aspirations—to keep tabs on fellow students involved in protest activi-ties against the Vietnam War. Morris says that the young Clinton indulged in some low-level spying in Norway in 1969, visiting the Oslo Peace Institute and submitting a CIA informant's report on American peace activists who had taken refuge in Scandinavia to avoid the draft. 'An officer in the CIA station in Stockholm confirmed that,' said Morris. The Washington Establishment would like to dismiss this troubling book as the work of a fevered conspiracy theorist. But Morris is no light-weight. He worked at the White House in both the Johnson and Nixon administrations, resigning from the National Security Council in 1970 in protest over the US invasion of Cambodia. He went on to become an acclaimed biographer of Richard Nixon."
3. A.E. Hotchner, *Blown Away: A No-Holds-Barred Portrait of the Rolling Stones and the Sixties Told by the Voices of the Generation*, New York: Fireside, 1990, pp. 218–19.
4. Mae Brussell, "Operation CHAOS," unpublished ms.
5. A.E. Hotchner, p. 232.
6. Bill Wyman with Bill Coleman, *Stone Alone*, New York: Viking, 1990, pp. 404–5.
7. Ibid.
8. Hotchner, pp. 232–33.
9. Wyman.
11. Hotchner, p. 233.
12. Hotchner, p. 234.
13. See Bill Landis, *Anger: The Unauthorized Biography of Kenneth Anger*, New York: Harper Collins, 1995.
14. Wyman, pp. 437–38.
15. Pete Hamill, "Long Night's Journey Into Day: A Conversation with John Lennon," *Rolling Stone*, no. 188, June 5, 1975, p. 73. Lennon: "I went on the Dick Cavett show and said they were followin' me. . . . [And] when they were followin' me, they wanted me to see when they were followin' me."
16. Landis, p. 167.
17. Davin Seay, *Mick Jagger: The Story Behind the Rolling Stone*, New York: Birch Lane, 1993, p. 98.
18. Hotchner, pp. 231–32.
19. Brussell.
20. Wyman.

21. Hotchner, p. 296. Psychological pressure of this sort put Jones in a hyper-vigilant state, tactics common in mind control operations. The Manson Family attempted to bully and cajole Los Angeles studio musician Terry Melcher and Dennis Wilson of the Beach Boys into forking over "travel expenses." The shakedown of guitarist Gary Hinman ended in his murder by torture. Brian Jones was also murdered after an argument over money with Thorogood. Jones had been stalked by the workmen for months. The psychological intimidations led, according to Jones' friend Robert Hattrell, to "odd mental behavior, paranoiac, afraid there were people after him, out to get him."
22. Wyman, p. 428.
23. Brussell.
24. "Murder Claims Raise Doubt over Rolling Stone's Death," *Independent*, April 4, 1994, p. 2.
25. Hotchner, pp. 297–99.
26. Laura Jackson, *Golden Stone: The Untold Life and Tragic Death of Brian Jones*, New York: St. Martin's, 1992, p. 217.
27. R. Gary Patterson, *Hellhounds on Their Trail: Tales from the Rock 'n' Roll Graveyard*, Nashville, Tennessee: Dowling Press, 1998, pp. 202–3.
28. Jackson, pp. 225–26.
29. Hotchner, p. 299.
30. Jackson, pp. 224–25.
31. Burk Uzzle, "Rock & Roll Heaven," *Rolling Stone*, June 12, 1980, p. 45.

CHAPTER SIX
Portraits in Carnage:
The End of the Rock Festivals

Five months after the drowning death of Brian Jones, a music festival held near San Francisco turned murderous, smothering Aquarius and its political anthems with a handful of apocalyptic screen images, "restless youth" seemingly devouring itself. The Rolling Stones were the centerpiece of the hellish fiasco at Altamont on December 6, 1969. The band would forevermore be tainted by the surreal violence of *Gimme Shelter*, the documentary film that chronicled the disaster, and so would the counterculture the Stones had done much to inspire.

The festival was conceived in the first place to redeem the group's flagging image. The press had laid into Jagger and crew, emphasizing their greed. "The stories of the Stones' avarice spread," journalist Robert Sam Anson reported, and critics pointed to Mick's $250,000 townhouse, the collection of glittering Rolls Royces, "and [they] wondered how revolutionary 'a man of wealth and taste' could be. A token free appearance would still those critics. The concert, problems and all, was going to happen. For the Stones' sake, it had to."

The group's management set out to select a site for the event. They consulted Jan Wenner, the editor of *Rolling Stone*, who sent them to several professional concert promoters, and they in turn put them in touch with famed San Francisco attorney Melvin Belli, fixture of California's well-heeled "conservative" power base.

This was the first Big Mistake. Belli was summed up at his funeral in July, 1996 by Bishop William Swing, in a eulogy stitched with irony in the context of Operation CHAOS, at Grace Cathedral. Over the infamous attorney's pale cadaver, the Bishop bid farewell to Belli.

A man of law against the chaos of life,
A man of chaos against the laws of life.[1]

A cartoon that appeared after Belli's death in the *San Diego Union Tribune* was an eloquent expression of his ethical standards.

It depicted St. Peter on the telephone, reporting, "I've got a guy here claiming he was struck and injured by one of the Pearly Gates," and there, smiling like an angel, stood a well-groomed soul identified by the nametag on his briefcase: "M. Belli."[2] The *San Francisco Chronicle* bid him farewell with a letter to the editor that appeared on the Op-Ed page: "Melvin Belli helped establish the principles of the plaintiff attorney: avarice, immunity to logic, self-aggrandizement and perfect contempt for the interests of society."[3]

He was not only an ambulance chaser par excellence. The legendary Melvin Belli was one of the CIA's most trusted courtroom wonders until hypertension and cardiovascular disease claimed him on July 9, 1996. His client roster included Jack Ruby, Sirhan Sirhan, Martha Mitchell and Jim Bakker. His first high-profile client was Errol Flynn, who, according to thousands of FBI and military intelligence documents released under FOIA to biographer Charles Higham, was an avid admirer of Adolf Hitler, recruited by Dr. Hermann Friedrich Erben, an Abwher intelligence agent, to spy on the United States. The FBI, Higham discovered in the midst of poring through the many boxes of FOIA documents dropped on his doorstep, pestered Flynn and the studio employing him over his wartime association with a Nazi, "but there was little doubt that Will Hays and Colonel William Guthrie, a high-ranking Army officer on the studio payroll as Jack Warner's troubleshoot in all matters connected with politics, were responsible for the cover-up. . . . Hays and Guthrie managed to smother the numerous inquiries that began seriously to threaten Errol's career."[4] Melvin Belli, Flynn's attorney, could also be counted on to button his lip, and he did repeatedly as a CIA-Mafia legal counsel in a number of assassination cover-ups.[5]

It was Melvin Belli who chose the speedway at Altamont for the festival. "As a staging ground for a rock concert," Anson concluded, "especially one expected to draw 300,000 people or more, Altamont could hardly have been worse. The raceway, which was on the brink of bankruptcy, was small, cramped, and difficult to reach. Its acres were littered with the rusting hulks of junked automobiles and thousands of shards of broken glass. In appearance, it had all the charm of a graveyard. Worst of all, though, the deal for its use had not been sealed until the final moment. Whereas Woodstock had taken months to prepare, Altamont had to be ready within twenty-four hours."[6]

The second Big Mistake of Altamont was the hiring of Ralph "Sonny" Barger and a contingent of Hell's Angels to keep the peace.

Barger, it has since been divulged, was an informant and hit man on the payroll of the Department of Alcohol, Tobacco and Firearms

(ATF). When Black Panther Eldridge Cleaver fled the country for Algeria, the ATF negotiated with Barger to "bring Cleaver home in a box." He often made deals with law enforcement in exchange for dismissal of charges against fellow Angels. Barger was even hired by federal agents to kill immigrant farm labor activist Cesar Chavez, and may well have if Barger hadn't first been arrested by police in the Bay area on a prior homicide charge.[7]

The accusation arose in the death of Servio Winston Agero, a drug dealer. In a surprise courtroom maneuver, Sonny took the witness stand and confessed to his arrangement with local police and federal agents. Over a period of several years, he testified, he had brokered deals with Oakland authorities to give up the location of hidden cachés of automatic weapons, mortars and dynamite in exchange for the dismissal of all charges against members of his motorcycle gang. This was a deal he had brokered with Edward Hilliard, then a sergeant at the Oakland Police Department's vice squad. Hilliard refused to comment when questioned by reporters. The defendant admitted for the record that he sold narcotics for a living, forged IDs, and slept with a pistol under his pillow. On seven occasions, though, Barger refused to respond to questioning and was fined $3,500 by Judge William J. Hayes for each demurral.

Deputy prosecutor Donald Whyte asked the "spiritual" leader of the Hell's Angels, an admitted federal operative, to name officers who asked him to "kill someone." Barger squirmed and claimed that he could not recall, exactly, but attempted several phonetic variations of a possible name.[8] Even in the courtroom, it seems, he was not about to risk retaliation by government contacts.

But the deal was exposed anyway by ATF whistle-blower Larry Shears. The agent told his story to narcotics agents, and they gathered evidence on the murder plan before talking to the press. Shears announced that Barger had been contracted to kill Chavez, an assassination ordered by agribusiness magnates in the San Joaquin Valley. Chavez was only alive, Shears reported, because there had been delays. The first came when ATF agents insisted that certain files first be stolen from the farm union. The arson of union offices was attempted by hired hands, another delay. Confirmation of these allegations came three weeks later when union officials complained to reporters that there had been recent "arson attempts against [farm] union offices. Others have been riddled with bullet holes, and on at least two occasions attempts were made to steal records in the union offices."

The next glitch in the Chavez assassination, Shears said, came when the hit man, Sonny Barger, was arrested for the Agero murder.

To support his statements, Shears waved a federal voucher at reporters signed by Senator Edward Kennedy, a payment of $10,000 to Shears for services rendered as an informant to narcotics agents and the IRS.[9]

In March 1989, according to wire releases, Sonny Barger was convicted with four other Angels for conspiracy to violate federal firearms and explosives laws in a variety of plots to kill members of rival motorcycle clubs. Barger and Michael Vincent O'Farrell were sentenced in US District Court, Louisville, Kentucky, for their part in the transport of explosives with intent to kill. Barger and three others were slapped with additional counts for "dealing with a stolen government manual." Barger was freed on parole three years later. The mystery of his early release was dispelled by the *Tucson Weekly* in 1996—it seems Barger had a political guardian: "You can talk about the biker tradition," a law enforcement source explained, "the Harley, the patch that they've killed for, but in the end, what's most important is money. Hell's Angels is represented in 18 countries now. They're probably the largest organized crime family that we export from the US. At the center of this global expansion is Oakland-based International President "Sonny" Barger, who's had his hand on the throttle of Hells Angels' money and mayhem machine since the late '50s, despite occasional prison stints. When Barger was released from prison in 1992, an estimated 3,000 people attended his party. . . . Some influential people might get bought. I can't tell you that Colorado Senator Ben Nighthorse Campbell received any money. . . . I do know that he used his influence to try to get Sonny Barger out of prison."[10]

Barger's booze-swaggling, two-wheeling entourage were paid killers. And since the carnage at Altamont, the Hell's Angels have twice attempted to *kill* the Rolling Stones. In March, 1983, a witness calling himself "Butch," his true identity protected by the federal witness program, testified before a Senate Judiciary Committee about plots to kill the Stones. "There's always been a contract on the band," he admitted under questioning. There were "two attempts to kill them that I know about. They will some day. They swear they will do it." The vendetta, Butch said, originated with the killing at the Speedway concert, and was motivated by the failure of the Stones to back the Angel prosecuted for the killing. The first attempt to assassinate the entire band took place in the mid-'70s. "They sent a member with a gun and a silencer" to a hotel where the Stones were staying. The hit-man "staked out the hotel, but [the Stones] never showed up," said the government informant. And in 1979, the Angels' New York chapter "were going to put a bomb in the house and blow everybody up and kill everybody at the party." But this conspiracy sank with a caché of plastic explosives, accidentally dropped overboard from a rubber raft. Killing the Stones, he testified, was an "obsession" with the bike gang.[11]

Who in 1969 suspected that the Hell's Angel was in reality a death squad leader in the pay of "conservative" political operatives? The swastika tattoos and gothic jewelry? Window dressing. The roughing up of peace demonstrators? The shootouts? The terrorizing of small towns? The rapings? The drugs? A refreshing break from the status quo.

A supplier from Berkeley donated 1,000 hits of LSD laced with speed to Barger's Altamont security force, and the Angels toted along several cases of red wine and a generous supply of barbiturates. The concert commenced at 1 PM with a set by Santana, and before long the beatings began. By the time Santana ripped to a close, the first casualties limped into the first aid station. There were broken arms, open wounds, shattered jaws and ribs, and bad LSD trips that left joy-seekers screaming in terror. There were so many of these that the Thorazine caché ran dry within a few hours, leaving the overdosed untreated.[12]

The Jefferson Airplane played songs about social unity and revolution and a flung beer bottle fractured a woman's skull. She reeled, fell, stood and collapsed again.

Jagger arrived in a helicopter. Anson writes: "Kids got up, yelled, and started running, bursting past the Angels to get close to him. Jagger emerged, smiling, waving, calling greetings, with Timothy Leary at his side flashing the peace symbol."[13]

Jagger hurried to the safety of his trailer. The Angels resumed beating concert-goers. A photographer was told to stop shooting the violence and give up the film. He refused and an Angel smashed him in the face with his camera.

Crosby, Stills and Nash preceded the Stones, but the escalating violence forced them to cut their set short. The Stones would not play until the sun went down and delayed their appearance some 90 minutes, aggravating the macabre tension of the event. The Angels, riding on electric currents of methamphetamine and lysergic acid, bludgeoned the audience with lead-filled pool cues. At long last, Jagger strutted across the stage, sporting a red, white and blue stovepipe hat, silver pants, black boots, an Omega symbol emblazoned on his chest.

The Rolling Stones packaged the occult education they had received from Satanist Kenneth Anger. "The top hat," explains Anger biographer Bill Landis, "was snatched from the legend of [Bobby]

Beausoleil," the Mansonite killer of L.A. guitarist Gary Hinman. "The Crowleyan personal power tripping" was amplified by "pop iconography and massive amounts of cocaine to fuel Jagger's attempt at incarnating Lucifer."[14]

The Stones managed to lumber through "Jumpin' Jack Flash" and "Carol," but "Sympathy for the Devil" was accompanied by howls from the crowd directly in front of the stage. Jagger urged the audience repeatedly to "cool down, cool down, now. . . ." Another outbreak accompanied "Under My Thumb." The source of the commotion was the stabbing death of Meredith Hunter, 18, who pulled a gun and reportedly took aim at Jagger.

"As Mick peered out," Ben Fong-Torres recalls, "there were kids staring at him in incredulous silence, mouthing the word, 'Why?'"

After the concert, reports Anson, "there was a mysterious shakeup in the Angel hierarchy, and the suicide of one Angel who had been particularly close to the rock scene." Alan David Passaro, 24, one of Barger's soldiers and an ex-convict, was charged with Hunter's murder. But Barger himself was unapologetic. "I'm no peace creep by any sense of the word. Ain't nobody gonna kick my motorcycle."[15] Passaro, already serving a prison sentence on an unrelated offense when served, was eventually acquitted on grounds of self-defense.

A platoon of cinematographers was assembled by directors Albert and David Maysles to shoot *Gimme Shelter*, the Altamont documentary. They were directed to concentrate on the violence, not the performances on stage. A recent *TV Guide* review of the the video complains that the crew "focused resolutely on the mayhem and discord."[16]

"Sympathy for the Devil" was the last-gasp anthem of the festival scene in America. A repeat of the disaster was visited upon Louisiana a few months later, when an excess of 50,000 young people turned out for a "Celebration of Life" on the Atchafalaya River. The Galloping Gooses motorcycle club, hired to attend to security, chain-whipped the celebrants, leaving three dead and many wounded.[17]

A cancer was growing on the counter-culture.

NOTES

1. Herb Caen, "Above and Beyond," *San Francisco Chronicle*, July 24, 1996, p. B-1.
2. Ibid.
3. Letter to the editor, *San Francisco Chronicle*, July 19, 1996, p. A-16.

4. Charles Higham, *Errol Flynn: The Untold Story*, New York: Doubleday, 1980, pp. 91–92. Background on Higham and the government documents released to him come from author's interviews of Higham.

5. San Francisco columnist Herb Caen reminisced about Belli's bosom friendship with the screen idol, both of whom had a keen interest in teenage girls: "When he and his close friend and client, Errol Flynn, were out on the town, no young lady was safe. Two Rogue Scholars on the loose, both exceedingly handsome and dangerous to know too well. Every time I saw Mel on the make I thought of Dorothy Parker's line about the girl who lost her virginity sliding down a barrister. One night at Cal-Neva, the Tahoe gambling joint with the California-Nevada state line running through the lobby, I saw Mel crossing that line with a very young girl. Referring to the then-statute against crossing a state line with a minor for immoral purposes, I asked him 'Does she know about the Mann Act?' 'Know about it?' he whooped. 'She loves it!'" Herb Caen, "Friday's Fractured Flicker," *San Francisco Chronicle*, July 12, 1996, p. C-1.

   For background on Melvin Belli's interaction with the Central Intelligence Agency and the Mafia, see: Constantine, A., *Psychic Dictatorship in the U.S.A.*, 1995, p. 191; Diamond, S., *Spiritual Warfare*, 1989, p. 30; Hinckle, W., *If You Have a Lemon, Make Lemonade*, 1990, p. 200; Johnson, R.W., *Shootdown*, 1987, pp. 377–8, 394–5; Kantor, S.,*The Ruby Cover-up*, 1992, pp. 224–35, 415–6; Marrs, J., *Crossfire*, 1990, pp. 414, 424; Piper, M.C., *Final Judgment*, 1993, pp. 161, 172–5; Ragano, F. Raab, S., *Mob Lawyer*, 1994, pp. 241–8, 360, Scheim, D., *Contract on America*, 1988, p. 154, Scott, P.D., *Deep Politics*, 1993, p. 233.

6. Robert Sam Anson, *Gone Crazy and Back Again*, New York: Doubleday, 1981, p. 141.

7. Account of Larry Shears, ATF agent, alleging that Barger was recruited by ATF agents—at a time when G. Gordon Liddy worked for the ATF, a division of the Treasury Department—to assassinate Eldridge Cleaver: December 17, 1971 news broadcast, Channel 23, Los Angeles, CA.

8. Drew McKillips, "Amazing Story by Hells' Angels Chief," *San Francisco Chronicle*, December 12, 1972, p. 1.

9. "ATF Agent Says He Was Part of Coast Plot to Kill Cesar Chavez," *New York Times*, January 2, 1972, p. 31).

10. Karen Brandel, "Angels In Arizona," *Tucson Weekly*, Aug. 15, 1996, p. 1.

11. Hotchner, p. 320.

12. Anson, p. 148.

13. Anson, p. 149.

14. Bill Landis, *Anger: The Unauthorized Biography of Kenneth Anger*, New York: Harper Collins, 1995, p. 177. It is ironic that with *Scorpio Rising* (1964), Anger the satanist had launched the popular mythos surrounding the Hell's Angels. Anger's cultural oddity, Landis writes, "made them seem more lyrical after all the media reports on gang rapes, chain whipping and stomping they were doing." (pp. 118–19).

15. Anson, pp. 156–57.

16. "Gimme Shelter, 1970," *TV Guide* Movie Database, Internet posting.

17. David P. Szatmary, *Rockin' in Time: A Social History of Rock and Roll*, New Jersey: Prentice-Hall, 1987, p. 149.

CHAPTER SEVEN
I Don't Live Today:
The Jimi Hendrix Political Harassment, Kidnap and Murder Experience

I DON'T BELIEVE FOR ONE MINUTE THAT HE KILLED HIMSELF. THAT WAS OUT OF THE QUESTION. **CHAS CHANDLER, HENDRIX PRODUCER**

I BELIEVE THE CIRCUMSTANCES SURROUNDING HIS DEATH ARE SUSPICIOUS AND I THINK HE WAS MURDERED. **ED CHALPIN, PROPRIETOR OF STUDIO 76**

I FEEL HE WAS MURDERED, FRANKLY. SOMEBODY GAVE HIM SOMETHING. SOMEBODY GAVE HIM SOMETHING THEY SHOULDN'T HAVE. **JOHN MCLAUGHLIN, GUITARIST, MAHAVISHNU ORCHESTRA**

HE DIDN'T DIE FROM A DRUG OVERDOSE. HE WAS NOT AN OUT-OF-CONTROL DOPE FIEND. JIMI HENDRIX WAS NOT A JUNKIE. AND ANYONE WHO WOULD USE HIS DEATH AS A WARNING TO STAY AWAY FROM DRUGS SHOULD WARN PEOPLE AGAINST THE OTHER THINGS THAT KILLED JIMI—THE STRESSES OF DEALING WITH THE MUSIC INDUSTRY, THE CRAZINESS OF BEING ON THE ROAD, AND ESPECIALLY, THE DANGERS OF INVOLVING ONESELF IN A RADICAL, OR EVEN UNPOPULAR, POLITICAL MOVEMENTS.

COINTELPRO WAS OUT TO DO MORE THAN PREVENT A COMMUNIST MENACE FROM OVERTAKING THE UNITED STATES, OR KEEP THE BLACK POWER MOVEMENT FROM BURNING DOWN CITIES. COINTELPRO WAS OUT TO OBLITERATE ITS OPPOSITION AND RUIN THE REPUTATIONS OF THE PEOPLE INVOLVED IN THE ANTIWAR MOVEMENT, THE CIVIL RIGHTS MOVEMENT, AND THE ROCK REVOLUTION. WHENEVER JIMI HENDRIX'S DEATH IS BLAMED ON DRUGS, IT ACCOMPLISHES THE GOALS OF THE FBI'S PROGRAM. IT NOT ONLY SLANDERS JIMI'S PERSONAL AND PROFESSIONAL REPUTATION, BUT THE ENTIRE ROCK REVOLUTION IN THE 1960S. **JOHN HOLMSTROM, "WHO KILLED JIMI?"** [1]

As the music of youth and resistance fell under the cross-hairs of the CHAOS war, it is not unthinkable that Jimi Hendrix—the tripping, peacenik "Black Elvis" of the '60s—found himself a target.

Agents of the pathologically nationalistic FBI opened a file on Hendrix in 1969 after his appearance at several benefits for "subversive" causes. His most cutting insult to the state was participation in a concert for Jerry Rubin, Abbie Hoffman, Tom Hayden, Bobby Seale and the other defendants of the Chicago Seven conspiracy trial.[2] "[We have to] get the Black Panthers not to kill anybody," he told a reporter for a teen magazine, "but to scare [federal officials]. . . . I know it sounds like war, but that's what's gonna have to happen. It has to be a war. . . . You come back to reality and there are some evil folks around and they want you to be passive and weak and peaceful so that they can just overtake you like jelly on bread. . . . You have to fight fire with fire."[3]

On tour in Liesburg, Sweden, Hendrix was interviewed by Tommy Rander, a reporter for the *Gotesborgs-Tidningen*. "In the USA, you have to decide which side you're on," Hendrix explained. "You are either a rebel or like Frank Sinatra."[4]

In 1979, college students at the campus newspaper of Santa Barbara University (USB) filed for release of FBI files on Hendrix. Six heavily inked-out pages were released to the student reporters. (The deletions nixed information "currently and properly classified pursuant to Executive Order 11652, in the interest of national defense of foreign policy.") On appeal, seven more pages were reluctantly turned over to the USB students. The file revealed that Hendrix had been placed on the federal "Security Index," a list of "subversives" to be rounded up and placed in detainment camps in the event of a national emergency.

If the intelligence agencies had their reasons to keep tabs on Hendrix, they couldn't have picked a better man for the job than Hendrix's manager, Mike Jeffrey. Jeffrey, by his own admission an intelligence agent,[5] was born in South London in 1933, the sole child of postal workers. He completed his education in 1949, took a job as a clerk for Mobil Oil, was drafted to the National Service two years later. Jeffrey's scores in science took him to the Educational Corps. He signed on as a professional soldier, joined the Intelligence Corps, and at this point his career enters an obscure phase.

JIMI HENDRIX

Hendix biographers Shapiro and Glebeek report that Jeffrey often boasted of "undercover work against the Russians, of murder, mayhem and torture in foreign cities. . . . His father says Mike rarely spoke about what he did—itself perhaps indicative of the sensitive nature of his work—but confirms that much of Mike's military career was spent in 'civvies,' that he was stationed in Egypt and that he could speak Russian." [6]

There was, however, another, equally intriguing side of Mike Jeffrey. He frequently hinted that he had powerful underworld connections. It was common knowledge that he had had an abiding professional relationship with Steve Weiss, the attorney for both the Hendrix Experience and the Mafia-managed Vanilla Fudge, hailing from the law firm of Seingarten, Wedeen & Weiss. On one occasion, when drummer Mitch Mitchell found himself in a fix with police over a boat he'd rented and wrecked, mobsters from the Fudge management office intervened and pried him loose. [7]

Organized crime has had fingers in the recording industry since the jukebox wars. Mafioso Michael Franzene testified in open court in the late 1980s that "Sonny" Franzene, his stepfather, was a silent investor in Buddah Records. [8] At this industry oddity, the inane, nasal, apolitical 1960s "bubblegum" song was blown from the goo of adolescent mating fantasies. The most popular of Buddah's acts were the 1910 Fruitgum Company and Ohio Express. These bands shared a lead singer, Joey Levine. Some cultural contributions from the Buddha label: "Yummy, Yummy, Yummy," "Simon Says," and "1-2-3 Red Light."

In 1971, Buddha Records' Bobby Bloom was killed in a shooting sometimes described as "accidental," sometimes "suicide," at the age of 28. Bloom made a number of solo records, including "Love Don't Let Me Down," and "Count On Me." He formed a partnership with composer Jeff Barry and they wrote songs for the Monkees in their late period. Bloom made the Top 10 with the effervescent "Montego Bay" in 1970. Other Mafia-managed acts of the late 1960s were equally apolitical: Vanilla Fudge ("You Keep Me Hangin' On," "Bang, Bang"), [9] or Motown's Gladys Knight and the Pips. [10] In the '60s and beyond, organized crime wrenched unto itself control of industry workers via the Teamster's Union. Trucking was Mob controlled. So were stadium concessions. No rock bands toured unless money exchanged hands to see that a band's instruments weren't delivered to the wrong airport. [11]

Intelligence agent or representative of the mob? Whether Jeffrey was either or both—and the evidence is clear that a CIA/Mafia combination has exercised considerable influence in the music industry for decades—at a certain point, Hendrix must have seen something that made him desperately want out of his management contract with Jeffrey.

Monika Dannemann, Hendrix's fiancé at the time of his death, describes Mike Jeffrey's control tactics, his attempts to isolate and manipulate Hendrix, with observations of his evolving awareness that Jeffrey was a covert operator bent on dominating his life and mind:

> Jimi felt more and more unsafe in New York, the city where he used to feel so much at home. It had begun to serve as a prison to him, and a place where he had to watch his back all the time.
>
> In May 1969 Jimi was arrested at Toronto for possession of drugs. He later told me he believed Jeffrey had used a third person to plant the drugs on him—as a warning, to teach him a lesson.
>
> Jeffrey had realized not only that Jimi was looking for ways of breaking out of their contract, but also that Jimi might have calculated that the Toronto arrest would be an easy way to silence Jimi. . . . Jeffrey did not like Jimi to have friends who would put ideas in his head and give him strength. He preferred Jimi to be more isolated, or to mix with certain people whom Jeffrey could use to influence and try to manipulate him.
>
> So in New York, Jimi felt at times that he was under surveillance, and others around him noticed the same. He tried desperately to get out of his management contract, and asked several people for advice on the best way to do it. Jimi started to understand the people around him could not be trusted, as things he had told them in confidence now filtered through to Jeffrey. Obviously some people informed his manager of Jimi's plans, possibly having been bought or promised advantages by Jeffrey. Jimi had always been a trusting and open person, but now he had reason to become suspicious of people he didn't know well, becoming quite secretive and keeping very much to himself.[12]

Five years after the death of the virtuoso, *Crawdaddy* reported that friends of Hendrix felt "he was very unhappy and confused before his death. Buddy Miles recalled numerous times he complained about his managers." His chief roadie, Gerry Stickells, told Welch, "he became frustrated . . . by a lot of people around him."[13]

Hendrix was obsessed with the troubles that Jeffrey and company brought to his life and career. The band's finances were entirely controlled by management and were depleted by a tax haven in the Bahamas founded in 1965 by Michael Jeffrey called Yameta Co., a subsidiary of the Bank of New Providence, with accounts at the Naussau branch of the Bank of Nova Scotia and the Chemical Bank in New York.[14] A substantial share of the band's earnings had been quietly drained by Yameta. The banks where Jeffrey opened accounts have been officially charged with the laundering of drug proceeds, a universal theme of CIA/Mafia activity. The Chemical Bank was forced to plead guilty to 445 misdemeanors in 1980 when a federal investigation found that bank officials had failed to report transactions they knew to derive from drug trafficking.[15] The Bank of Nova Scotia was a key investor in the Bank of Commerce and Credit International, (BCCI), once described by *Time* magazine as "the most pervasive money-laundering operation and financial supermarket ever created," with ties to the upper echelons of several governments, the CIA, the Pentagon, and the Vatican.[16] BCCI maintained warm relationships with international terrorists, and investigators turned up accounts for Libya, Syria and the PLO at BCCI's London branch, recalling Mike Jeffrey's military intelligence interest in the Middle East. And then there were bank records from Panama City relating to General Noriega. These "disappeared" en route to the District of Columbia under heavy DEA guard. An internal investigation later, DEA officials admitted they were at a loss to explain the theft.[17]

Friends of Hendrix, according to *Electric Gypsy*, confiscated financial documents from his New York office and turned them over to Jimi: "One showed that what was supposed to be a $10,000 gig was in fact grossing $50,000."

"Jimi Hendrix was upset that large amounts of his money were missing," reports rock historian R. Gary Patterson. Hendrix had discovered the financial diversions and took legal action to recover them.[18]

But there was another factor also involving funds.

Some of Hendrix's friends have concluded that "Jeffrey stood to make a greater sum of money from a dead Jimi Hendrix than a living one. There was also mention of a one million dollar insurance policy covering Hendrix's life made out with Jeffrey as the beneficiary." The manager of the Experience constructed "a financial empire based on the posthumous releases of Hendrix's previously unreleased recordings."[19] Crushing musical voices of dissent was proving to be an immensely profitable enterprise because a dead rocker leaves behind a fortune in publishing rights and royalties.

Roadies couldn't help but notice that Mike Jeffrey, the seasoned military intelligence officer, was capable of "subtle acts of sabotage against them," reports Shapiro. Jeffrey booked the Experience for a concert tour with the Monkees and Hendrix was forced to cancel when the agony of playing to hordes of 12-year-old children, and fear of a parental backlash, convinced him to bail out.

As for the arrest in Toronto, Hendrix confidantes also blame Jeffrey for the planted heroin. The charges were dropped after Hendrix argued that the unopened container of dope had been dropped into his travel bag upon departure by a girl who claimed that it was cold medicine.[20]

In July, 1970, one month before his death, at precisely the time Hendrix stopped all communications with Jeffrey, he told Chuck Wein, a film director at Andy Warhol's Factory: "The next time I go to Seattle will be in a pine box."[21]

And he knew who would drop him in it. Producer Alan Douglas recalls that Hendrix "had a hang-up about the word 'manager.'" The guitarist had pled with Douglas, the proprietor of his own jazz label, to handle the band's business affairs. One of the most popular musicians in the world was desperate. He appealed to a dozen business contacts to handle his bookings and finances, to no avail.[22]

Meanwhile, the sabotage continued in every possible form. Douglas: "Regardless of whatever else Jimi wanted to do, Mike would keep pulling him back or pushing him back. . . . And the way the gigs were routed! I mean, one nighters—he would do Ontario one night, Miami the next night, California the next night. He used to waste [Hendrix] on a tour—and never make too much money because the expenses were ridiculous."[23]

The obits were a jumbled lot of skewed, contradictory eulogies: DRUGS KILL JIMI HENDRIX AT 24, ROCK STAR IS DEAD IN LONDON AT 27, OVERDOSE. Many of the obituaries dwelt on the "wild man of rock" image, but there were also many personal commentaries from reporters who followed his career closely, and they dismissed as hype reports of chronic drug abuse. Mike Ledgerwood, a writer for *Disc* and *Music Echo*, offered a portrait that the closest friends of Jimi Hendrix confirm: "Despite his fame and fortune—plus the inevitable hang-ups and hustles which beset his incredible career—he remained a quiet and almost timid individual. He was naturally helpful and honest." *Sounds* magazine "found a man of quite remarkable charm, an almost old-world courtesy."

Hendrix biographer Tony Brown has, since the mid-'70s, collected all the testimony he could find relating to Hendrix's death, and finds it "tragic" but "predictable." The official cause of death was asphyxiation caused by inhaling his own vomit, but in the days and weeks leading up to the tragedy anyone with an ounce of common sense could see that Hendrix was heading for a terrible fall. Unfortunately, no one close to him managed to steer him clear of the maelstrom that was closing in. Brown sent a report based on his own investigation to the Attorney General's office in February, 1992, "in the hope that they would reopen the inquest into Jimi's death. The evidence was so strong that they ordered Scotland Yard detectives to conduct their own investigation." Months later, detectives at the Yard responded to Sir Nicholas Lyle at the Attorney General's office, rejecting the proposal to revive the inquest.[24]

The pathologist's report left the cause of death "open." Monika Dannemann had long insisted that Hendrix was murdered. At the time of her own death, she had brought media attention to the case in a bitter and highly-publicized court battle with former Hendrix girlfriend Kathy Etchingham. On April 5, 1996, her body was discovered in a fume-filled car near her home in Seaford, Sussex, south England. Police dismissed the death as a "suicide" and the corporate press took dictation. But the *Eastern Daily Press*, a newspaper that circulates in the East Anglian region of the UK, raised another possibility: "Musician Uli Jon Roth, speaking at the thatched cottage where Miss Dannemann lived, said last night: 'The thing looks suspicious. She had a lot of death threats against her over the years. . . . I always felt that she was really being crucified in front of everybody, and there was nothing anyone could do about it.' Mr. Roth, formerly with the group The Scorpions, said Miss Danneman 'is not a person to do something to herself.'" Roth threw one more inconsistency on the lot: "She didn't believe in the concept of suicide."

Devon Wilson, another Hendrix paramour, in Experience drummer Mitch Mitchell's view, "died under mysterious circumstances herself a few years later."[25]

Red, Red Wine

Was Hendrix murdered while under the influence? Stanton Steele, an authority on addiction, offers a seemingly plausible explanation, "Extremely intoxicated people while asleep often lose the reflexive tendency to clear one's throat of mucus, or they may strangle in their vomit. This appeared to have happened to Jimi Hendrix, who had taken both alcohol and prescription barbiturates the night of his death."[26]

Evidence has recently come to light clarifying the cause of death—extreme alcohol consumption aggravated by the barbiturates in Hendrix's bloodstream—*drowning*. Hendrix is said to have choked to death after swallowing nine Vesperax sleeping tablets. This is not

I'm shattered says Mick Jagger

DRUGS KILL JIMI HENDRIX

AT 24

Evening News Reporter
POP STAR Jimi Hendrix died in London today after being taken to hospital suffering from an overdose of drugs.

Hendrix, aged 24, was taken to St. Mary Abbots Hospital, Kensington, but was certified dead by a doctor who examined him in the back of the ambulance.

OBITUARY

JIMI HENDRIX

A key figure in the development of pop music

PRESS REPORTS ON THE DEATH OF JIMI HENDRIX CLAIMED FALSELY THAT THE VIRTUOSO OVERDOSED ON HEROIN.

the lethal dose he'd have taken if suicide was the intent—he surely would have swallowed the remaining 40 or so pills in the packets Dannemann gave him if this was the idea—as Eric Burdon, the Animals' vocalist and a friend of Hendrix, has suggested over the years.

Hendrix was not felled by a drug overdose, as many news reports claimed. The pills were a sleeping aid, and not a very effective one at that. The two Vesperax that Dannemann saw him take before she fell asleep at 3 AM failed to put him under. He had taken a Durophet 20 amphetamine capsule at a dinner party the evening before. And then Hendrix, a chronic insomniac with an escalated tolerance level for barbiturates, had tried the Vesperax before and they proved ineffective. He apparently believed nine tablets would do him no harm.

At 10 AM, Dannemann awoke and went out for a pack of cigarettes, according to her inquest testimony. When she returned, he was sick. She phoned Eric Bridges, a friend, and informed him that Hendrix wasn't well. "Half asleep," Bridges reported in his autobiography, "I suggested she give him hot coffee and slap his face. If she needed any more help to call me back." Dannemann called the ambulance at 18 minutes past 11 AM. The ambulance arrived nine minutes later. Hendrix was not, she claimed, in critical condition. She said the paramedics checked his pulse and breathing, and stated there was "nothing to worry about."

But a direct contradiction came in an interview with Reg Jones, one of the attendants, who insisted that Dannemann wasn't at the flat when they arrived, and that Hendrix was already dead. "It was horrific," Jones said. "We arrived at the flat and the door was flung wide open. . . . I knew he was dead as soon as I walked into the room." Ambulance attendant John Suau confirmed, "We knew it was hopeless. There was no pulse, no respiration."[27]

The testimonies of Dannemann and medical personnel at the 1970 inquest are disturbingly contradictory. Hendrix, the medical personnel stated, had been dead for at least seven hours by the time the ambulance arrived. Dr. Rufus Compson at the Department of Forensic Medicine at St. George's Medical School undertook his own investigation. He referred to the original medical examiner's report and discovered that there were rice remains in Hendrix's stomach. It takes three-four hours for the stomach to empty, he reasoned, and the deceased ate Chinese food at a dinner party hosted by Pete Cameron between the hours of 11 PM and midnight, placing the time of death no later than 4 AM.[28] This is consistent with the report of Dr. Bannister, the surgical registrar, that "the inside of his mouth and mucous membranes were black because he had been dead for some time." Dr. Bannister told the *London Times*, "Hendrix had been dead for hours rather than minutes when he was admitted to the hospital."[29]

The inquest itself was "unusual," Tony Brown notes, because "none of the other witnesses involved were called to give their evidence, nor was any attempt made to ascertain the exact time of death," as if the subject was to be avoided. The result was that the public record on this basic fact in the case may have been incorrectly cited by scores of reporters and biographers. Tony Brown: "Even [medical examiner] Professor Teare made no attempt to ascertain the exact time of death. The inquest appeared to be conducted merely as a formality and had not been treated by the coroner as a serious investigation."[30]

In *'Scuse Me While I Kiss the Sky* (1996), Bill Henderson describes the inquest and its aftermath: "Those who followed his death . . . noticed many inconsistencies in the official inquest. It has been an open and shut affair that managed to hide its racist intent behind the public perceptual hoax of Hendrix as a substance abuser. . . . As a result, millions of people all over the world thought that Hendrix had died that typical rock star's death: drug OD amid fame, opulence, decadence. But it seems that Hendrix could very well have been the victim not of decadence, but of foul play."[31]

Forensic tests submitted at the inquest have been supplemented over the years by new evidence that makes a reconstruction of the murder possible. In October, 1991, Steve Roby, publisher of *Straight Ahead*, a Hendrix fanzine, asked, "What Really Happened?": "Kathy Etchingham, a close friend/lover of Jimi's, and Dee Mitchell, Mitch Mitchell's wife, spent many months tracking down former friends and associates of Hendrix, and are convinced they have solved the mystery of the final hours." Central to reconstructing Hendrix's death is red wine. Dr. Bannister reports that after the esophagus had been cleared, *"masses"* of red wine were "coming out of his nose and out of his mouth." The wine gushing up in great volume from Hendrix's lungs "is very vivid because you don't often see people who have *drowned in their own red wine*. He had something around him—whether it was a towel or a jumper—around his neck and that was *saturated with red wine*. His hair was matted. He was completely cold. I personally think he probably died a long time before. . . . He was cold and he was blue."[32]

Henderson writes:

> The abstract morbidity of Hendrix's body upon discovery may indicate a more complex scenario than has been commonly held. Hendrix was not a red wine guzzler, especially in the amounts found in and around his body. He was known to be moderate in his consumption. If he was 'sleeping normally,' then why was he fully clothed? And how could the ambulance attendants have missed seeing someone who was supposed to be there? The garment, or towel, around his neck is totally mysterious given the scenario so widely distributed. But it is consistent with the doctor's statement that he drowned. Was he drowned by force? In a radio interview broadcast out of Holland in the early 1970s, an unnamed girlfriend answered 'yes' to the question, 'Was Hendrix killed by the Mafia?'[33]

Tony Brown, in *Hendrix: The Final Days* (1997), correlates the consumption of the wine to the approximate time of death: "Jimi must have drunk a large quantity of red wine just prior to his death," suggesting, the quantity of alcohol in his lungs was the direct cause.[34]

The revised time of death, 3–4 AM, contradicts the gap in the official record, and so does the revelation that Jimi Hendrix *drowned* in red wine. While it is common knowledge that Hendrix choked to death, it has only recently come to light that the wine—not the

Verparex—was the primary catalyst of death. Hendrix was, the evidence suggests, forced to drink a quantity of wine. The barbiturates, as Brown notes, "seriously inhibited Jimi's normal cough reflex." Unable to cough the wine back up, "it went straight down into his lungs. . . . It is quite possible that he thrashed about for some time, fighting unsuccessfully to gain his breath." [35] It is doubtful that Hendrix would have continued to swallow the wine in "massive" volumes had it begun to fill his lungs. One explanation that explains the forensic evidence is that Jimi Hendrix was restrained, wine *forced* down his throat until his thrashings ceased. All of this must have taken place quickly, before the alcohol had time to enter his bloodstream. The post mortem report states that the blood alcohol level was not excessive, about 20 mg over the legal drinking limit. He died before his stomach absorbed much of the wine. Jimi Hendrix choked to death. That much of the general understanding of his demise is correct, and little else.

The kidnapping, embezzling, and numerous shady deceptions would make Jeffrey the leading suspect in any proper police investigation. And his reaction at the news of Hendrix's death did little to dispel any suspicions that associates may have harbored. Jim Marron, a nightclub owner from Manhattan, was vacationing with Jeffrey in Spain when word of the musician's death reached him. "We were supposed to have dinner that night in Majorca," Marron recalls. Jeffrey "called me from his club in Palma saying that we would have to cancel. . . . I've just got word from London. Jimi's dead." The manager of the Hendrix Experience took the news completely in stride. "I always knew that son of a bitch would pull a quickie," Jeffrey told Marron. "Basically, he had lost a major property. You had the feeling that he had just lost a couple of million dollars—and was the first to realize it. My first reaction was, Oh my God, my friend is dead." [36] But Jeffrey reacted coldly, comparing the fatality to a fleeting sexual romp in the afternoon.

His odd behavior continued in the days following the death of Hendrix. He appeared to be consumed by guilt, and on one occasion "confessed." On September 20, recording engineer Alan Douglas received a call from Jeffrey, who wanted to see him. Douglas drove to the hotel where Jeffrey was staying. "He was bent over, in misery from a recent back injury. We started talking and he let it all out. It was like a confession."

"In my opinion," Douglas observed, "Jeffrey hated Hendrix."

Bob Levine, the band's merchandising manager, was perplexed by Jeffrey's response to the tragedy. First, Hendrix's manager dropped completely out of sight. "We tried calling all of Jeffrey's contacts . . .

trying to reach him. We were getting frustrated because Hendrix's body was going to be held up in London for two weeks and we wanted Jeffrey's input on the funeral service. A full week after Hendrix's death, he finally called. Hearing his voice, I immediately asked what his plans were and would he be going to Seattle. 'What plans?' he asked. I said, 'The funeral.' 'What funeral?' he replied. I was exasperated: 'Jimi's!' The phone went quiet for a while and then he hung up. The whole office was staring at me, unable to believe that with all the coverage on radio, print and television, Jeffrey didn't know that Jimi had died." As noted, Jeffrey had been notified and almost grieved, in his fashion. "He called back in five minutes and we talked quietly. He said, 'Bob, I didn't know,' and was asking about what had happened. While I didn't confront him, I knew he was lying." [37]

It was reported that Michael Jeffrey "paid his respects" sitting in a limousine parked outside Dunlap Baptist Church in Seattle. He refused to go inside for the eulogy.[38] Hendrix was buried at the family plot at Greenwood Cemetary in Renton.

Screenwriter Alan Greenberg was hired to write a screenplay for a film on the life of Jimi Hendrix. He traveled to England and taped an interview with Dannemann shortly before her death in April, 1996. In that interview, Dannemann sketched in more details of Jeffrey's skullduggery, which continued after Hendrix's death and has long been concealed behind a wall of misconceptions. On the Greenberg tapes, Dannemann denied allegations of heroin use, as do others close to Hendrix: "You should put that into the right perspective since all of the youngsters still think he was a drug addict. The problem was, when he died, I was told by the coroner not to talk until after the inquest, so that's why all these wild stories came out that he overdosed from heroin." The coroner found no injection tracks on Hendrix's body. That he snorted the opiate, a charge advanced by biographer Chris Welch in *Hendrix*, is disputed by Jimi's closest friends. He indulged primarily in marijuana and LSD. The popular misconception that Hendrix was a heroin addict lingers on but should have been buried with him. One of rock's greatest talents was maliciously smeared by the press on this count.

At times, the public has been deliberately misled about Hendrix's drug habits. Kathy Etchingham, a former girlfriend, was deceived into giving an article about Jimi to a friend in the corporate media, and it was snatched up by a newspaper, rewritten, and the story that emerged depicted the guitarist as a violent and drug-infested lunatic. The editor later apologized in writing to Kathy for falsifying the record, but failed to retract in print.[39] Media swipes at

Hendrix to this day are often unreasonably vicious, as in this transparent attempt to shape public opinion from London's *Times* on December 14, 1993:

> Not only did [Hendrix] leave several memorable compositions behind him; he left a good-looking corpse. Kathy Etchingham, a middle-class mother of two, who used to be one of Hendrix's lovers, still mourns his passing and is seeking to persuade the police that there is something suspicious about the circumstances in which he died. Quite why she should bother is hard to say. Perhaps she is bored.

Hendrix, we are advised, "lived an absurdly self-indulgent life and died, in essence, of stupidity."

Close friends of Jimi Hendrix suggest that Jeffrey was the front man for a surreptitious sponsor, the FBI, CIA, or Mafia. In 1975, *Crawdaddy* magazine launched its own investigation and concluded that a death squad of some kind had targeted him: "Hendrix is not the only artist to have had his career sabotaged by unscrupulous sharks and leeches." The recent memory of the death of Average White Band drummer Robby McIntosh from strychnine-laced heroin circulating at a party in Los Angeles "only serves to update this fact of rock 'n' roll life. But an industry that accepts these tragedies in cold blood demonstrates its true nature—and the Jimi Hendrix music machine cranks on, unencumbered by the absence of Hendrix himself. One wonders who'll be the next in line?"[40]

On March 5, as if in reply, Michael Jeffrey, every musician's nightmare, was blown out of the sky in an airplane collision over France, enroute to a court appearance in London related to Hendrix. Jeffrey was returning from Palma aboard an Iberia DC-9 in the midst of a French civil air traffic control strike. Military controllers were called in as contingency replacements for the controllers. Hendrix biographer Bill Henderson considers the midair collision fuel for "paranoia." The nature of military airline control "necessitated rigorous planning, limited traffic on each sector, and strict compliance with regulations. The DC-9 however was assigned to the same flight over Nantes as a Spantax Coronado, which 'created a source of conflict.' And because of imprecise navigation, lack of complete radar coverage, and imperfect radio communications, the two planes collided. The Coronado was damaged but remained airworthy; no one was injured. The DC-9 crashed, killing all 61 passengers and seven crew. . . ." There are theories that Jeffrey was merely a tool, a mouthpiece for the real villains lurking in the wings, that he was "the target of assassination."[41]

A quarter-century after Hendrix died, his father finally won control of the musical legacy. Under a settlement signed in 1995, the rights to his son's music were granted to 76-year-old Al Hendrix, the sole heir to the estate. The agreement, settled in court, forced Hendrix to drop a fraud suit filed two years earlier against Leo Branton Jr., the L.A. civil rights attorney who represented Angela Davis and Nat King Cole. Hendrix accused his lawyer of selling the rights to the late rock star's publishing catalogue without consent.

Hendrix, Sr. filed the suit on April 19, 1993, after learning that MCA Music Entertainment—a company rife with Mafia connections—was readying to snatch up his son's recording and publishing rights from two international companies that claimed to own them. The MCA deal, estimated to be worth $40 million, was put on hold after objections were raised in a letter to the Hollywood firm from Hendrix. By this time, Experience albums generated more than $3 million per annum in royalties, and $1 million worth of garments, posters and paraphernalia bearing his name and likeness are sold each year. All told, Al Hendrix should receive $2 million over 20 years.[42]

NOTES
1. John Holstrom, "Who Killed Jimi?" Lions Gate Media Works, http://lionsgate.com/Music/hendrix/I_ Dont_Live_Today.html.
2. John Raymond and Marv Glass, "The FBI Investigated Jimi Hendrix," *Common Ground*, University of Santa Barbara, CA student newspaper, vol. iv, no. 9, June 7, 1979, p. 1.
3. "Jimi Hendrix, Black Power and Money," *Teenset*, January, 1969.
4. Tony Brown, *Hendrix: The Final Days*, London: Rogan House, 1997, p. 43.
5. On Mike Jeffrey's undefined politics, see: John McDermott with Eddie Kramer, *Hendrix: Setting the Record Straight*, New York: Warner, 1992, p. 180.
6. Harry Shapiro and Ceasar Glebbeek, *Jimi Hendrix, Electric Gypsy*, New York: St. Martin's, 1990, p. 120.
7. Bill Henderson, "IT'S LIKE TRYING TO GET OUT OF A ROOM FULL OF MIRRORS," Jimi Hendrix web page, http://www.rockmine. music.co.uk/jimih. html.
8. Fredric Dannen, *Hit Men: Power Brokers and Fast Money Inside the Music Industry*, New York: Times Books, 1990, p. 164–5.
9. Shapiro and Glebbeek, *Jimi Hendrix, Electric Gypsy*, New York: St. Martin's, 1990, p. 294. The Fudge once booked a tour with Jimi Hendrix, per arrangement between the band's mobbed-up management and Michael Jeffrey, Hendrix's manager.
10. Dannen, p. 165.
11. Shapiro and Glebbeek, p. 295.
12. Monika Dannemann, *The Inner World of Jimi Hendrix*, New York: St. Martin's Press, 1995, pp. 76–8.

13. John Swenson, "The Last Days of Jimi Hendrix," *Crawdaddy*, January, 1975, p. 43.
14. Ibid., p. 488.
15. "Banks and Narcotics Money Flow in South Florida," *US Senate Banking Committee report*, 96th Congress, June 5–6, 1980, p. 201.
16. Jonathon Kwitny, *The Crimes of Patriots: A True Tale of Dope, Dirty Money, and the CIA*, New York: Touchstone, 1987, p. 153.
17. Josh Rodin, "BANK OF CROOKS AND CRIMINALS?" Topic 105, *Christic News*, August 6, 1991.
18. R. Gary Patterson, *Hellhounds on Their Trail: Tales from the Rock 'n' Roll Graveyard*, Nashville, Tennessee: Dowling Press, 1998, p. 208.
19. Ibid.
20. Shapiro and Glebbeek, p. 473.
21. Shapiro and Glebeek, p. 477.
22. Swenson. In *Crosstown Traffic* (1989), Charles Murray reports that Hendrix "began consulting independent lawyers and accountants with a view of sorting out his tangled finances and freeing himself from Mike Jeffrey," p. 55.
23. Henderson website.
24. Brown, p. 7.
25. Mitch Mitchell with John Platt, *Jimi Hendrix—Inside the Experience*, New York: St. Martin's, 1990, p. 160.
26. E. Stanton Steele, "The Human Side Of Addiction: What caused John Belushi's death?" *US Journal of Drug and Alcohol Dependence*, April 1982, p. 7.
27. David Henderson, *'Scuse Me While I Kiss the Sky*, New York: Bantam, 1996, pp. 389–90.
28. Brown, p. 164.
29. Henderson, p. 392.
30. Brown, p. 163.
31. Henderson, p. 388.
32. Ibid., p. 392.
33. Henderson, *'Scuse Me While I Kiss the Sky*, p. 393. If the Mafia did indeed participate, Hendrix wasn't the first African-American musician to have a contract on his head. In May 1955, jazz saxman Wardell Gray was murdered, probably by Mafia hitmen. Gray had toured with Benny Goodman and Count Basie in 1948. His remarkable recording sessions of the late 1940s, especially with Dexter Gordon, brought him fame. Bill Moody, a jazz drummer and disk jockey, published a novel in 1996, *Death of a Tenor Man*, based on the life and death of Grey. "It's strange," a publisher's press release comments, "that 1950s Las Vegas, a town in which the Mob and corrupt police worked hand in glove, became the home of the first integrated nightclub in the country. The Moulin Rouge was owned by blacks and had the honor of being the only casino hotel in Vegas that allowed African-Americans to mingle with white customers. On opening night, Nat King Cole and Frank Sinatra sat in with Benny Carter's band. The second night, Wardell Gray, a black sax player in the Carter band with a growing reputation, was beaten to death. The police said he overdosed and 'fell out of bed,' dying later 'of complications.' Some suspected Gray's death was the Mob's way of telling the African-American businessmen who backed the Moulin Rouge that 'this town isn't big enough for the both of us.'" Gray's murder has never been investigated. It "hung over the Moulin Rouge

like a storm cloud" and remains unsolved. The casino went out of business a few months later.

And the 1961 attempt on the life of soul singer Jackie Wilson has never been rationally explained. Wilson was shot in the stomach by a fan supposedly trying to "prevent a fan from killing herself." He recovered from the assault and went on to release "No Pity (In the Naked City)" and "Higher and Higher."

The Halloween 1975 murder of Al Jackson, percussionist for Booker T. and the MGs, at the age of 39, also appeared to be a premeditated hit. Barbara Jackson, his wife, was the sole eyewitness. She told police, according to *Rolling Stone*, that she "arrived home on the night of the shooting and was met by a gun-wielding burglar who tied her hands behind her back with an ironing cord." Al Jackson, who'd been taking in a closed circuit telecast of the Muhammad Ali-Joe Frazier fight, arrived an hour later. Any burglar would have collected valuables in the house and fled by this time, but he waited a full hour for Jackson to return home. Babara Jackson was freed from the ropes and the "burglar" ordered her at gunpoint to open the door for him. "After confronting Jackson and asking him for money, the intruder forced him to lie on the floor. He then shot Jackson five times in the back and left." (*Rolling Stone*, November 1975).

34. Brown, p. 165.
35. Brown, pp. 165–66.
36. McDermott and Kramer, pp. 286–87.
37. Ibid.
38. Ibid.
39. Shapiro and Glebeek, p. 474.
40. Swenson, p. 45.
41. Henderson web ite.
42. Chuck Philips, "Father to Get Hendrix Song, Image Rights," *Los Angeles Times* (home edition), July 26, 1995, p. 1. Also named as defendants were producer Alan Douglas and several firms that have profited from the Hendrix catalogue since 1974 under contracts negotiated by Branton: New York-based Bella Godiva Music Inc; Presentaciones Musicales SA (PMSA), a Panamanian corporation; Bureau Voor Muzeikrechten Elber B.V. in the Netherlands; and Interlit, based in the Virgin Islands.

Branton negotiated two contracts in early 1974—signed by Al Hendrix—that relinquished all rights to his son's "unmastered" tapes for $50,000 to PMSA and all his stock in Bella Godiva, his son's music publishing company, for $50,000. "PMSA and the other overseas companies were later discovered to be part of a tax shelter system created by Harry Margolis," reported the *Los Angeles Times*, "a Saratoga attorney whom federal prosecutors charged but never convicted of tax fraud. The tax shelter plan collapsed after Margolis' death in 1987, and also [prompted] complaints from the estates of other entertainment clients, including singer Nat King Cole, screenwriter Larry Hauben as well as from followers of New Age philosopher Werner Erhard, who allegedly stashed revenues from his EST enterprise in the foreign account."

CHAPTER EIGHT
When You're a Stranger:
Fragrance dé CHAOS – Investigative
Findings on the Death of Jim Morrison

THERE IS MENACE UNDER THE MUSIC, BUT SOMETHING IS BEING HELD BACK. A
SENSE OF ANGER, RAGE AND BETRAYAL. BENT OVER THE MIKE, MORRISON, WHO
FOUR DAYS LATER WOULD GIVE HIS LAST CONCERT THEN ABANDON THE BAND,
LEAVING ROCK BEHIND, IS AT HIS PROVOCATIVE, INFLAMMATORY, CONFRONTATIONAL
BEST, REPEATING HIMSELF OVER AND OVER AGAIN. "ROCK IS DEAD. ROCK IS DEAD.
IT'S DYING. IT'S OVER. IT'S OVER. ROCK 'N' ROLL IS DEAD."

IF NOSTALGIA ISN'T WHAT IT USED TO BE, NEITHER IS ROCK. WEIGHED DOWN BY
ITS OWN MYTHOLOGICAL PAST, TOP-HEAVY BECAUSE OF THE UNNATURAL LONGEVITY
OF TOO MANY BANDS, BLOATED BECAUSE OF THE SIZE OF THE CORPORATIONS THAT
DOMINATE THE INDUSTRY, ROCK MUSIC HAS BEEN WAY TOO SUCCESSFUL FOR ITS
OWN GOOD. **MICHAEL EPIS, AUSTRALIAN CRITIC**

Jim Morrison's body was
found by Pamela Courson, Morrison's common-law wife,
in the bathtub at their flat in Paris, France in the early
morning hours of July 3, 1971—exactly two years after the death
of Brian Jones.[1] The New York Times reported, "Jim Morrison, lead
singer of The Doors rock group, died last Saturday in Paris, his
public relations firm said today." The death was initially attributed
to "natural causes," "pneumonia," and finally (but by no means con-
clusively) "heart failure."[2] "Details were withheld pending the
return of Mr. Morrison's agent from France. Funeral services were
held in Paris today. In his black leather jacket and skin-tight vinyl
pants, Jim Morrison personified rock music's image of superstar as
sullen, mystical sexual poet."

The surviving Doors, Robbie Krieger, Ray Manzarek and John
Densmore, discussed Morrison's death in an interview conducted on
February 11, 1983 by BBC-2's Robin Denselow at the Institute of
Contemporary Arts in London. Manzarek recalled his state of denial
upon learning of Jim Morrison's death, and weighed the possibility of
political assassination:

Manzarek: We got a phone call. I got a phone call Saturday morning
saying Jim Morrison is dead in Paris . . . Yeah, yeah, yeah . . . sure, right.

John had talked to him a couple of weeks beforehand and he's dead . . .

Q: What about CIA involvement?

Manzarek : Well, I've heard that theory, yeah, Janis Joplin, Jim Morrison, Jimi Hendrix. Black man, white man, white woman. You know, the flowering of American youth in poetry and art and music . . . trying to stop it all. It's conceivable . . .

Densmore: There was definitely some political weirdness at Miami, that [obscenity charge] coming down.

Krieger: And there was an FBI file on Morrison that we got a hold of, so the government was aware of The Doors . . .

Morrison's spontaneous political outbursts in rock press interviews attracted FBI attention: "I like ideas about the breaking away or overthrowing of established order," he announced. "I am interested in anything about revolt, disorder, chaos—especially activity that seems to have no meaning. It seems to me to be the road toward freedom—external revolt is a way to bring about internal freedom."[3]

In another interview, Manzarek considered possible motives for eliminating the anarchistic Lizard King:

They were going to stop all of rock 'n' roll by stopping The Doors. As far as Americans were concerned, he was the most dangerous . . . . Janis Joplin was just a white woman singing about getting drunk and laid a lot, and Jimi Hendrix was a black guy singing, 'Let's get high.' Morrison was singing, "We want the world and we want it now." There was plenty of hounding.[4]

FBI harassment, in fact, rendered Morrison so anxiety-ridden that he contracted an ulcer by his mid-'20s—a condition not exactly conducive to overthrowing the established order. "Paranoia" struck deep, and biographers James Riordan and Jerry Prochnicky confirm that Morrison was a "marked" man.

The busts took their toll on Morrison. . . . By 1970 he was still reeling from the effects of one federal trial and about to face another. And the FBI had marked him. It was they who made the charges in Miami stick. . . . Morrison was guilty before he was arrested. But the particular crimes were not the problem. The real issue was because he was guilty of being Jim Morrison, a larger-than-life symbol of rebellion to the youth of America, and thereby a threat.

The busts cost Morrison a great deal of money, but more than that they wore him down and sapped his enthusiasm for life. "The vice squad would be at the side of the stage with our names filled in on the warrants, just waiting to write in the offense," Manzarek recollected. "Narks to the left, vice squad to the right, into the valley of death rode the four. . . . They wanted to stop Morrison. They wanted to show him that he couldn't get away with it.[5]

Like Brian Jones and Jimi Hendrix before him, and many rock musicians to follow, Morrison was consumed by "paranoia," as historian Marianne Sinclair observes:

Inevitably, Morrison and The Doors became a focus for attack and victimization by the conventional forces of society . . . Doors' performances were frequently canceled at the last minute through the efforts of local do-gooders, and audiences were regularly clubbed by policemen during concerts . . . This was too much for Morrison, within whom the forces of destruction had already been long at work. A heavy user of LSD and an alcoholic who could get drunk at any time of the day or night on whatever happened to be handy, Morrison seemed hell-bent on killing himself young. He once described his drinking as 'not suicide, but slow capitulation.' What he was capitulating to was his own need to block out the sense of frustration, despair and growing *paranoia*.[6]

Morrison's death was followed by press reports noting federal interest in Morrison's life, political views and, significantly, all independent investigations of his death.

Researcher Thomas Lyttle gathered up leads in the international press:

One of the more explicit appeared in the Scandinavian magazine *Dagblatte*. This article detailed French intelligence efforts to assassinate Jim Morrison in Paris.[7]

In France, the Documentation Exterieure et De Contre Espionage (SDECE) performs internal security functions. Under DeGaulle, it was SDECE's policy to resist and oppose the CIA, with the exception of a small contingent within the bureau enlisted to collaborate secretly with Langley. Under Pompidou and d'Estang, the domestic French intelligence service was ordered to cooperate fully with US intelligence agents and would have been drawn into any assassination plans in Paris conceived by the CIA.[8]

SDECE assassins are highly-trained and were certainly capable of killing Morrison discreetly, leaving no trace of their complicity.

There are precedents. In 1962, an SDECE agent code-named Laurent rigged the Rome-bound flight of a plane, and Italian oil millionaire Enrico Mattei died in the crash. The magnate's offense: a planned take-over of French interests in Algerian oil. *Time* magazine reporter William McHale was also killed.[9] At the behest of their American counterparts in Virginia, the "murder committee" of de Centre Espionage was undeniably capable of eliminating a troublesome rock celebrity and burying the evidence.

Bob Seymore pieced together official documents for *The End*, his book on the peculiar circumstances surrounding Morrison's death, and soon found himself immersed in a sea of contradictions and unanswered questions. One of the most troubling was his belief that Pamela Courson withheld evidence, and that friends Alan Ronay, Agnes Varda and Bill Siddons "know more than they have revealed in public." Morrison biographer Danny Sugarman told Seymore that he had government documents through Freedom of Information Act request for files pertaining to Morrison's death. Seymore writes:

> I asked if Danny had seen such documents, then why were there no details of any of them in his book? He said that Pamela had told him things about Jim's death that he promised her he would never divulge. . . .[1]

Sugarman is married to indicted Contragate co-conspirator Fawn Hall, Oliver North's secretary at the National Security Council, who shredded an 18-inch file of documents linking the Reagan administration to the diversion of funds from Iran arms sales to the Nicaraguan contras on November 21, 1986, and quipped before a Congressional committee, "Sometimes you have to go above the law" (ironic in light of her admission to the DEA during a federal drug investigation in 1989 that she "used cocaine many times" in her three years as an NSC staffer)—and he has concealed evidence that would shed light on Morrison's death.

Why suppress evidence of this significance to the historical record? Supposedly because Sugarman "promised Pam" he would conceal and suppress certain facts, as he explained to Seymore. Danny Sugarman predictably rejects all "conspiracy theories" out of hand, but he is himself is involved in a conspiracy of silence, ignoring not only official intelligence files but the aforementioned public reports on prior attempts by French intelligence agents to murder Jim Morrison—a documented "finger on the trigger," a conspiracy—and instead stating that Morrison did, per the official verdict, suffer some sort of cardiopulmonary arrest at the tender age of 27 in Paris. But when pressed to account for the gaping discrepancies in the case—

for instance, heart failure causes anguished thrashing and ordinarily does not leave a smile, such as the one reported by Courson and the paramedics, on the victim's face—Sugarman concedes that Morrison's death "could have involved a number of factors," and when cornered by Seymore, reluctantly conceded:

> You could say that the CIA and other intelligence agencies may have had a hand in the deaths of Hendrix, Janis Joplin and then Morrison. Simply for the reason that they were leaders of a generation during the 1960s.[11]

You could also say that Morrison was viewed as an anarchistic defiler of "restless youth" in some loops on the Washington Beltway, according to Sugarman's own best-selling biography:

> Jim was certainly popular enough, and more threateningly, smart enough to cause the powers that be ample reason to take some sort of action to prevent his subversive influence. Surely the authorities were wary of him.[12]

Doors of Deception

How wary? Enough to keep secret files on Morrison. Enough to spread false rumors to the effect that he had faked his own death to deflect attention from political assassination. The "conspiracy," as charted by Sugarman and others, was a hoax hatched by Morrison to "fake his own death." A book, The Bank of America of Louisiana, appeared in 1975, supposedly written by Morrison, the source of the rumor.[13] In No One Here Gets Out Alive, a sensational history larded with drug-and-sex debauchery, Sugarman and Hopkins devote an entire chapter to "evidence" that Morrison had survived Paris and launched a new life free from the encumbrances of celebrity and the FBI.

The rumor was a deliberate obfuscation concocted by unknown covert operators. The proper question is "Who killed Morrison?" not "Is he still alive and working for the Bank of America?"

Author Thomas Lyttle writes:

> In the first few years after Morrison's death, the owner of B of A Communications, named James Douglas Morrison, claimed to be operating as an intelligence agent for a number of domestic and international groups including the CIA, NSA, Interpol, Swedish

Intelligence and others. There are also connections between James Douglas Morrison and various occult groups with probable intelligence connections. . . . JM2 also claims to be the "dead" rock star and former singer for The Doors. The new JM2 dropped the old JM1 rock and roll identity to become "James Bond."

This author has in fact seen what appear to be stacks of official-looking documents and letters between the CIA, various government agencies, national news groups like CNN and NBC and JM2, involving what looked like personal meetings, projects and ephemera. Of special interest is that when I viewed parts of the

THE PUBLICATION OF **THE BANK OF AMERICA OF LOUISIANA** IN 1975 PROMPTED FALSE RUMORS THAT JIM MORRISON FAKED HIS OWN DEMISE, AN ALLEGATION THAT SURVIVES TO THIS DAY.

files, all the reports had a paper-thin metallic band affixed to them with colored UPC bar codes. There is no way for me to authenticate the claims of JM2, but everything looked extremely official and very elaborate. . . .

A courtroom transcript which I have seen implicates the FBI and CIA in several coverups regarding JM2's intelligence career. These show that there seems to be a systematic destruction of files relating to JM2's spy activities. . . . Also in my possession are files concerning JM2's rogue financial activities with the Bank of America, and news reports regarding lawsuits by and against JM2 for bank fraud and espionage.

There also appear to be hundreds if not thousands of miscellaneous files. . . . These involve the CIA, Danish intelligence, and others. There are also an active passport and banking IDs under the name James Douglas Morrison.

Is this all for real or is this an elaborate hoax? . . . The important thing to note for the sake of this study is that someone or some group is actively pursuing and setting up a mass "urban legend" regarding James Morrison. They are painstakingly documenting it also. Whether this is a hoax or not is not as important as the fact that a lot of official-looking information is being generated surrounding the myth and legend of Jim Morrison.[14]

Any account of the second Morrison's career (according to Daniel Brandt's NameBase website, an index of names related to intelligence activity, the CIA employs one James Douglas Morrison, an active agent stationed in France) would be incomplete without the names of the Morrison double's Agency contacts, particularly William Colby, a CIA director under Richard Nixon. Since 1972, Morrison's double has left a surreal international trail of paper. The documents include letters to and from Louisiana Governor Edwin Edwards and late CIA Director William Colby, through the Washington, DC law firm of Colby, Miller and Hanes.

The day before his death, the original Jim Morrison sent a telegram to Jonathan Dolger, a publishing contact in New York, about changing the cover of a book of poetry written by the Door. Bob Seymore, trying to piece together Morrison's final days in Paris, phoned Dolger and discovered that someone else was interested in that telegram:

> "Oh, my God," [Dolger] said. It was as though he had been woken up from an old nightmare. I asked him about the telegram but he said he no longer had it. At first he thought maybe his former employers had it in their files. . . . Then he realized that a man whose name he had forgotten contacted him to ask if he could have the telegram Jim sent. This was a month after Jim died and the person said he was with Jim when he died. . . .[15]

There are a score of unknowns to resolve before writing Morrison off as a crazed narco-rocker bent on self-destruction:

- ◆ The cause of Jim Morrison's death was an unspecified "heart failure," so states the forensic examiner's report, not an "attack" or "seizure." The heart failed, quit. Dr. Vasille noted "a little blood round the nostrils," indicating a hemorrhage, inconsistent with heart failure. Paramedics from the local Fire Brigade reported that Morrison was still smiling when they arrived, also not consistent with the officially-stated cause of death.
- ◆ Dr. Derwin, the singer's personal physician, told representatives of the media industry: "Jim Morrison was in excellent health before

JIM MORRISON'S CURSORY REPORT, PREPARED BY DR. MAX VASSILLE, PARIS, ON JULY 3, 1971. NO OFFICIAL AUTOPSY WAS CONDUCTED, IN VIOLATION OF FRENCH LEGAL STRICTURES.

traveling to Paris."[16] Pam Courson, the last person to see him alive, wrote in her signed statement to Paris police that the night before his death, Morrison "looked in good health, he seemed very happy."[17]

♦ No autopsy was performed—a probable violation of French law and certain violation of French custom.

♦ Two persons could answer questions about the odd death: Ms. Courson died of "apparent overdose" herself on April 24, 1974— a few days before a judge would have ruled in her favor concerning a dispute over the distribution of the Morrison inheritance, a decision that would have brought her, as Morrison's common-law wife and sole heir, a quarter of the Doors' income and an immediate payment of half a million dollars[18]—and Dr. Max Vassille, the medical examiner, consistently turns down all interviews related to Morrison's death.[19]

♦ Pamela's friends, James Riordan reports in *Break On Through*, believe she was murdered: some "suspect foul play, saying that although Pam had been using heroin, she could not shoot herself up. She always had to have someone else do it. Whoever did it, they claim, knew he or she was injecting her with a lethal [dose]," a "hot-shot."[20]

Jim Morrison died in a bathtub, this much is certain based on the statements of Courson, friends of Morrison close to the case, and Paris officials.

Dr. Vassille estimated the time of death to be 5:00 AM. Paramedics arrived at the flat at exactly 9:24 AM, an interval of nearly four and a half hours, but the bath water, they reported, was still "lukewarm." So Morrison probably died two-three hours later than the death certificate claims. This would place the time of death closer to 7–8 AM.

Pamela Courson told police that Morrison had choked in his sleep, that she shook him awake. He was in wretched condition and told her that a bath might make him feel better. This was roughly 2:30 in the morning. Courson told police that she fell asleep and awoke to discover the body in the bathtub at about 5 AM. The timeline revised by water temperature leads to the inescapable conclusion that he was alive after the estimated time of death.

The statements of witnesses and officials clash, and this often happens when fear or coercion forces them to fabricate cover stories. It's entirely possible that Courson was threatened, or feared to implicate others, and this is why Sugarman mumbles that she and all close to the case "knew more about Morrison's death" than they ever revealed—exactly as witnesses to the murder of Brian Jones did under duress for thirty years. Dr. Vassille may have been forced by Pamela Courson's statements to find the time of death at 5 AM. This and his refusal to talk to the press suggest that the medical examiner was also under pressure—orders from superiors, threats to himself or his family—and suppressed information regarding Morrison's death.

What were they concealing? Patricia Kennealy Morrison believes that her husband-by-pagan-ceremony overdosed on heroin. She sides with the late Albert Goldman on this particular point, although in general she steadfastly rejects the "noxious lie-o-rama" allegations that "Albert Goldigger" made concerning the deceased Door.

Dr. John Morgan written more than 100 articles and books on clinical pharmacology, and "declares Jim to have quite likely died, in his opinion, of a prolonged heroin overdose, an overdose drawn out into respiratory depression over several hours because Jim did not shoot the smack but snorted it," Patricia wrote in 1997. Other medical specialists consulted by her agreed with this diagnosis, finding "nasal or esophageal varices as the likely cause of Jim's reported profuse bleeding." Dr. Morgan: "Pam's versions certainly indicate that he was snorting heroin. A nasal or oral dose would delay the decline into respiratory death."[21] The OD was gradual and evidently not traumatic, to judge by the smile on his face when found.

The consensus among most investigative reporters, medical consultants, and Morrison's circle of friends is also that he overdosed on heroin. Pamela's closest friend at the time of Morrison's death, Diane Gardiner, told biographer James Riordan that Courson had "confessed" to her. Courson "told me a lot about Jim's death. It's true that he got into some of Pam's drugs and overdosed."[22]

Pamela told Sugarman that Morrison—who mortally feared the narcotic after the death of Janis Joplin and ordinarily avoided it—was deeply depressed and intended to numb the pain by helping himself to her provisions: "She started telling me something about Jim's death being her fault and that he had found out that she was doing heroin, and 'You know Jim, of course he wanted to try it.' Then she looked at me and said, 'It was my stash—Jim didn't know how to score. He knew how to drink.' She said that later he didn't feel well and decided to take a bath and she nodded out. But when I pressed her for details she suddenly denied the whole thing."[23]

A similar account was told by Alan Ronay, a friend of Jim Morrison's since UCLA film school, one of the last to see the rocker alive. Ronay told a reporter for *Paris Match* in 1991 that Morrison was still alive when Pam awoke and found him in the bath, a version that conforms to the revised timeline. Ronay said that Pamela pulled him aside after the medical examiners arrived and confided that Morrison had been snorting heroin for 48 hours when she and Morrison fell asleep listening to the first Doors LP. He was choking in his sleep and struggling for air, and she woke him up and helped him to the bath. She fell asleep and woke up again to find that he hadn't returned to bed, discovered him bleeding from the nose and vomiting blood into a pot. Then he told her that he felt better and she should go back to bed. He died shortly thereafter. Pamela told Ronay, "Jim looked so calm. He was smiling."[24]

Did he ingest poisoned opiate or a "hot shot?" If the posthumous revelations are correct, Jim Morrison and Pamela Courson were both killed by lethal doses of heroin. The absence of an autopsy report precludes any attempt to determine the true cause of Morrison's death, and some of the troubling questions raised here may never be resolved completely if Danny Sugarman, the CIA rumor mongers, and an indifferent press have their way, which raises one more pertinent question: What's it to them?

NOTES

1. Laura Jackson, *Golden Stone: The Untold Life and Tragic Death of Brian Jones*, New York: St. Martin's, 1992, p. 214. Jackson places the exact time of death sometime between 11:30 on July 2 and midnight on July 3, the official date.
2. Doctor Max Vassille, forensic doctor, stated in his medical report that Morrison's death was "natural due to heart failure."—Bob Seymore, *The End: The Death of Jim Morrison*, London: Omnibus Press, 1991, pp. 61, 63.
3. Quoted in the original Elektra Records bio release, 1967.
4. James Riordan and Jerry Prochnicky, *Break On Through: The Life and Death of Jim Morrison*, New York: William Morrow, 1991, p. 375.
5. Riordan and Prochnicky, p. 376.
6. Marianne Sinclair, *Those Who Died Young*, London: Plexus Publishing, 1979.
7. Thomas Lyttle, "Rumors, Myths, and Urban Legends Surrounding the Death of Jim Morrison," in *Secret and Suppressed*, Jim Keith, ed., Portland: Feral House, 1993, p. 117.
8. Henrik Krüger, *The Great Heroin Coup: Drugs, Intelligence & International Fascism*, Boston: South End Press, 1980, p. 49.
9. Krüger, p. 47.
10. Seymore, p. 44, 78.
11. Ibid.
12. Jerry Hopkins and Danny Sugarman, *No One Here Gets Out Alive*, New York: Warner, 1981, p. 372.
13. Jim Morrison, *The Bank of America of Louisiana*, [no city listed]: Zeppelin Publishing Corp., 1975.
14. Lyttle, pp. 117–18. The impersonations, Lyttle explains, "were part of sociological experiments like Artichoke or MKULTRA" (p. 119), CIA mind control projects of the 1950s.
15. Seymore, p. 77.
16. Lyttle.
17. Seymore, p. 56.
18. Hopkins and Sugarman, pp. 376–77. Also, Pamela des Barres, *Rock Bottom: Dark Moments in Music Babylon*, New York: St. Martin's, 1996, p. 211.
19. Seymore, p. 77.
20. Riordan and Prochnicky, p. 484.
21. Patricia Kennealy Morrison, "An Open Letter to Jim's Fans," October, 1997.
22. Riordan and Prochnicky, p. 458.
23. Ibid.
24. des Barres, p. 211.

CHAPTER NINE
Like Coffins in a Cage:
The Baez Contras and the Death of
Phil Ochs

THE TEMPTATION FOR POWER IS SO GREAT, AND UNFORTUNATELY, WHAT ONE'S POWER HAS ALWAYS MEANT IS ONE'S ABILITY . . . TO MURDER ONE'S NEIGHBOR.

JOAN BAEZ

I STARTED OUT WITH INFORMATION KIND OF REMOTE. WHEN A PATRIOTIC MOTHER DRAGGED ME DOWN BY THE THROAT. WHEN [HUAC INVESTIGATORS] ASK YOU A QUESTION, THEY EXPECT A REPLY! DOESN'T MATTER IF YOU'RE FIXIN' TO DIE.

RICHARD FARIÑA

Folk singer Joan Baez, a distinguished critic of the Sturm and Drang in Southeast Asia, survived the CHAOS backlash. Unlike many of the musicians who fell under the heel of the mammoth inter-agency operation, she fully understood that political assassination could be her reward for openly castigating military-industrial masters of war.

Her close friend Martin Luther King, Jr. climbed to the "mountaintop." She met him on the descent. The world's most honored civil rights leader explained to Baez and a group of activist supporters before delivering the famed speech how he came to scale the "mountaintop": "[He] told us how it happened. It was when he was in solitary confinement in Alabama or someplace. [The police] had dumped him in the hole, and it was black, he couldn't see. And they shoved food into the room, but he was afraid to eat it. Starving, afraid—he said he got on his knees for hours. 'And when I stood up,' he said, 'it didn't matter anymore.'"

King's entourage hid their pain "when we knew what he meant—we knew he was going to die. And he was ready to die, and he was ready to make his commitment about Vietnam—which is *why* he died. 'I've been to the mountaintop, and I've seen the promised land, and it doesn't matter anymore.'" [1]

King's example left Baez with a personal and highly instructive vantage point to view the pathological drives of the intelligence sector's bloodhounds, but she already had a jump on most activists—she was to the national security state born. Baez wrote in a memoir, *And a Voice to Sing With* (1987), of her childhood and her father, a "bright young Stanford scientist" who settled in Los Alamos, New Mexico, the incubation chamber of the atomic bomb. Albert Baez "recognized the potential destructive power of the unleashed atom even in those early days. So he took a job as a research physicist at Cornell University in Ithaca, New York." Cornell was the home base of the CIA's mind control experiments, and Joan Baez is a survivor of ritual child abuse and a multiple personality, according to letters she has written to researchers and other survivors, a common cover for trauma-based mind control programming (she has sung about it: "I'm paying for protection/Smoking out the truth/Chasing recollections/Nailing down the proof . . ."[2]).

Baez entertained no delusions about the CIA. In San Francisco, she once promoted *State of Seige*, a film, she said later, that "exposed, among other things, the corrupt element in the AID program which funded the teaching of torture techniques in Latin America. We solicited signatures against the use of torture." She informed these signatories, "Torture was more prevalent than it had been since the middle ages, thus the danger was its common use as government policy," and, "though at one remove, the hands of the US government were far from clean."[3]

The psychological cost of ritual abuse/mind control experimentation as a child, and decades of civil rights activism, has been years of intensive therapy to confront her "inner demons," her fears, insomnias, panic attacks, phobias, and anxieties. Therapists kept Baez "glued together, to get me to the next gig, or to the next march."[4]

Joan's father, a Quaker by religious conversion, "was invited to become Head of Operations Research at Cornell." This position and a security pass would almost certainly bring him into contact with the CIA's Human Ecology Fund, the contract base for all classified academic mind control studies sequestered behind the privet fences of Ivy League campuses across the country. "Exactly what the job entailed was classified information," Baez recalls, but her father was "offered a three-week cruise on an aircraft carrier as an introduction to the project and promised a huge salary. As it turned out, he would be overseeing Project Portrex, a vast amphibious exercise which among other things involved testing fighter jets, then a relatively new phenomenon. Millions of dollars would be poured into the project, about which he was to know little and say less."[5] After high school, her father moved on to MIT, another fount of classified military research.[6] At the age of ten, she lived in Baghdad, Iraq with her family. Upon their return to the US, the Baez family moved to California.

SOME RIGHT-WINGERS FOUND THE MUSIC OF JOAN BAEZ LESS THAN INSPIRATIONAL . . .

She was not buried by CHAOS, but she lived under its intolerant eye and it could silence her: "An American," the *New York Times* reported on February 21, 1967, "identifying himself as Harold Cooper, a CIA man, had ordered the Japanese interpreter, Ichiro Takasaki, to substitute an innocuous translation in Japanese for Miss Baez' remarks in English on Vietnam and Nagasaki's atom bomb survivors." Cooper asked Takasaki to revise political statements made by the folk singer, and warned, "If you don't cooperate, you will have trouble in your work in the future." The interpreter cooperated and mistranslated her statements.

"It was a most strange case," Takasaki told reporters. "I knew that Miss Baez was a marked person who was opposed to the Vietnam War and who had been tacitly boycotted by the broadcasting companies in the United States. American friends also repeatedly advised me not to take on the job, but I took it on as a business proposition, since the Japanese fans were coming not to hear her political statements, but her music. I met Mr. Cooper once in the presence of a *Times* reporter in Japan, but even in that meeting he openly demanded that I mistranslate. I tried to reject the absurd demands, but he knew the name of my child and the contents of my work very well. I became afraid and agreed."[7]

A year later the European Exchange System announced that the sale of Joan Baez records had been banned from all Army PXs. And in 1969, Baez denounced the draft on *The Smothers Brothers Comedy Hour*. She was censored by CBS—her comments cut from the video tape when the program aired. Shortly thereafter, CBS canceled the troublesome *Smothers Brothers* for good. This was the same year that David Harris, her then-husband, was sentenced to a three-year prison term for draft evasion.

Baez also fell under the baleful eye of Mississippi's Sovereign Commission, a secret agency operating behind a pro-segregationist public relations facade, as revealed in 132,000 pages of documents declassified in 1998. The Commission spied on and smeared civil rights activists by falsely linking them to communist organizations. Among the estimated 80,000 names contained in the files: Baez, Sidney Poitier, Washington attorney Vernon Jordan, James Brown, Harry Belafonte, and jazz musician Dave Brubeck. "It's more disappointing than angering," Jordon told CNN on March 17, 1998. "It's disgraceful to have been spied on for doing your duty and trying to become first-class citizens." But Horace Harned of Starkville, a former state legislator and two-term member of the commission, defended the CIA-backed group. "We were under the threat of being overrun by an alien force led by the communists. . . . This was a time when the Freedom Riders were marching and burning things from New Jersey to California. They threatened to march through Mississippi," Harned declaimed. "Whether it was legal or not . . . never bothered me. We needed to have those spies. . . . A lot of [civil rights activists] were misguided, not realizing who was leading them and putting up the money."[8]

In April 1961, Baez met Bob Dylan at Gerde's Folk City, then opening for bluesman John Lee Hooker. Dylan, writes rock historian Wayne Hampton, would lead "the surge of folk protest into the popular mainstream of American culture. . . . Never before had songs of such stark political intensity reached into the realm of popular culture."[9] Dylan, of course, nearly died in 1966 after a motorcycle accident. Three months earlier, Joan's brother-in-law, Richard Farina, a folksinger and novelist of Irish-Cuban descent, *did* die in a motorcycle accident on his way home from a promotional party for his book, *Been Down So Long it Looks Like Up to Me*. Farina died on April 30, 1966, his wife Mimi's birthday. "He'd been riding on the back of a motorcycle on Carmel Valley Road," his friend Thomas Pynchon— who dedicated the labyrinthian *Gravity's Rainbow* to Farina—wrote in a memoir, "where a prudent speed would have been thirty-five. Police estimated that they must have been doing ninety, and failed to make a curve." Farina was thrown and killed. Before his death he had been producing an album of contemporary songs performed by Joan Baez. The recording was shelved after Farina died.[10]

Ninety miles per hour on a slow turn? How to account for the breakneck motorcycle ride? Was Farina in a reckless mood or had someone fiddled with the throttle? The government had no use for Richard Farina. The notorious HUAC Committee attempted to demonize him after a joyously rebellious trip to Cuba and his earthy political performances on college campuses. Farina's dissident lyrics—"It was the red, white and blue making war on the poor/Lying mother justice on a pile of manure"—undoubtedly cost him fans in the District of Columbia.

Dylan nearly followed Farina through the mists of American Pie oblivion but took a hard turn instead. He dropped the broadside lyrics grating on the nerves of the establishment. In 1963, Dylan was informed by censors that he would not be allowed to sing a ditty lampooning the distant-right John Birch Society on the *Ed Sullivan Show*.[11] Three years later, rock critic Ralph J. Gleason, writing in *Ramparts*, could argue that the most serious threat to the American Order came "not from the armed might of a foreign power but from a frail, slender, elusive lad, whose weapons are words and music, a burning imagination and an apocalyptic vision of the world."[12]

But after his motorcycle accident and a slow recovery from concussion and a number of broken vertebrae, Dylan underwent a political change. He retreated to Nashville and recorded *John Wesley Harding*, an allegoric collection of songs about his life situation, and in 1969 cut *Nashville Skyline*, a politically-innocuous country-and-western album. "He no longer wished to play radical politics with his music," observes Hampton. Dylan was suddenly apolitical. "Perhaps it was the accident, or perhaps he had already lost his nerve and used the accident as a cover." His sudden departure from radical politics outraged some critics and many of his fans. There were calls for a boycott.[13] Only five years after the accident did he appease his detractors with "George Jackson," a fiercely-driven ballad about the Black Panther leader viciously murdered by a prison guard. But by and large, he announced, "I don't want to write for people anymore. You know, be a spokesman."[14]

JOAN BAEZ AND BOB DYLAN COMPOSED THE NUCLEUS OF A FOLK MOVEMENT. THEY DID MUCH TO TRANSFORM AND MOVE THIS SUBCULTURE INTO DIRECT CONFRONTATION WITH EISENHOWER'S "COMPLEX."

Dylan shied away from communal politics in general, preferring to align himself with the individual tormented by the evils of American culture. He was a symbol of the '60s. Mark Edmundson, in *Civilization* magazine, writes:

> He wasn't ruined by drugs or the lure of easy transcendence, though he never sneers at the prospect of happiness. Dylan's work combines art and politics, the drive for pleasure with the urge to know the harshest truth about the world and then to try doing something about it. And ultimately this is the 1960s idea that has been lost from view. The accounts we have that are unsympathetic to the 1960s tell the story of people who have been addicted to power or pleasure and were ruined by those addictions. But there was, and is, a middle ground, where Dylan's work unfolds. The Dylan who moved audiences in the 1960s and continues to do so is not a "protest singer," nor is he just another episode in the disposable culture of American pop. He is, in the major phase of his work, a visionary skeptic. . . . Dylan, like the post-1865 Whitman, loves the promise of America and yet is disgusted by much of its reality.[15]

Dylan and Baez became intimate in 1963, a time, critic Tom Smucker wrote in the October 31, 1969 issue of *Fusion*, when, "due to factors I do not understand, having something to do with post WWII America, the breakdown of the socializing forces of schooling, affluence, the Cold War, and the beginnings of the Black revolt as a vital semi-alternative, some white kids began: 1. listening to black music on the radio, or eventually their own derivative of that: Rock 'n' Roll; 2. participating in what was then called the Civil Rights movement." They met at the Monterey Folk Festival and joined forces. Farina sketched one of their performances a year later: "They claimed to be there not as virtuosos in the field of concretized folk music but as purveyors of an enjoined social consciousness and responsibility. They felt the intolerability of bigoted opposition to Civil Rights. . . . When they left the stage to a whirlwind of enthusiastic cheers, it seemed that the previously unspoken word of protest, like the torch of President Kennedy's inaugural address, had most certainly been passed."[16]

The stories that Dylan spun over his dangling harmonica were not traditional folk music, Farina—his first wife launched Dylan's career—observed. The songs "had nothing to do with unrequited Appalachian love affairs or idealized whorehouses in New Orleans. They told about the cane murder of Negro servant Hattie Carroll, the death of boxer Davey Moore, the unbroken chains of injustice waiting for the hammers of a crusading era. They went right to the heart of his decade's most recurring preoccupation: that in a time of irreversible technological progress, moral civilization has pathetically faltered; that no matter how much international attention is focused on macrocosmic affairs, the plight of the individual must be considered."[17]

Phil Ochs, the "Outlaw" and his Brain

U.S. AGENTS WERE ABLE TO DESTROY ANY PERSON'S REPUTATION BY INDUCING HYSTERIA OR EXCESSIVE EMOTIONAL RESPONSES, TEMPORARY OR PERMANENT INSANITY, SUGGEST OR ENCOURAGE SUICIDE, ERASE MEMORY, INVENT DOUBLE OR TRIPLE PERSONALITIES INSIDE ONE MIND. . . . **MAE BRUSSELL, "OPERATION CHAOS"**

Yippie cherub Phil Ochs, for instance. Ochs was a close chum of Dylan's, and the nearest competitor for the folk-rock mantle. Life in another's shadow stung him. Yet he considered Dylan the "greatest poet ever" and often talked about his songs.

Dylan, Ochs and Farina set out on the folk minstrel's path in the Village of the early '60s at The Bitter End, the Gaslight, and other Greenwich Village clubs with Tom Paxton, Eric Anderson, Buffy Saint-Marie, John Sebastian, Eric Anderson, Dave Van Ronk, and a clutch of other then unknowns dubbed by Seeger "Woody's Children." There was an invigorating charge in the air, a sense of social rage finding and redefining itself after the cultural stagnation of the Eisenhower decade. Dylan crooned "Masters of War," Phil Ochs belted out an anguished "Too Many Martyrs." Together, they dragged folk music away from the migrant camps and union halls into direct confrontation with the boardroom of Eisenhower's looming "military-industrial complex."

Dylan, Baez, and Ochs strummed a path to the bill of the 1963 Newport Festival. Folksinging made an overnight comeback and immediately altered course to meet the path of extreme resistance. Ochs denounced American geopolitics in "Cops of the World."

PHIL OCHS, FOLK REVOLUTIONARY AND MULTIPLE PERSONALITY.

And when we've butchered your sons, boys,
Have a stick of our gum, boys!
We own half the world, "Oh, say can you see."
And the name for our profits is democracy. . .

He was the ultimate dissident . . .

The comic and the beauty queen are dancing on the stage.
The raw recruits are lining up like coffins in a cage.

A prophet on the barricades . . .

Oh, we're fighting in a war we lost before the war began . . .

Ochs was appalled by the corruption flourishing in the District of Columbia under Richard Nixon. One evening toward the end of his life, at a concert on West Third Street, Ochs knocked back a few tumblers of rum and drew down on CIA Director William Colby, formerly director of the murderous Phoenix program in Vietnam. "I put out a contract on Colby," Ochs spat, "for a hundred thousand dollars. I told Colby he's got a half year to get out or he's dead. They can kill me but he's dead. He's a dead man now. William Colby is *dead*."

Before the concert was over, sobriety was a distant memory, but he ranted on about his distrust of Patty Hearst ("Tanya . . . it's like a CIA code word"), the execution of Che Guevara, the media ("That awful cunt paper *Ms*., run by that CIA agent—what's her name?—Steinem, CIA Steinem . . .").[18]

Ochs rose to prominence as a performer with Baez and Dylan after the killing of John Kennedy. He was a founder of the Yippie Party, sang for the embattled ranks of protesters at the nightmarish 1968 Democratic convention in Chicago, appeared as a witness, guitar in tow, at the Chicago Seven Trial. His lyrics were considered so inflammatory that he was banned from the airwaves.

Ochs despised Nixon and the war. Music conveyed his obsessions, and so "Here's to the State of Richard Nixon":

Nixon's gone and taught you lies
A face that screams out for replies . . .
If ever there was a crook, he's it
Perversion is the soul of wit
Pack your shovel, he's full of shit,
The tides are risin.'

The bursts of rage did not pass unnoticed by J. Edgar Hoover, who whipped off anxious memoranda to the executive branch implying that Ochs was gunning for Nixon. A recently declassified Justice Department memo, originating with the FBI office in Little Rock, Arkansas on October 22, 1969, reveals that "paranoia" was a two-way street:

PHONOGRAPH RECORD ENTITLED "REHEARSALS FOR RETIRE-MENT" BY PHIL OCHS, THREAT AGAINST THE PRESIDENT
[Name redacted] made available a phonograph record entitled, "Rehearsals for Retirement" by PHIL OCHS, distributed by A&M Records, 1416 North La Brea, Hollywood, California. The record was purchased by her 14-year-old son, Stanley Thomas, at Osco Drugs, Southwest Shopping Center, Little Rock, Arkansas.

This record was monitored on October 20, 1969, and on side one the first song, entitled "Pretty Smart On My Part," states in song what appears to be: "I can see them coming. They are training in the mountains. They talk Chinese and spread disease [the CIA]. They will hurt me, bring me down . . . Sometime later, when I feel a little better, we will assassinate the President and take over the government. We will fry them."

A disclaimer attached to the memo notes, "this document contains neither recommendations nor conclusions of the FBI, and in keeping with that we will refrain from drawing conclusions." But the Bureau did not refrain from amassing a huge file on Ochs, and the feeling that he was never alone unnerved him. In "My Life," he addressed the federal agents shadowing him:

Take everything I own,
Take your tap from my phone
And leave my life alone,
My life alone.

But he wasn't left alone. The name Phil Ochs was listed on Hoover's Security Index, a catalogue of "subversives" considered a threat to national defense. He was tarred as a "Communist."[19] The fear, the "paranoia" that had gripped Brian Jones, Jimi Hendrix, and other ill-fated musicians before him took hold. His friend John Berendt recalls that Ochs was "convinced he would be assassinated, probably onstage. Once, while he was waiting in the wings in Baltimore, the performer ahead of him dropped his guitar on the floor with a bang. Ochs ducked, positive the shooting had begun."

After the Chicago police riot, his life underwent an erratic, tormented decline. He was cursed by lengthy spells of depression. The tombstone on the cover of *Rehearsals for Retirement* (1969) was one of the many intimations of his pending death scattered around.[20] The album's title track reflected the despair that sank in after Chicago, a nagging sense of doom:

This then is the death of the American imprisoned by paranoia,
And all his diseases of his innocent inventions.
He plunges to the drugs of the devil to find his gods.
So the poet swordsmen and their lost generation
Must divorce themselves from their very motherland.
While I stumble through this paradise, considering several suicides.
My responsibilities are done, let them come, let them come,
And I realize these last days these trials and tragedies
Were after all only our rehearsals for retirement.

He was driven to drink by the radio blackballing of his music, hounded by the authorities and a series of unexplained mishaps. His nerves gave out. He lived in a perpetual state of "paranoia." In Hong Kong, tagging along on a lecture tour with underground cartoonist Ron Cobb in 1971, Ochs returned to his hotel room to find that it had been forcibly entered and all of his cash stolen. Ochs was convinced the CIA had robbed him to prevent his entry to Vietnam, the ultimate destination of Cobb's tour, and had no choice but to catch the next flight back to the States on an American Express card.[21]

And there was the crushing of his vocal chords by thugs in Tanzania. Ochs was drawn to Africa by its music, language, and political potential. While strolling on the beach at Dar es Salaam, Ochs was mugged by three black men. One of them held Ochs with a strangling forearm while another searched his pockets. The forearm compressed his throat so tightly that he was unable to scream or even breathe. He struggled, the arm tightened. Ochs passed out and the thieves beat him before they fled with his cash. The injuries were largely flesh wounds but his vocal chords were permanently damaged.[22] The muggers who quashed his career have never been identified.

His injuries, the pressures of political confrontation, and the death of the movement may have conspired in his retreat to leave him with a right-wing pseudo-personality, "John Train." Or was he, like his friend Joan Baez, the victim of CIA mind control experimentation? What are the odds that two activists in a small circle of friends would develop dissociative identity disorder, multiple personalities? The transformation—into a pathological

CIA agent, no less—is one of the most incredible declines of the American Pie mortality chart.

"On the first day of summer 1975, Phil Ochs was murdered in the Chelsea Hotel by John Train," he claimed in a taped interview. "For the good of societies, public and *secret*, he needed to be gotten rid of."[23]

Ochs made allusions to his pseudo-personality in song fragments of an album he planned, but never recorded:

> Phil Ochs checked into the Chelsea Hotel.
> There was blood on his clothes . . .
> Train, Train, Train, the outlaw and his brain . . .

"He actually believed he was a member of the CIA," writes biographer Marc Eliot. Ochs, reborn as Train, began compiling mysterious lists: "shellfish toxin, Fort Dietrich, cobra venom, Chantilly Race Track, hollow silver dollars, New York Cornell Hospital . . ."[24]

Ochs biographer Michael Schumacher interpreted the transformation as an escape from deep depression to living martyrdom. The singer's death at the hands of an alter-personality "assured him of the status of having a heroic figure in the mind of the 'public' society that admired his activism," and incidentally ended the harassment by the 'secret' societies (the FBI, CIA, Mafia, etc.) that wanted him silenced. "Or so Train hoped."[25]

John Train, a drinking, brawling right-wing thug, boasted in a filmed interview that he had "killed" Phil Ochs. The motive: Ochs was "some kind of genius but he drank too much and was a boring old fart." But Train hinted that if Ochs had been a commercial success, "they" [the CIA] would have killed his host personality. "Colby and Company would be more than happy to put a slug through his head at that point."[26] Colby did not have Ochs shot for "innocent inventions" but his slow death at the hand of a "CIA agent" alter-ego does raise the specter of mind control.

Ochs committed suicide on April 9, 1976 by hanging. This was the same year *The Control of Candy Jones*, by Donald Bain, a case study of CIA mind control experimentation, was published.[27] Jones also had a dual personality. Psychiatrists on the Agency payroll, according to Bain, secretly drugged and hypnotized the professional model, transformed her into a civilian Manchurian Candidate, a marionette with an inner-Nazi personality who carried out covert assignments. Any memory of these adventures, some of them hazardous, was erased when the host personality was recalled under hypnosis. Candy Jones worked without her knowledge as a CIA operative for twelve years, throughout the '60s into the early '70s. Her final post-hypnotic command was suicide, and she might well have gone through with it if not for the intervention of her husband, talk-show host Long John Nebel. This was the same federal "thought control" program that columnist Dorothy Kilgallen had stumbled upon in 1965, shortly before her own murder was misinterpreted as an accidental overdose of barbiturates.

The body of Phil Ochs was found but a few years after the culmination of the Candy Jones experiment. There was no evidence of foul play. It's very probable that Ochs did, in fact, end his life and that he, or rather "John Train," was programmed to kill Ochs, the host personality. The folksinger was left alone but for a few minutes, and clearly took the opportunity to end his own life. There was no evidence of foul play—unless Candy Jones-style, programmed multiplicity is considered and explored.

NOTES

1. Kurt Loder, "Joan Baez" (interview), *The Rolling Stone Interviews* New York: St. Martin's Press, 1989, p. 90.

2. Lyrics to the title track of Baez's *Play Me Backwards*, LP, Virgin Records, 1992. The album was nominated for a Grammy. Baez has discussed the trauma-based programming she endured as a child with activists who subsequently contacted me, requesting anonymity.

   Another popular musician with repressed memories of childhood trauma was Who guitarist Pete Townshend. Townshend began "chasing recollections" and "nailing down the truth" himself in 1991, when it occurred to him that certain phrases from the band's rock opera *Tommy* were echoes of submerged memories of his childhood. He had broken an arm in a bicycle accident and recuperated at his mother's house. Biographer Geoffrey Giuliano described the musician's confrontation with his hidden past: "She had just started work on her autobiography, and Pete asked her about the time frame between the ages of four and six, which, except for a few isolated incidents, was a mystifying blank." She filled in the two-year maw in his memories. Townshend isn't specific about the missing years. "It didn't contain the kind of trauma Tommy went through," Townshend reported, "seeing his mother's lover shot by his father, but it was pretty damn close." The memories surfaced gradually. The culmination of his struggle to remember came while working with *Tommy* director Des McAnuff on Broadway. It dawned on Townshend in the middle of a script conference, "I hadn't written a fantasy at all. I'd written my own life story." McAnuff recalls Townshend "striding around the room, ranting about [his] childhood." The director used the backdrop of Townshend's youth, Giuliano notes, "as fodder for [*Tommy's*] darkly surreal setting." Geoffrey Giuliano, *Behind Blue Eyes: The Life of Pete Townshend*, New York: Plume, 1996, p. 4.

3. Joan Baez, *And a Voice to Sing With*, New York: New American Library, 1987, pp. 182–83.
4. Kevin Ransom, "Joan Baez brings her life and music into the '90s," *Detroit News*, February 22, 1996.
5. Baez, p. 22.
6. Ibid., p. 49.
7. Ibid., p. 144.
8. Brian Cabell, AP, "Mississippi segregation spy agency records now public," CNN, March 17, 1998.
9. Wayne Hampton, *Guerrilla Minstrels*, Knoxville: University of Tennessee Press, 1986, p. 160.
10. Jeff Pike, *The Death of Rock 'n' Roll: Untimely Demises, Morbid Preoccupations and Premature Forecasts of Doom in Popular Music*, Boston: Faber and Faber, 1993, pp. 89–90.
11. Ralph J. Gleason, "The Children's Crusade," in *Bob Dylan: The Early Years*, Craig McGregor, ed., New York: Da Capo, 1972, p. 36.
12. Ibid., p. 173.
13. Hampton, pp. 185–89.
14. Anonymous, "The Genius Who Went Underground," 1967 *Chicago Tribune* story, reprinted in McGregor, p. 194.
15. Mark Edmundson, "Tangled Up In Truth," *Civilization: The Magazine of the Library of Congress*, October/November, 1997, p. 50.
16. Richard Farina, "Baez and Dylan: A Generation Singing Out," *Mademoiselle*, August 1964.
17. Ibid.
18. John Berendt, "Phil Ochs Ain't Marchin' Anymore," *Esquire*, vol. 86, October, 1976, p. 132.
19. Marc Eliot, *Death of a Rebel: A Biography of Phil Ochs*, New York: Carol, 1995, p. xi–xii.
20. Ibid., p. 334.
21. Eliot, pp. 234–35.
22. Ibid., p. 243.
23. Michael Schumacher, *There But for Justice: The Life of Phil Ochs*, New York: Hyperion, 1996, p. 313.
24. Eliot, pp. 295–96.
25. Schumacher, p. 314.
26. Eliot, pp. 179–80.
27. Donald Bain, *The Control of Candy Jones*, Chicago: Playboy Press, 1976, p. 267.

CHAPTER TEN
Who Killed the Kennedys?
(and Sal Mineo?)

I PLAY RUSSIAN ROULETTE EVERY TIME I GET UP IN THE MORNING. BUT I JUST DON'T
CARE. THERE'S NOTHING I COULD DO ABOUT IT ANYWAY. THIS ISN'T REALLY SUCH A
HAPPY EXISTENCE, IS IT? **ROBERT F. KENNEDY, "KENNEDY EXPECTED TRAGEDY
TO STRIKE," DALLAS TIMES HERALD, JUNE 6, 1968**

Sal Mineo was stabbed to
death in the parking garage beneath his apartment
complex just below Sunset Strip in West Hollywood on
February 12, 1976, a building then owned by divorce attorney
Marvin Mitchelson. There was no evidence of a robbery but a great
deal of speculation concerning motive. West Hollywood has a
sizable gay population. *Newsweek* reported after the actor's murder
that "long-whispered reports of the actor's alleged bisexuality and
fondness for sadomasochistic ritual quickly surrounded his murder." [1]
The press reveled in Mineo's rumored secret life. Local gay papers
were rife with claims of sadomasochistic sex and satanism. [2] Fear
ripped through the homosexual community. Gay bars in Los Angeles
closed and many a Hollywood star took refuge behind locked doors.

The former teen idol had signed on, according to friends, to play
Sirhan Sirhan in a film about the murder of Robert F. Kennedy—in
it, CIA assassination and post-hypnotic programming were to be
prominently-featured themes. Mineo and a friend, Elliot Mintz—
then a talk show host for the local ABC affiliate, later Bob Dylan's
publicist and spokesman for John Lennon and Yoko Ono—had
"buried themselves in research, asking questions everywhere about
the [Robert Kennedy] killing." The more they learned, "the more
convinced they became that Sirhan was innocent. [3] But the producer
had disagreed with that interpretation and Mineo pulled out of the
picture." [4]

Mineo felt an affinity with the Kennedys. "You know what day
they killed me? The same day as Kennedy—November 22." On this
day in motion picture history, Mineo was in Monument Valley for
the making of John Ford's *Cheyenne Autumn*. "Ricardo Montalban
shoots me," Mineo told friends at a party a year later. "I fall down.
Ford says, 'That's swell,' and they do something else. A couple

of hours later we hear the President's been murdered and Ford calls a wrap for the rest of the day. Somebody else figured out that at the same time Ricardo was shooting me, Oswald was shooting Kennedy."[5]

Facts emerged in his research concealed by

SAL MINEO IN **REBEL WITHOUT A CAUSE**. WHEN HIS ACTING CAREER WAS GUTTERED, HE TURNED TO POP MUSIC, WITH LESS THAN SPECTACULAR RESULTS. THE SAME MIGHT BE SAID FOR HIS ATTEMPT TO BRING SUPPRESSED FACTS CONCERNING THE MURDER OF ROBERT KENNEDY TO THE SILVER SCREEN.

the LAPD's "Special Unit Senator" (SUS), a CIA-linked police cadré assigned to an "investigation" of the shooting directed by Lieutenant Manuel Pena. On November 13, 1967—seven months before the RFK murder—the *San Fernando Valley Times* ran a brief on Lt. Pena's retirement from the Los Angeles police force. A testimonial dinner was held for him at the Sportsmen's Lodge in Encino, "a rousing and emotion-packed affair." Pena, we learn, "retired from the police force to advance his career. He has accepted a position with the Agency for International Development (AID) Office of the State Department" (a common front for CIA operations overseas). Pena hired on to AID as a "public safety advisor" to train foreign police forces. "After nine weeks of training and orientation, he will be assigned to his post, possibly a Latin American country, judging by the fact that he speaks Spanish fluently," the *Times* reported.

One month before the Robert Kennedy assassination, Pena returned to the LAPD and directed the SUS investigation away from the CIA and Mafia toward Sirhan, a feat that required mass destruction of evidence, the seizure of photos of the killing, much eyewitness badgering, attempts on the lives of forensic specialists (William H. Harper identified the second gun drawn in Kennedy's assassination only to be shot at himself the day before he was to testify) and other "clean-up" operations.

Pena's colleagues in the SUS unit were a curious lot, as Lisa Pease, a reporter for *Probe*, discovered in her own examination of the case:

> SUS members predominantly came from military backgrounds. Charles Higbie, who controlled a good portion of the investigation, had been in the Marine Corps for five years and in Intelligence in the Marine Corp Reserve for eight more. Frank Patchett, the man who turned the Kennedy "head bullet" over to DeWayne Wolfer after it had taken a trip to Washington with an FBI man, had spent four years in the Navy, where his specialty was cryptography.
>
> The Navy and Marines figured prominently in the background of a good many of the SUS investigators. The editor of the SUS Final Report, however, had spent eight years of active duty with the Air Force, as a Squadron Commander and Electronics Officer.
>
> Two SUS members were in a unique position within the LAPD to control the investigation and the determination of witness credibility: Manuel Pena and Hank Hernandez. Pena had quite the catbird seat. A chart from the LAPD shows that all investigations were funneled through a process whereby all reports came at some point to him. He then had the sole authority for "approving" the interviews, and for deciding whether or not to do a further interview with each and every witness.
>
> In a similarly powerful position, Sgt. Enrique "Hank" Hernandez was the sole polygraph operator for the SUS unit. In other words, whether a witness was lying or telling the truth was left to the sole discretion of Hernandez.
>
> Pena's brother told the TV newsman Stan Bohrman that Manny was proud of his service to the CIA. Pena had gone to a "special training unit" of the CIA's in Virginia. On some assignments Pena worked with Dan Mitrione, the CIA man assassinated by rebels in Uruguay for his role in teaching torture to the police forces there.[6]

No mention of hypnosis or behavior modification appears in the official report, but Michael Ruppert, a former LAPD officer who left the department to expose his CIA trainers, speaks of it: "Sirhan Sirhan was hypno-programmed using hypnosis, drugs and torture by, among others, the Reverend Jerry Owen and CIA mind-control specialist William Bryan at a stable where he worked months before the shooting. Also working there at the same time was Thomas Bremer, the brother of Arthur Bremer, who in 1972 shot Presidential contender George Wallace."[7] Arthur Bremer's sister, Gail Aiken, was nearly called by the prosecution to testify in the trial of Sirhan—that is, defense attorney Mike Wayland informed the judge that he intended to grill the witness on the stand—but she briskly left town.[8] "Ask yourself what you believe about the existence of democracy in this country," Ruppert suggests, "and what you believe about the fate of ANY Presidential candidate not sanctioned by the powers that be before the 'race' is run."

Did the LAPD's concealment of evidence implicating the CIA in the shooting at the Ambassador Hotel in 1968 extend to the murder of Sal Mineo eight years later? For evidence linking the murders, look to Robert Duke Hall—a private investigator who tailed Mineo on the day of his death[9]—but pack a Kevlar vest.

The subterranean channels of the intelligence world swarmed with crooks and killers. When agents veered over the top and into the headlines, they were sometimes shown the door by the CIA, and many entered the private investigations business. This is the industry that belched forth the late Robert Hall, Robert Vesco's security chief and a security contractor for Howard Hughes (who died on April 6, 1976, a few months before Hall himself was found dead). Jim Hougan, an investigative reporter and former editor of *Harper's*, describes the Burbank private investigator as a "sleaze," a pathological lowlife, "decidedly larcenous . . . a father, a wire-tapper, an informer, a dope peddler and a double agent."[10] He was also a gun-toting paranoiac, nagged by the perennial belief that someone wanted him dead.

The late Bobby Hall loved his work, but a Jewish pornographer and drug dealer from Shanghai ended all that. Hall was obsessed with intrigue, and, notes Hougan, "unchecked intrigue can certainly get even the most seasoned investigator into situations that quickly become questionable." Hall blackmailed Robert Vesco and was involved in a burglary at Summa Corporation, the inner sanctum of the Howard Hughes empire.

He believed that fugitive financier Vesco wanted him dead, but there were scores of L.A. fixers, trigger-men and covert operators, each nursing a grudge, who would have happily disposed of him. Prominent among Angelenos harboring homicidal feelings toward Hall count those hooked on his famous "Happy Shots," potent methamphetamine mixed with vitamin B-12. L.A. prosecutors suspected that the corrupt private investigator was blackmailing these clients and many others.

So it came as a complete surprise to no one when, on July 22, 1976, six months after Sal Mineo was murdered, Hall himself was gunned down. Hall's body was discovered on the floor of his kitchen. A .38 slug had penetrated the back of his skull. Jack Ginsburgs, a

Jewish pornographer with well-documented connections to corrupt L.A. police officials, was convicted for the murder.

Local and federal law enforcement agencies, the *Los Angeles Times* reported, were "scrutinizing Hall's dealings with a number of present and former police officers to determine if his death was linked to one such relationship." Few in his orbit had a kind word for his eulogy, but "even his most ardent detractors are vocal in praise of his talents for wire-tapping and electronic eavesdropping."[11]

Police searched Hall's house for clues to his murder. Instead, they stumbled upon Ian Fleming's techno-dreams: several cases of electronic bugging and debugging equipment, a tranquilizer dart gun, drug-tipped darts, tear-gas canisters, syringes, ampules of narcotics, lock-picking devices, and cartons filled with more than two-hundred audio tapes, an archive of corruption implicating powerful politicians and popular celebrities in drug trafficking, prostitution, blackmail and all varieties of criminal and political shenanigans. Some of Hall's best friends were interviewed by police—among them crooner Eddie Fisher.

Hall had once been retained by the managers of seven rock bands to investigate physicians who'd slipped their clients fraudulent prescriptions, mega-potency drugs that altered their personalities, sabotaged public appearances, and hampered their lives and music. Hall reported back that two doctors and a dentist had prescribed the pharmaceuticals. This information was turned over to the authorities. No action was taken.[12]

Hall was gunned down shortly thereafter. The homicide investigation turned up tapes of bugged conversations recorded by Robert Hall. Captain Jack Egger of the Beverly Hills Police Department abruptly resigned, citing "health" reasons, his underworld connections caught on the 300 tapes confiscated from L.A. stockbroker and gunrunner Thomas P. Richardson, a crony of Hall's convicted to a six-year prison term for stealing millions from a long list of banks, brokerage houses and Ivy League college funds.[13]

Egger's sudden departure from the Beverly Hills police force, the *Los Angeles Times* noted, "was precipitated by Burbank detectives playing selected tape recordings [from Hall's collection] for Beverly Hills Police Chief Edward Kreina."[14]

The press linked the detective to Washington politicians, famed Hollywood celebs embroiled in corrosive drug and sex scandals, cocaine traffic from L.A. to Malibu, international sporting events, and the LAPD. It was George Yocham, a former police lieutenant, retired, chairman of the Police Science Department at L.A. Valley College, and Robert Hall himself who had given the five-shot, .38 Caliber Centennial Special used in his murder to alleged trigger-man

Jack Ginsberg, alias Jack Ginsburgs.[15] Yocham was employed as a private detective for Hall's agency after leaving the Beverly Hills Police Department in 1971, after 25 years of service.

Ginsburgs was Hall's business partner and a consultant to Richardson. Also a pornographer with connections to organized crime, the proprietor of XXX, Inc. on Prairie Street in Chatsworth, California. Hougan: "The son of a White Russian émigré, he'd spent his youth inside the decadent Shanghai Bund—that romantic foreign colony which [was] a meld of opium, kinky sex and intrigue." The transcript of Richardson's trial reveals that Captain Egger enlisted Ginsburgs as a police informant. He also made Hall a "double agent" in the Richardson stock fraud case. Gene LeBell, the famed ex-wrestler, karate expert and Hollywood stunt man, was charged in Hall's murder as well. LeBell is well-known in any gymnasium, the son of Aileen Eaton, the famed Olympic Auditorium boxing pro-moter. It was Eaton who refereed the bout between heavyweight pugilist Muhammed Ali and martial arts star Antonio Inoki.[16]

Lebell was a third partner in Hall's private detective firm, and owned a pharmacy in Hollywood—the same pharmacy that distrib-uted tainted drugs to rock musicians—and Hall had blown the whistle.[17] Tommy Richardson, Hall's partner and Robert Vesco's pimp (he once reportedly flew Elizabeth "The Hollywood Madam" Adams and a plane loaded with prostitutes to Costa Rica to service the fugi-tive), told LAPD Detective Richard Schmidt that he believed Jack Ginsburgs "may have killed Hall because of Hall's activities against Ginsburgs,"[18] turning evidence on the poisoned prescriptions and other criminal enterprises.

The Hall slaying was not the only bullet-perforated door that led to the suites of corrupt public servants and wealthy military-industri-alists. L.A.'s "premiere gangster," gambling czar Mickey Cohen, was a friend of Sal Mineo's, or so the mobster claimed, and possibly the critical link to the killing of Robert Kennedy. Cohen was moved to contact the press immediately after the murder of Mineo to remi-nisce about his "old friend," and his appearance in news reports of the slaying was morbidly incongruous, because the former hit-man had no place in the story except to boast, "Sal was my pal." Unlike the average "former" underworld figure, he enjoyed the spotlight and maintained amiable relations with the press. But there was a whiff of mordant irony in this impromptu appearance in the very first *Los Angeles Times* report on Sal Mineo's murder. They met when the actor was in his 20s, Cohen boasted to the *Times*. Well . . . they weren't exactly "close" friends, he conceded, but still "friends." The actor/singer once frequented a Brentwood ice-cream shop, The

Carousel, owned by Cohen' sister, a thriving mob hangout in the mid-'50s until Cohen took a sabbatical to McNeil Island Penitentiary.[19] The Mafioso and the actor remained friendly till the day Mineo was cut down in a dark carport.[20]

Cohen was chummy with Nixon and his entourage. In 1968, Cohen, then imprisoned, said that Mob attorney Murray Chotiner had solicited campaign contributions from him on behalf of Richard Nixon. In 1970, Chotiner was appointed to the office of Nixon's special counsel. A year later, in private practice, he lobbied for a prison pardon on behalf of Teamster heavy Jimmy Hoffa.[21]

Cohen was the undisputed godfather of all West Coast Mafia gambling operations, a Meyer Lansky lieutenant. The gangster's *sub rosa* political exploits were the topic of his confessions in July 1975, at UCLA Medical Center, where he lay convalescing. One of these, heard only by investigative reporter Chuck Ashman, concerned Cohen's contribution to the rapturous rise of arch-conservative evangelist Billy Graham, President Nixon's celebrated "spiritual advisor."

> Mickey and I had met several times, but it wasn't until his last illness that he really began to open up. He said he had one final Big One that he had been saving for the end.
>
> When he told me the tale of his being paid off to fake a dose of Christianity for Billy Graham's early New York Crusade, I didn't take it all that seriously. Then I started checking—and I found enough documentation from federal investigators, tax agents, prosecutors and Mickey's pals, together with a Graham defector, to piece the story together. It was true! Two of Billy Graham's key disciples had passed more than $10,000 to Mickey and his family in exchange for his staged "conversion" to Christ for the benefit of the first official Billy Graham Crusade in New York City 20 years ago. We found the dates and amounts and even the checks.[22]

The former pugilist and trigger-man's numerous links to the Nixon circle were cast immediately after WWII. In 1946, Nixon made his first bid for Congress. Chotiner, then a defense attorney for mobsters, managed the Nixon campaign with the backing of Mickey Cohen, who contributed $5,000 from his own pocket to the California Republican's first congressional campaign. When Nixon ran for the Senate, Cohen kicked in $75,000 gathered from Las Vegas mobsters. Thus began the long and mutually-enhancing partnership of Nixon's political mob and the Mob,[23] and the merger would prove fatal to two Kennedy brothers.

Mickey Cohen was the first bridge linking the killers of Robert Kennedy and Sal Mineo. And much more. The gangster was on friendly terms with Carlos Marcello, the mob boss who ran with David Ferrie—one of the corrupt CIA operatives investigated by New Orleans prosecutor Jim Garrison in connection with the killing of JFK—in drug smuggling, the illicit import-export arms trade, and other underworld activities. Cohen was also Jack Ruby's chum. Cohen and Ruby were both fixated on a local stripper, Ms. "Candy Bar," an ex-convict, and shared her sexual favors. "Ruby often boasted of his friendship with the legendary Mickey Cohen," mob investigator John Davis notes, "and took pride in the fact that he had an affair with a woman who had been engaged to the Los Angeles mobster. That Robert Kennedy was shot in a city whose underworld was dominated by a friend of Carlos Marcello and Jack Ruby has to be regarded as potentially significant."[24] Marcello and Cohen had an enduring friendship that began in 1959, when they were both hauled before the McClellan Committee hearings on organized crime to face the interrogations of an openly contemptuous Robert Kennedy. As attorney general, Kennedy singled Cohen out as the principal target of his organized crime probe and concentrated his prosecutorial flame-throwing talents on the L.A. Mafioso.

Cohen was also a friend of Melvin Belli, Jack Ruby's defense attorney. Cherita Cutting, a researcher specializing in JFK murder minutiae, reports that Belli "once played a practical joke on a conference of tax lawyers. Belli, the featured speaker, introduced to the crowd a man with a phony name who Belli claimed was an expert on reducing your taxes. It turned out to be Mickey Cohen, who didn't pay taxes because the government couldn't prove he earned money."

Cohen dominated the West Coast rackets by 1968, the year of Robert Kennedy's death. He also controlled the Santa Anita racetrack, where Sirhan was employed as a groom and exercise boy.[25]

Cohen had close business connections to the Ambassador Hotel for many years. But one of the most damning indictments against him was his tie to Thane Eugene Cesar—in the opinion of most impartial and independent investigators, the unindicted killer of Robert Kennedy, a security guard from Lockheed with a security clearance and a registered .22 caliber firearm of the type used in the assassination—through a close mutual friend of both, John Alessio, the shah of gambling operations in San Diego.[26]

Mickey Cohen's circle of friends, his presence among the superpartiot cadrés of Kennedy's enemies, and that peculiar appearance in the limelight immediately after the Mineo killing, beg more questions about Hollywood power brokers than they put to rest.

They go on:

Sirhan, while tending horses at Santa Anita, had been befriended by horse trainer "Frank Donneroumas," an alias for Henry Ramistella, fugitive small-time gangster from New Jersey. Ramistella, Sirhan and Cohen were all close to Hollywood producer and anti-Castro Cuban exile leader Desi Arnaz.[27] (In 1966, Sirhan scrawled in his notebook that he had landed a job at Corona Breeding Farm, co-owned by Arnaz. Terry Welch, one of Sirhan's co-workers at the race track, told the FBI, "Desi Arnaz, Buddy Ebsen, and Dale Robertson, prominent television personalities . . . were well acquainted with Sirhan."[28] All three were ultra-conservatives. "Sol" Sirhan, as he was known in this circle, was also a fierce anti-Communist.)

But the most telling Cohen link to Sirhan was Russell E. Parsons, Sirhan's "defense" attorney. Parsons achieved notoriety as *consigliere* of the Cohen gang.[29] The Mob attorney had once written a letter of recommendation for him. Parson's syndicate connections were once dissected by the McClellen committee and its chief counsel, Robert F. Kennedy. Parsons dropped the ball in his "defense" of Sirhan. John Davis writes, "He made no effort to show that Sirhan might have been the tool of someone else and downplayed his association with racetrack gambling."[30] Worse, Parsons never objected to the prosecution's argument that the fatal shot was fired by Sirhan despite a statement from the Los Angeles coroner that the accused was in the wrong position to kill the Senator, who was shot from behind, not from the front where Sirhan stood.

Sirhan was railroaded by his own lawyers. The chief defense counsel in the Robert Kennedy case was Grant Cooper. At the time, Cooper also represented Johnny Rosselli, the mobster and Bay of Pigs veteran, in a card-cheating case and would soon be sentenced to prison himself for perjury for his courtroom performance in that case. Cooper threw Sirhan's defense by suppressing vital evidence. He never cited the autopsy report that would have cleared his client, revealing that the shot that killed Kennedy was not fired by Sirhan.

Nixon had certain tasks to perform best handled by gangland cutouts. One declassified FBI memo notes that a domestic Nazi leader and rancher in Southern California pledged up to $750,000 to the Mafia for a contract on the life of Robert Kennedy.[31] Larry Jividen, a former Marine pilot and Justice Department informant who mixed with Nixon's business associates, discovered organized crime with an emphasis on drug smuggling. The word "Rosemark," Jividen reported in a confidential letter to the Justice Department, was a code word used by this clique in reference to "funds contained in the Union Bank of Switzerland and the Investment and Trade Exchange Central

Bank in Zurich, Switzerland. Large amounts of money from under-world operations are funneled into these banks (casino skims, narcotics profits, prostitution income, etc.)." It was from this account that Howard Hughes—whose network, a clearinghouse of CIA/Mafia miscreants, comprises the second bridge connecting the Kennedy and Mineo killings—was loaned the capital to buy TWA in 4 1961, Jividen noted. "Puerto Rico and Santo Domingo appear to have been points for gold bullion pickups. During one flight, Donald Nixon was a passenger. My employers claim their influence permeated the highest levels of government."[32]

Howard Hughes, the scheming apparition of corporate power on CIA contract, another secret investor in Nixon's campaign, was never far from this circle of corrupt spies and racketeers. Robert Hall, the wire-tapping extortionist, doubled as a security contractor for the Summa Corporation in Los Angeles at 7020 Romaine Street, the communications hub of the decaying millionaire's worldwide corporate holdings. Security at Summa was overseen by Vince Kelley, formerly the ranking officer of the LAPD's notorious "Glass House," the intelligence center of the police department, and much more, a nest of domestic spies who infiltrated prisons and leftist political organizations to gather information, disrupt their activities, and in general cripple organized resistance. George Yocham, the former police lieutenant who kicked in the murder weapon used to kill Hall, reported to Kelley, and so did Robert Hall.

It's possible that Sal Mineo, in his homework on the Robert Kennedy murder, learned of Bill Stout, the CBS correspondent, who through then DA John Van De Camp contacted the FBI to inquire about certain fully-annotated Bureau photos the reporter had obtained of the murder scene at the Ambassador Hotel in Los Angeles. In the photos of the pantry, unexplained bullet holes appeared. The FBI returned that forensic examiners had not conducted a ballistics investigation of the scene, an answer that did not address the question. A Bureau official assured Stout that he would investigate the matter thoroughly and "get back with him." Stout is still waiting.

Someone else was agitated about the bullet holes in the Ambassador Hotel pantry. In August 1971, criminalist William Harper narrowly escaped an attempt on his life by a pair of gunmen pecking away at his automobile. The attempt to silence Harper occurred the day before he was to testify before a grand jury investigating ballistics evidence in the RFK assassination.[33] Harper testified in a sworn affidavit that "Senator Kennedy was fired upon from two distinct firing positions while he was walking through the kitchen pantry." Further, "no test bullets recovered from the Sirhan gun are in evidence. The gun was never identified scientifically as having fired any of the bullets removed from any of the victims." The firearm forcibly pried from Sirhan's grip "has not been connected by microscopic examinations or other scientific testing to the actual shooting."

Eight years later . . .

Pop music heaven admitted a number of rock celebrities in 1976, including: Mal Evans, 40, the Beatles' road manager, shot dead on January 5; Florence Ballard of the Supremes, 32, dead of "natural causes" on February 22; Free's Paul Kossoff, 25, drug overdose, March 19; Duster Bennett, 29, in a March 26 car crash; Phil Ochs, 35, suicide by hanging, April; Keith Relf of the Yardbirds, 33, electrocuted on May 14; Tommy Bolin, 25, of Deep Purple and the James Gang, heroin overdose in December. Flo and Eddie were forced to cancel a tour of America and the UK booked a year in advance after their lead guitarist dropped nine stories from his room at the Salt Lake City Hilton and was killed. On November 9, 1976 *San Francisco Chronicle* columnist John Austin commented, "The accident has not yet been reported." The police, he observed, were "trying to keep the lid on it." Was the media blackout of the "accidental" fatality related to the death threat that Jim Martin, the band's manager, received a few days earlier?

On February 13, 1976, the front page of the *Los Angeles Times* teemed with political upheaval. A bomb exploded at the Hearst Castle. A fiercely-delivered denunciation was leveled by a "strained" Secretary of State Henry Kissinger at congressional investigators. Nixon's ranking foreign policy advisor cursed a newly-released report from the House Intelligence Committee enumerating a litany of CIA abuses. "A vicious lie," he spat. Kissinger soundly excoriated the document, *The Pike Report*. It was "flagrant," "a disgrace," a "new version of McCarthyism" that "can only do damage to the foreign policy of the United States."

The swelling hordes of American conservatism heard, rallied, and dogged Pike into political obscurity for his "vicious lies" about the CIA.

Next to Kissinger's throes, the *Times* ran the obituary of veteran actor-singer Sal Mineo, stabbed to death in his carport at Hollywood Manor at roughly 9:15 PM. Neighbors heard the cries for help. The body was found by Ray Evans, a neighbor in the complex, a retired actor in the real estate business. "I saw a man in the fetus position, lying on his side," Evans told police. "Because of an incline, blood seemed to be coming from his head. I turned him over and I said, 'Sal, my God,' and I saw his whole chest covered with blood on the left side."

Witnesses gave homicide detectives a partial description. A white man with long brown or blond hair fled the murder scene in a yellow compact.[34]

The autopsy transcript states that Mineo suffered "a massive hemorrhage due to a stab wound to the chest, penetrating the heart." The murder weapon was a "heavy-type knife." There were, officially, no other injuries apparent. This observation clashed head-on with the testimony of eyewitnesses, who reported that Mineo had been stabbed repeatedly. This and other absurd contradictions were telltale signs that the fix was in. The name Robert Hall or one of his associates may have fit the profile, but his name would never surface in the ensuing investigation.

Homicide detectives installed a 24-hour hotline for information about the Mineo murder on February 17, five days after the knife attack. The delay may have sabotaged the entire investigation.

The Hollywood press handled the story with its usual dearth of aplomb. Kimberly Hartman, in an unpublished Mineo biography, recalls, "a powerful battle had begun—the image of Sal-the-Good-Son vs. Sal-the-Weirdo. Sal-the-Weirdo won out. [The] tabloid journalism did nothing to help the case. Some cops simply labeled it a 'fag killing' like the Navarro case only eight years before, and simply did not want to deal with it. The ones who did care were swamped with easily hundreds of tips, most of them fantasy and speculation."[35]

Back in Mamaroneck, friends of Mineo's from Hollywood fought with his family at O'Neil Mortuary. "Michael Mason seemed to have been the center of all debates," Hartman recalls. "He claimed that money was the first thing Sal's family asked about." It didn't occur to Mason that money had weighed heavily on his own mind and others who'd been close to Mineo. A small cabal headed by Mason tried to ostracize the family from the burial. "Michael Mason told Sal's brother, 'It's too bad you didn't know him well enough to find these answers out for yourself. But I see why he didn't like you or have anything to do with you in recent years.' That statement was a low blow to Sal's family which he had always loved. Mason did not have his facts correct—he was no better than anyone else in Sal's life." It seemed that even in death, "Sal Mineo was being pulled apart, and Michael Mason's selfishness fueled the tug-of-war. Sal's family suffered more than anyone can know—even more than 'friends' like Mason who took advantage of the good-natured actor."

Police still had no murder weapon, no suspects, motive or witnesses.

Mineo's body was flown to Mamaroneck, New York for the funeral at Holy Trinity Roman Catholic Church, with 250 paying respects. Many more stood quietly outside, and some 300 onlookers surged in the street. Sal Mineo was buried on February 17, 1976, at Heaven Cemetery in Hawthorne, New York.

On the same day the body was flown east, detectives revised their description of the suspect: He was a 20–30 year old white male, dark clothing, roughly 5' 7" to 10' tall, average build, dark hair.

Nearly a year and a half passed before the case was "solved." Burton S. Katz—a prosecutor in the Manson murders, the district attorney who convicted Bobby Beausoleil and Steve "Clem" Grogan for the slayings of Gary Hinman and Donald "Shorty" Shea—nailed down a grand jury indictment in the Mineo case in May 1977.[36] LAPD detectives questioned Theresa Williams, an L.A. hooker. As the police told it, Ms. Williams confessed that her husband had returned home on the night Mineo was killed, smeared with blood. He allegedly told her, "I just killed this dude in Hollywood." Police were skeptical at first. They were looking for a white male, and Lionel Ray Williams was African-American. But an examination of his arrest records turned up a fascinating detail: Williams had been arrested on forgery and robbery charges shortly after the Mineo murder, and was already incarcerated in Michigan.

The police claim that Ms. Williams called and freely offered to turn state's evidence against her husband. Mr. Williams responds from prison: "That's all crap. That's not true. Police went to her. She had a prostitution case, and [the police] were going to take my kid from her." Williams maintains that continual police harassment drove his wife to attempt suicide. She was pressured "to the point where she put a bullet in her head," Williams said. "She tried to kill herself." [37]

Williams did have one connection to the case. In exchange for clemency, he had offered information about the Mineo case to Michigan police who notified the LAPD—and by stepping forward with the first break in the investigation, Williams may have become the man who knew too much. He said that Mineo had been murdered "in a dispute with a drug dealer." (Bobby Hall with his amphetamine concession?) Williams was freed, the charges against him dropped with a proviso that he gather more information on the Mineo murder and get back with the Los Angeles homicide detail.[38]

The former pizza delivery man was charged on an L.A. County grand jury indictment. Williams pled not guilty to ten counts of robbery, one count of armed robbery—the latter mysteriously overturned despite the Los Angeles Times report that Williams "was armed with a gun or knife in all the robberies except one."[39] The 21 year-old pizza delivery man was held on $500,000 bail and ordered to stand trial before Superior Court Judge Edward A. Heinz, Jr.

At trial, Hartman says, defense attorney Mort Herbert called two witnesses to the stand, both of whom claimed to have seen a white man running from the scene. "He produced written accounts from many of Sal Mineo's neighbors who had claimed to have seen a white man running away. He cited that even the police had been looking for a white man. Next, he pointed out the obvious—Lionel Ray Williams was a black man. Another eyewitness verified that they had seen 'a swarthy white man, perhaps an Italian or a Mexican,' running down the driveway to of the apartment building. All in all, Herbert punched many a hole in the prosecution's case."

The DA's office drafted a murder complaint. This was attached to ten complaints of robbery already attributed to Williams. It was a completely circumstantial case, but soon the Sheriff's Department filed a declaration in Beverly Hills Municipal Court claiming that Williams had confessed to fellow inmates. This development was overheard, police claimed, by a bug planted in Williams' cell. But transcripts of the bugging were withheld from the defense and even the judge.

Allwyn Williams (no relation to Lionel), a prison inmate, was the prosecution's star witness, purchased with a plea bargain. He testified: "We came to the discussion that he had killed someone famous. I wondered who. 'Sal Mineo,' he replied. He started talking about it. He said he was in Hollywood, driving around below Sunset. He was going to rob someone for money." No money was stolen. "He stabbed someone. And he told me how he done it. He demonstrated."

"Allwyn Williams," Hartman reports, "under cross-examination, admitted that he made up testimony about Williams driving a Lincoln Continental and using a pearl-handled knife in some attacks because he allegedly felt his statement, which linked Williams to the Sal Mineo murder, was not strong enough to get himself out of jail" (Allwyn Williams was provided immunity for an L.A. robbery which he had participated in with the defendant). "Mort Herbert attempted to show that Allwyn Williams had a motive for testifying against the defendant—his own fear of going to prison. Herbert also was able to make Allwyn admit that if necessary he would have lied even further to get his felony conviction reduced to a misdemeanor. The prosecution's key witness also admitted that he had been taking drugs w hen the defendant supposedly discussed the murder. A following witness for the defense further discounted the prosecution's key witness by claiming that he had never heard L.R. Williams admit to the Mineo murder in the supposed conversation with Allywn Williams."

NOTES

1. Dennis Williams and Martin Kashdorf, "The Outcast," *Newsweek*, February 23, 1976, p. 25.
2. Susan Braudy, *Who Killed Sal Mineo?*, New York: Wyndham Books, 1982, p. 32—a novel based on the case. Mineo's closest friends insist that these reports were exagerrated, that he was drawn to the gay community because he found it exotic. But "Sal had some strange tastes," producer Peter Bogdonovich acknowledged, and "he was totally unaffected by it. The murder was so shocking because as a person he was so innocent." But bisexual and innocent are not mutually exclusive qualities. The Hollywood Paparazzi press, most notably Boze Hadleigh, reports that Mineo was bisexual, counting Rock Hudson among his paramours. See Boze Hadleigh, *Conversations with My Elders*, New York: St. Martin's Press, 1987.
3. Elliot Mintz resurfaces in this mortal inventory to witness the unfolding of a covert operation designed to discredit the Beatle and his widow. Mintz was a thorough and highly credible historian of the 1960s, recalls Jim Ladd, a colleague at RADIO KAOS, an underground station in Los Angeles: "During his ten years in the business, Elliot had logged over two thousand interviews and more than 50,000 telephone calls over the air. He explored the entire gamut of the movement during his time in the glass booth, from Baba Ram Dass to Buffy Sainte-Marie, from Jane Fonda to Jack Nicholson, from Norman Mailer to Abbie Hoffman. A self-taught intellectual, and one of the most well-read humans on the planet, Elliot was the counterculture's answer to William F. Buckley." Jim Ladd, *Radio Waves: Life After the Revolution on the FM Dial*, New York: St. Martin's, 1991, p. 187.
4. Hartman. Also, Mae Brussell, "Operation CHAOS" unpublished ms. And, Tim Hunter, "Who Done It," *Chic*, June 1977, p. 88.
5. Peter Bogdanovich, "The Murder of Sal Mineo," *Esquire*, March 1, 1978, p. 116.
6. Lisa Pease, "Sirhan and the RFK Assassination, Pt. II—Rubrick's Cube," *Probe*, vol. 5, no. 4, May–June, 1998.
7. Michael C. Ruppert, Internet posting.
8. William W. Turner and John G. Christian, *The Assassination of Robert F. Kennedy*, New York: Random House, 1978, p. 265.
9. Hunter and Brussell.
10. Jim Hougan, *Spooks: The Haunting of America—The Private Use of Secret Agents*, New York: William Morrow, 1978, p. 243.
11. Bill Farr and Bill Hazlett, "Tapes Raise Questions in Detective's Death," *Los Angeles Times*, September 10, 1976, p. B-1.
13. Farr and Hazlett, p.B-1.
12. For the questioning of Eddie Fisher, see Hougan, p. 245. On the pharmacy connection, Mae Brussell, "Operation Chaos," unpublished ms.
14. Hougan, p. 247.
15. William Farr, "Defense Attorneys in Killing of Detective Ask Access to Files," *Los Angeles Times*, November 13, 1976, p. A-22.
16. Gene LeBell, a Hollywood actor and stunt man in Hollywood. Among his long list of credits: *As Good As It Gets* (1997) *Dante's Peak* (1997), *L.A. Confidential*, *CIA II Target: Alexa* (1994), *Darkman* (1990), *Die Hard 2* (1990), *Total Recall* (1990), among others.
17. Brussell.
18. Farr and Hazlett, p. B-1.

19. Sam Kashner and Nancy Schoenberger, *Hollywood Kryptonite: Accident, Suicide, or Cold-Blooded Murder—The Truth About the Death of TV's Superman,* New York: St. Martin's, 1996, pp. 9.

20. John Kendall, "Motive in Sal Mineo Slaying Baffles Police," *Los Angeles Times,* February 13, 1976, p. A-3.

21. A.J. Weberman, Coup D'Etat in America Data Base http://Weberman.com. FBI FOIA Request #72,182 approx. 500 pp.; HSCA OCR 11.2.78 Brady.

22. Chuck Ashman, "The Conversion of Mickey Cohen," *Chic,* Vol. 1, no. 8, June 1977, p. 56.

23. Hougan, pp. 251–52.

24. John H. Davis, *Mafia Kingfish: Carlos Marcello and the Assassination of John F. Kennedy,* New York: McGraw-Hill, 1989, p. 346.

25. Ibid.

26. Davis, p. 356. In 1968, novice "underground" journalist Lowell Bergman discovered that Alessio had enormous influence in southern California right-wing circles and a possible motive for wanting Robert Kennedy out of the way. Bergman went on to write for *60 Minutes* in 1983, but in his youth lived in a commune and wrote for the resident underground newspaper: "What we were trying to do was break the monopoly on information. We tried to approach it from an academic point of view. Some of us had experience in what was called 'power-structure research.' What we were looking for was: Who ran San Diego? What we discovered was that the richest guy in town, [financier] C. Arnholt Smith, was in reality in partnership with John Alessio. The second-largest landowner, next to the Navy, at that time, was the Teamsters' Central States Pension Fund, which had been called by Robert Kennedy, the attorney general at the time, the 'piggy-bank' for the Mob." [John Freeman, "Lowell Bergman, Television-Radio Writer" (interview), *San Diego Union-Tribune,* May 26, 1996, p. E-1.]

    Like Cohen, C. Arnholt Smith and his San Diego business clique made illegal campaign contributions to the Nixon campaign in 1968. Harry D. Steward, the U.S. attorney in San Diego, ran an investigation of the contributions—and was forced to resign in December, 1974 after the Senate Judiciary Committee charged him with obstructing its probe. One of Steward's career highlights was the 1970 conviction of Alessio, described by federal officials as the largest case of income-tax evasion at the time. But Alessio received a light sentence, three years in federal prison, and was paroled in two.

27. Davis, p.352. Also see, John G. Christian and William W. Turner, *The Assassination of Robert F. Kennedy: A Searching Look At the Conspiracy and Cover-Up, 1968–1978,* New York: Random House, 1978, p. 220.

28. Christian and Turner, pp. 220–21.

29. Dan E. Moldea, *The Killing of Robert F. Kennedy,* New York: W.W. Norton, 1995, p. 116.

30. Davis, p. 354.

31. Christian and Turner, p. 320.

32. Hougan., p. 253.

33. Turner and Christian, p. 315. Harper also reported that Sirhan's prosecutors "attempted to establish that the Sirhan gun, and no other, was involved in the assassination. It is a fact, however, that the only gun actually linked scientifically with the shooting is a second gun, not the Sirhan gun."

34. Ellen Hume and Ted Thackrey, Jr., "Sal Mineo Knifed to Death," *Los Angeles Times*, February 13, 1976, p. A-1.
35. Kimberly Hartman, "Pretty Boys Make Graves," unpublished ms., ch. 20.
36. "Judge Burton S. Katz," press release, Santa Barbara Speaker's Bureau, P.O. Box 30768, Santa Barbara, CA 93130-0768. Katz went on to be a judge, in which capacity he presided over the murder trial of John Sweeney—convicted on minor charges of simple assault and voluntary manslaughter for the strangulation murder of actress Dominique Dunne. He has taught at law schools, police academies, and the California Specialized Training Institute. "Menendez. Simpson. Bobbit. King," boasts the Bureau's release. "Everyone immediately recognizes these names because of their high-profile cases—and controversial verdicts."
37. "Sal Mineo," *Mysteries and Scandals*, E! Channel, February 14, 1999.
38. Ibid.
39. Bill Farr, "Mineo Slaying Suspect Charged," *Los Angeles Times*, May 4, 1978, p. B-8.

CHAPTER ELEVEN

"Project Walrus"
and Holden Caulfield's Warm Gun

AT THE MORGUE, THE ENTRANCE WAS SEALED SHUT WITH A LOCK AND CHAIN. ATTENDANTS WITH GREEN MORTUARY MASKS MOVED AROUND IN A DUMB SHOW, THEIR WORDS INAUDIBLE, OR TYPED OUT FORMS ON GRIM CIVIL-SERVICE TYPE-WRITERS. BEHIND THEM, IN A REFRIGERATOR, LAY THE SIXTIES. **PETE HAMILL, NEW YORK MAGAZINE, JOHN LENNON OBITUARY**

The "Catcher in the Rye of the present generation" confronted his judge on January 6, 1981. The courtroom antics that followed were a macabre illustration of the principle that the cover-up proves the crime. Justice Herbert Altman asked how Mark David Chapman chose to plead. "Not guilty," the prisoner—following the direction of his "voices"—responded. By law, the defendant decides the plea, guilty or not guilty by reason of insanity, one or the other, not the defense attorney. Nevertheless, Chapman's attorney Jonathan Marks punctuated the plea ". . . by reason of insanity."

The bench favored a motion from Marks to enlist three psychiatrists to provide opinions on Chapman's mental competence to stand trial. The first was Dr. Milton Kline, a prestigious clinical psychiatrist, an authority on hypnosis from New York,[1] and an esteemed consultant to the CIA on the creation of programmed killers while president of the American Society for Clinical and Experimental Hypnosis, a true believer in the "Manchurian Candidate" killing concept who once boasted that he was capable of creating a hypnotically-driven patsy in three months, a mind-controlled assassin in six.[2]

The second psychiatrist chosen to examine Chapman was Dr. Bernard Diamond from the University of California at Berkeley, a busy hive of illicit mind control experimentation in past decades. Dr. Diamond had provided the same service to Sirhan

Sirhan. The accused killer of Robert Kennedy told another psychiatrist, Dr. Eduard Simson-Kallas, a clinical psychologist assigned to the case, that he did not trust Dr. Diamond. As Sirhan explained to Dr. Simson-Kallas after the trial, "Whatever strange behavior I showed in court was the result of my outrage over Dr. Diamond's and other doctors' testimony. They were saying things about me that were grossly untrue, nor did I give them permission to testify [on] my behalf in court." [3]

The third psychiatrist entrusted to evaluating Chapman's hold on reality was Dr. Daniel Schwartz, director of forensic psychiatry at King's County Medical Center in Brooklyn. Dr. Schwartz had examined David "Son of Sam" Berkowitz, and offered that the accused serial killer believed he'd been commanded by "demons" to kill. Mark David Chapman had also been pushed by the "demons" of his dementia to shoot John Lennon, Dr. Schwartz opined from the stand. He testified that Chapman had admitted, "I can feel their thoughts. I hear their thoughts. I can hear them talking—but not from the outside, from the inside." Up to the moment he squeezed the trigger of his Charter Arms .38, Chapman "continued to operate under this primitive kind of thinking, in which he believed or believes that forces outside of him, supernatural or otherwise, determined his behavior." [4] The diagnosis was nearly identical to the one he gave Son of Sam.

Not one of these three mental health specialists explored the hint of mind control, in the opinion of Dr. Dorothy Lewis, a professor in psychiatric research at the Yale School of Medicine and a consultant to Marks. Dr. Lewis reported that the assassin may have acted in response to a "command hallucination." British barrister Fenton Bresler, in *Who Killed John Lennon?*, asks: "Could any term be more appropriate for a disturbed man operating under hypnotic programming?" [5]

In 1977, Chapman lost his religion. His fundamentalist indoctrination festered in a stew of self-loathing, devil-worship, and a killer's fantasies. Months before the murder, he visited satanist and filmmaker Kenneth Anger at a screening in Hawaii, shook hands and handed over two .38 caliber bullets. "These are for John Lennon," he explained to Anger. [6] Chapman may have felt a spiritual kinship with the satanist. He had attempted suicide, interpreted his survival as a sign, and thereafter addressed his prayers to Satan, [7] who responded with commands, mind control. And, as it happens, the CIA has been obsessed with mind control techniques since the dawn of the Cold War. Agency psychiatrists were eminently capable of transforming a hyper-religious nobody on the board of the Decatur, Georgia YMCA into a programmed killer, and the allegation has been made repeatedly since Lennon's murder.

Psychotronics was the topic of an August 22, 1994 *Newsweek* report on a secret Arlington, Virginia conference between behavioral specialists from the FBI's Counter-Terrorism Center and Dr. Smirnov, whose work was truly Frankensteinian: "Using electroencephalographs, Smirnov measures brain waves, then uses computers to create a map of the subconscious and various human impulses, such as anger or the sex drive. Then through taped subliminal suggestions, he claims to physically alter the landscape with the power of suggestion."

The CIA attained the same level of sophistication as Dr. Smirnov's EEG approach by the mid -'60s. In 1974, Ed Sanders, poet and author of *The Family*, a book that explores the totalitarian fantasies of Charles Manson, wrote a letter to the late political researcher Mae Brussell, describing federally-sponsored mind control operations in Hawaii, Chapman's home, conducted by the US military, most notably the creation of serial killers.[8] Northern Califonia mass murderer Herbert Mullen, Sanders wrote, worked at a Holiday Inn and flew to Hawaii in 1970 with Patricia Brown, a much older woman, against the wishes of his family. She told him that they would stay with a "church group," but Mullen was committed the day after his arrival to a mental hospital operated by the U.S. Army instead. He was given generous servings of LSD and other hallucinogenic drugs, not exactly standard therapeutic practice. In her December 20, 1980 broadcast, Brussell related that Sanders informed her how Lawrence Quong, a raving gunman who shot at a San Francisco radio personality while on the air, "was taken to Hawaii by a woman and brought back to San Francisco with a mysterious gun placed in his hand." The gun was unregistered, its origin unknown. Quong "went to a private detective many times and said he'd been programmed with electrodes and he was directed to this radio station. He couldn't control himself." Others, Sanders insisted, did.

Mind control researchers have long pointed to Chapman's relationship with World Visions, an evangelical charity that boasted John Hinckley, Sr., CEO of Vanderbilt Energy Corp., an oil exploration company, on its board. Hinckley was a close friend of George Bush, one path to the CIA.[9] (As in the Chapman case, CIA psychiatrists were summoned to evaluate John Hinckley, Jr. after his assault on Ronald Reagan. The prosecution's psychiatric expert was Dr. Sally Johnson, currently chief of psychiatric services at the Butner Federal Correctional Institute in North Carolina—for decades one of the foremost CIA mind control facilities in the country. Dr.

Johnson surfaced in the news weeklies in January, 1998 when she examined accused Unabomber Theodore Kacynzski—a subject of Agency-sponsored mind control experimentation while a student at Harvard—for the court. Her appearance raises the distinct possibility that the Unabomber was programmed. Dr. Johnson was calle d after Kacynzski tried to fire his attorneys and represent himself in court.) World Visions has collaborated with the CIA in past black operations, including the use of a camp in the Honduras where the organization fronted for a contra recruiting drive for the Nicaraguan rebellion. In Cuba, World Vision camps concealed the agitations of Alpha 66, the anti-Castro brigands of Bay of Pigs fame. Phalange fascists butchered Palestinians at the World Vision camp in Lebanon. These evangelicals also turned up in Guyana after the Jonestown massacre to plan a re-population of the area with Laotian mercenaries still reeking of raw opium, refined by the CIA into heroin for distribution to American GIs stationed in Vietnam and to the States via Air America and other criminalized Agency tentacles.

Some researchers consider Chapman's world travels suggestive of CIA support. In the summer of 1975, Chapman, then 19 years old, signed on to the YMCA's International Camp Counselor Program (ICCP) and asked to be sent to the Soviet Union—an odd request, since Chapman was a strident anti-Communist. He was packed off instead for a stint in Beirut, where, it is postulated, he received instruction in the lethal arts at a CIA training camp, or, depending on one's point of view, a school of terror (as did renegade Agency arms dealers Frank Terpil and George Korkola, and William Peter Blatty of *Exorcist* fame ran an experimental mind control unit for the Army in Lebanon[10]).

Chapman did in fact receive firearms training at the Atlanta Area Technical School after dropping out of Covenant College, a Presbyterian academy in Tennessee, and taking a job as a security guard. He passed the pistol-training course with flying colors. The job and course work were a marked departure from Chapman's prior ambition to lead the life of a missionary. They were suggested to him by a new circle of friends, and accompanied by a drastic change in his personality. The happy, hard-working Christian fundamentalist went sour. He moved to Hawaii to start a new life, but sank into a period of deep depression and attempted suicide. He was admitted to Castle Memorial Hospital in 1977, where he was diagnosed as suffering from severe depressive neurosis. Chapman was not considered pathological, however, and was released two weeks later. He had proven so popular with doctors at the clinic that Chapman was hired on in August 1977 through November 1979 as a maintenance worker with a promotion to the customer relations office. But he impulsively quit the job with a modest loan from the hospital credit union in his pocket, Chapman claimed, and set off on a world tour.[11]

In August 1980, he surfaced in New York and mailed a letter to an Italian addressee. The Dakota was given as the return address. It was a breezy note, nothing momentous—with the exception of a reference to his "mission" in New York. The "mission" could be interpreted as a "command hallucination," or possibly a boastful exaggeration if it weren't for the mysterious path the letter followed after Chapman dropped it in the mailbox. The Italian acquaintance could not be found and it was returned to New York, where it moldered in the dead-letter bin for three years and was finally delivered to the Dakota. Yoko Ono glanced at the returned letter, dropped it in her DERANGED file and forgot about it. In June 1983, Dan Mahoney, the head of security at the Ono household, was sorting through the file and found the letter, postmarked 1980. This was evidence of premeditated murder and possible conspiracy. Mahoney intended to give it to Yoko Ono and ultimately the police. But shortly thereafter the Chapman letter vanished, only to reappear again on Yoko's kitchen table, slightly altered. The postdate was now 1981. Turning the letter over to authorities was now out of the question. The revised letter was as breezy as the original, but now made no mention of Chapman's "mission" in New York.[12] (In conversation with Rev. Charles McGowan at Rikers Island a few days after the murder, the gunman also spoke of a "mission that I could not avoid."[13]) An infiltrator in Yoko's household had apparently altered the letter to protect the "lone" gunman's accomplices—and they were up to their own nostrils in a black operation the conspirators called "Project Walrus."

Elliot Mintz (last seen on this trail of murder and hypocrisy gathering information about the RFK assassination with his doomed friend Sal Mineo) was instrumental in exposing the Project. Mintz, Lennon's chum and publicist since 1971 until the arrival of Mark David Chapman, pins primary responsibility for the exploitation of Lennon on Fred Seaman, the Beatle's chauffeur and author of *The Last Days of John Lennon: A Personal Memoir*. Mintz laid out the plot in the December 1991 issue of *Instant Karma*, a Beatles 'zine.

"In the opening pages of Fred's book, he describes his arrest," Mintz says. "Now understand what led up to the arrest was all the circumstances of the Project." Fred's college roommate, Bob Rosen, a controlling psychiatrist, and a New York diamond dealer "all got together and decided to engage in this 'Project Walrus' conspiracy. [This] involved setting up an apartment as well as a warehouse in

Manhattan, have Fred steal as many things as he could—not just the journals, although the journals were the most important things—and for these four guys to: 1. sell the materials privately, because this was right after John's death and obviously the sky was the limit in terms of what one could charge for those kinds of things, and; 2. write a book that would corner the gossip market on John Lennon . . . and Yoko." [13]

Rosen, the project archivist, was nudged out of the operation. When entire filing cabinets stuffed with stolen Lennon material were discovered missing, the scheme came unraveled. Rosen turned evidence on Seaman and his accomplices in exchange for full immunity, Mintz recalls, "because now the district attorney's office was involved, now the New York City police department was involved. Obviously Rosen was getting a little anxious."

More than a little—Rosen told Ono that he feared for his life. [14]

Of his accomplices: "Fred was using drugs at the time [and] he was, I think, probably being manipulated by the psychiatrist," Dr. Francis DeBilio, a Brooklyn psychotherapist, "and the diamond dealer was feeding them cash." [15] Norman Schonfeld, the diamond trader and financier of Project Walrus, has refused to answer any questions about this coalition formed to destroy Lennon's reputation, a plan conceived months before Chapman arrived at the Dakota to ask for an autograph. In August 1980, Rick Dufay, a guitarist for Aerosmith, was recruited by the Project. Like the others, Dufay strolled into the conspiracy fully conscious that it was morally repugnant. Rosen wrote in his diary that he, Seaman, and Dufay "know how contemptible the other one is. Interesting contest, who is the most contemptible among us." [16]

Some insight into the operation might have been culled from Lennon's diary for the months preceding his death, but it vanished and has never been recovered.

Mintz recalls, "Some of Yoko's bodyguards were at the time New York City police officers. This is not unusual because New York has the Sullivan Law, which is the strictest anti-gun law in the United States. In New York City, it is very difficult for a private citizen to [legally] possess a weapon and keep it on his or her person secretly. The people who are allowed to do it are off-duty New York City police officers. So it's not unusual for a number of very well-known celebrities in New York to have this [bodyguard] arrangement. Naturally, some of the off-duty officers who were protecting Yoko and Sean at the time were aware of things that were disappearing. . . . You would go someplace to look for a file and the contents of whole file cabinets would be missing."

Fred Seaman, says Mintz, claims that "one or both of the officers physically assaulted him, beat him up, held a gun to his head, took him for a ride, parked under a bridge somewhere and made clear threats, then brought him to the police station where he was booked, mug shots were taken and he confessed on videotape. . . . I'm here to tell you that one of the people who he names as a police officer who arrested him . . . was never part of Fred's arrest, was never there that night. . . ."

Mintz accompanied police to the warehouse to identify Lennon's stolen files. "There were boxes of them, all inventoried as part of the public record. I heard Fred say to Geraldo [Rivera] for the first time that some of these things were planted in his apartment and presumably planted in the warehouse. These are lies. John would have had to have told him to take all of these things and he didn't. John didn't tell him to steal his journals. And by the way, even if John had, even if John's last wish to Fred if anything happened to him was to take the journals and bring them to Julian [Seaman's claim], why didn't he? He had traveled to Wales to see Julian. He had gone out to Cold Spring Harbor to spend some time with Julian. He had the journals in his possession for over a year and made no attempt to get them to Julian because that was not his intent. The intent in taking the journals was 'Project Walrus.' He lied about that."[17]

But the plan went far beyond the theft of Lennon's journals. Project Walrus was a full-blown surveillance, assassination and psychological operations program.

In March 1983, Mahoney found listening devices planted at the Dakota and swept the place clean. Another sweep a few days later detected more bugs. They had been quietly replaced when no one was looking, quite probably by someone on Ono's staff.[18]

And there have been numerous attempts on Ono's life. The first came on December 9, 1980, the day after Lennon was gunned down, with a call from a man in Los Angeles who announced that he was flying to New York to "finish the job that Chapman started." At the Los Angeles airport, the man was arrested when he swore to "get" Yoko, and punched a police officer in the fray. In November 1981, two strangers were stopped and questioned by bodyguards at the Dakota. They cut and ran. One of them escaped, the other was tackled. He was taken into custody by police and shouted that he had come to "get" Yoko and Sean Lennon. Ono received a letter in February 1983, warning, "I am going to kill you. You were not supposed to have survived." One of the two brothers responsible for the threat turned up outside the Dakota a few days later. He was arrested, admitted that he meant to "get" Yoko—and was released. A month later she received an anonymous call informing her that one of her bodyguards intended to kill her. In September, on a trip to San Francisco, she received a call at her hotel room from police. The officer told her that they'd arrested a sniper firing from his window a mile away. Police confiscated 700 rounds of ammunition and a collection of books about John Lennon and Yoko Ono.[19]

"I grew up afraid somebody was going to shoot my mom or me," Sean Lennon told *Newsweek* in 1996.[20] Two years later he informed *New Yorker*'s Rebecca Mead that he had a normal childhood, except, "I had two detectives with guns following me everywhere." He also said that his father's murder was a "government" conspiracy and attributed insanity, naiveté, or distorted thinking to anyone who didn't fathom this self-evident historical fact.[21]

In 1965, Ono designed a conceptual art piece she called the "Danger Box," a machine from which "you will never come back the same." The Dakota became a danger box the day Lennon was shot. The assassination was followed by organized operations undertaken to discredit Lennon and Ono, symbols of a generation that denounced war and the geopolitical Frankenstein's monster that American industry and government had created by merging and breeding rabid watchdogs in the intelligence establishment.

Sociologist Fred Fago writes in a study of media responses to the killing of Lennon that it occurred in the "larger context of social disturbance that calls into question fundamental social meanings and relationships and sets visibly into conflict forces of stability and change. The United States in the 1960s experienced the onset of a social drama as the nation divided angrily, often violently, over the Vietnam war, the civil rights movement and the rise of libertine lifestyles."[22] In posthumous Lennon hatchet jobs, the sixties are also sundered and trashed. Fago writes that Albert Goldman's *The Lives of John Lennon*, a book that depends almost entirely on defamations concocted by Project Walrus, "goes for the jugular of both the Lennons and the sixties generation in a dramatic refutation of the last happy image of Lennon presented in the media just before and just after his death." Goldman's is "one of a number of voices in the late 1980s that vilifies . . . the sixties generation."[23]

Many conservative media pundits praised his book. A review in the *London Times* written by critic Robert Sandall excoriated the peaceniks that John Lennon inspired, "in reality a far darker, more destructive, turbulent and antisocial thing than we now care to admit. Goldman has touched a nerve in reminding us that Lennon was a child of the other 1960s that we are now trying so hard to forget."[24]

The mewling, anorexic, irascible, weak-minded, heroin-addicted version of John Lennon depicted in *Lives*, Fago writes, is a deliberate historical revision, "what conservative voices of the 1980s character-ized as the destructive permissiveness of the sixties. Both Lennon and the sixties counterculture stand discredited. If the group is seen, and sees itself, as being totally discredited, then reintegration would seem to require an open rejection of sixties identity," a cynical exer-cise in molding mass opinion, discrediting a generation to rid the world of its "subversive" convictions. And what else is it when the gutting of Lennon's reputation leads, argues Fago, to a 'born again' conversion from left-wing error to right-wing 'enlightenment?' " The Goldman "revelations" spelled "the obliteration of sixties identity coordinates. Reentry into the social order would then be on terms dictated to the sixties generation by others, most prominently the voices of the conservative cultural and political revolution of the 1980s." At stake in the Goldman "debate" was nothing less than "identity, in this case cultural/historical identity, and the countercul-ture's sense of place in the social order." [25]

Dead Lennons = $$$$$

That sense of place was largely influenced by cultural spokesmen like John Lennon. After his assassination, the first priority of "Project Walrus" was the decimation of his reputation. Mintz was in a posi-tion to observe the inner-workings of Project Walrus more closely than anyone, and concluded that the assassination attempts, bugs, wiretaps, thefts, and forgeries were steps in the discrediting of Lennon and Ono. He does not speak about who was behind it, but allows that they are "extremely powerful." [26]

The FBI and its sibling big brother agencies come to mind. Lennon was unaware of the nationalistic depths some in the federal bureaucracy were willing to plumb. Jon Weiner, author of *Come Together: John Lennon in his Time*, observed in a 1984 interview that the Lennons "didn't realize what kind of a person Nixon was and the risks they were running in challenging him." The same could be said of Lennon's attitude toward the FBI. "John did believe that they were wiretapped and he complained about the aggressive surveillance that he was sometimes subject to in the spring of 1972," Weiner com-ments, "but it was hard to prove it and he wondered whether maybe he was just being paranoid. You know, 'don't despair, paranoia is everywhere.' After Watergate and after Nixon's resignation, John filed a lawsuit claiming that he had been subject to illegal wiretap-ping and surveillance and made some progress with the suit. The Justice Department never would admit that it actually did carry out wiretapping, and in fact maintained that they didn't, 'it could be that it was somebody else that was doing it; it could be that it was the New York City police; maybe it was the Immigration Service or Army intelligence.' So John had tried to find out with his lawsuit, but eventually after he got his green card, he gave up the suit. He could have filed a Freedom of Information Act request for his own files, but I think that once he got his permanent residency, that was enough." Lennon was worn out: "He'd been fighting for four years and now it was over and I think he just wanted to go back to leading a normal life. It had taken enough out of him." [27]

In a news story on Weiner's debacle over the suppressed FBI files, Eliot Mintz stated that memories of Hooverian overkill were too traumatic for Yoko to bear. She wasn't an obstacle to Weiner's struggle with the FBI over Lennon's files, but didn't care to be involved. "She'll say, 'it's incredible how much was going on,'" Weiner said. She told him that their friends in the Peace Movement "were always saying that they should've been doing more, but all of this stuff makes it clear that the government thought that they were doing way too much." [28]

The intelligence groups would revisit this thought again when, conceivably, Lennon overcame his fear of federal harassment and buggered the rising shadow of Reaganism with four-letter outbursts of anti-Republicanism.

Killing Lennon was only the first step. All that he signified must be defaced. This was the principal objective of Walrus.

The headquarters for Walrus was Bob Rosen's apartment on 169th Street. The key strategist was Dr. DeBilio. German-born Fred Seaman, the psychiatrist's pawn, was an avid Beatles "fan." Like Chapman, he was obsessed with John Lennon and sought to subvert his memory.

Defaming Lennon and revising history required "primary materials," so every Friday for a period of twelve months, at the end of his workday, Seaman strolled out of the Dakota with a grocery bag stuffed full of Lennon's diaries, folders, an unpublished Joycean novella, other manuscripts, love letters, song lyrics, photographs, everything that could secreted from the apartment complex.

The theft of the diaries, kept current by Lennon from 1975 until his death, was essential to the central purpose of Project Walrus, the defamation of Lennon, Ono, and their political views. When most of the diaries were recovered, it was found upon close examination that some entries were not in Lennon's handwriting, and others had been altered. This tampering with history by Lennon's "extremely powerful" detractors undermined forever the use of the diaries by future biographers and historians. These documents were the record of his most personal thoughts and concerns, defiled with no better justification than the scoring of a crude propaganda coup.

Once the project had possession of the diaries, it followed that a legal claim to them be made to void any litigation Yoko Ono might apply to force their return and stop the publication of the defamatory book on Lennon planned by Fred Seaman. The chauffeur wrote in a journal that he and Dr. DeBilio had an "intense talk about doctoring the diary to show Lennon's setting me up to write book . . . to build up [the appearance of] great intimacy."[29]

Seaman was to be the executor of John Lennon's archives, the dead Beatle's official biographer, co-opting Yoko Ono. Seaman told friends that he was going to "discredit Ono at all costs."

A number of assassination attempts failed, but did rattle her deeply. Further psychological pressure was applied to drive her to a nervous breakdown and thereby discredit her in any steps she might take to correct the public record.

The Walrus crew anticipated immense profits. As Rosen wrote in his diary, "Dead Lennons = $$$$$."

In the March 1984 Playboy, authors David and Victoria Sheff described "unexplained events" at the Dakota: "Passports are found to be missing and then turn up days later on the kitchen table; lyrics to new songs disappear and then just as mysteriously reappear; collages by Lennon . . . disappear and the reappear in unexpected places. It is beginning to sound like the movie Gaslight, in which a woman is made to feel she is going crazy." The Chapman letter was stolen and altered. Anonymous death threats by phone and mail were continuous. "There are precious few people to trust," observed the Sheffs, "and Ono is depending mostly on her bodyguards for any sense of security. So when an anonymous call is received saying one of her security men is working against her, the paranoia around the [Dakota] is almost palpable. . . . The idea that someone in her own home may kill her has been planted. She begins sleeping badly again." One of Ono's assistants, wracked by the stress, began packing a gun at all times. "You don't know how big this thing is. The people who are doing this are too big to fight."[30]

On May 7, 1983, Fred Seaman entered a guilty plea to grand larceny in the second degree. He was sentenced to five years' probation. But, the Sheffs reported, "Seaman's obsession has clearly become manic. He calls a reporter at odd hours, saying only, 'How does it feel to be useless?' then calls the Dakota with the same enigmatic message. He spreads stories about Ono's wickedness—that she is a drug addict, that she was having affairs before Lennon died, that she had McCartney arrested in Japan for possessing marijuana. Seaman will admit to friends that the smears are meant to 'discredit Ono at all costs.' "[31]

Albert Goldman, in a biography largely based on Seaman's distortions after Simon & Schuster rejected a manuscript penned by the former Lennon/Ono employee—the publishers found it replete with unfounded smears—was the most prominent of the post-assassination assassins of Lennon. A publisher's blurb promises that *The Lives of John Lennon* is the study of a "turbulent personality of labyrinthine complexity," a "tribute to his legendary achievements and a revelation of the true price he paid for them." In fact, the reader finds in Goldman's book a Lennon unrecognizable to his friends and followers. At every stop, Lennon's actions and motives are skewed. An instructive example is the claim that John and Yoko avoided visiting places of artistic or cultural significance while on tour in Japan in the late 1970s, preferring to fritter away their afternoons at amusement parks and shopping centers. In fact, as seen in *Imagine: John Lennon* (a documentary that premiered in New York on October 7, 1988, within weeks of the release of Goldman's book, untainted by Walrus, a criminal plot, the organized attempt to malign, to influence public opinion, to portray the late Beatle precisely as the "phony" that Mark David Chapman happened to despise, a "king," as Goldman had it, who "has no clothes"), the Lennons visited scores of Buddhist temples to meditate, and in general immersed themselves in Japanese culture. Goldman's journalistic practices in the preparation of the book were abysmal, obviously designed to sully Lennon and his generation. Tony Manero, a musician who knew Lennon briefly in the 1960s, reported to David and Victoria Sheff that Goldman offered to pay him for a story on his "homosexual liaison" with the Beatle— which, unfortunately for the author, Manero maintains never occurred.[29] *Rolling Stone*, in an October 20, 1988 commemorative issue honoring Lennon, found Goldman's biography "riddled with factual inaccuracies, embroidered accounts of true events that border on fiction and suspect information provided by tainted sources."

The discrediting of Lennon and the late peace movement was one facet of the Walrus plot. Another was the dissemination of false conspiracy theories, clouding public comprehension of John Lennon's murder. In Santa Cruz, California, and soon all across the state, Steven Lightfoot emerged to pester talk show hosts with his insistence that the true killer of John Lennon was author Stephen King. This revelation, Lightfoot contends, is "the biggest true story since Christ was discovered." His argument, repeated *ad nauseum* on California radio stations, is founded on "coded" language allegedly planted in headlines and photo captions printed in *Time* and *Newsweek*.

Lightfoot explains in a 1997 Internet posting that it was "hard not to spot strange behavior in the headlines of *Time* magazine, especially since the magazine I happened to pick up came out the day of the murder. The bold print headlines, with almost every turn of the page, seemed to plug into the murder of John Lennon and not just the more obvious intent of the article. When I turned to page 16 and saw the ominous headline 'Who's In?' Who's Out?' above just elected Reagan I began to think I was stumbling on to government codes and that the double meaning of this headline translated to 'Reagan's In,' 'Lennon's Out.' I looked closer and noticed the smaller headline below the photo that read 'Fitting together the pieces of a complicated jigsaw puzzle . . .' I looked at the picture and saw a vase of lillies, symbolic of death . . ." and so on. Bearing in mind that Lennon was the victim of an extreme right-wing plot, Lightfoot's own affinity with the Far Right is revealing. "Incidentally," he notes, "I am not an anti-semite. I am merely aware that a small, evil group of Jews want the destruction of America and are using the media and violence to bring about a hasty disintegration of our morals. I, in fact, think Moscow is behind this media monopoly under 90 percent Jewish control and that America's harboring of Nazis after WWII is one obvious reason."

European fascists brought to these shores after the war participated in political assassinations conceived by the intelligence community. American and German operatives are the beating heart of fascist conspiracies of the sort that claimed the life of John Lennon, so the appearance of a Jew-baiting anti-communist making unfounded claims on talk radio—to discredit legitimate researchers on the Lennon murder—is a predictable development.

NOTES

1. Fenton Bresler, *Who Killed John Lennon?*, New York: St. Martin's, 1989, p. 242.
2. John Marks, *The Search for the Manchurian Candidate*, New York: Times Books, 1979, pp. 187, 191.
3. Dr. Eduard Simson-Kallas, *Affidavit in Behalf of Sirhan Sirhan Serving Time in San Quentin*, March 9, 1973, pp. 13–14. The Sirhan trial, he concluded, "was, and will be remembered, as the psychiatric blunder of the century" (p. 22). But Simson caught a glimpse of conspiracy beyond the "blunders" when he examined the notebooks supposedly kept by Sirhan. Simson wrote: "A conclusion emerges from the study of court transcripts that Sirhan's 'notebooks' were modified . . . to support the improper diagnosis of paranoid schizophrenia. This is an assumption that should not

be ignored" (p. 14). "I strongly suspect that the notebooks are a forgery, for the thinking reflected in them is foreign to the Sirhan I carefully studied." (p. 18).

4. Bresler, p. 270.
5. Bresler, p. 240.
6. Bill Landis, *Anger: The Unauthorized Biography of Kenneth Anger*, New York: HarperCollins, 1995, p. 228.
7. Michael Newton, *Raising Hell: An Encyclopedia of Devil Worship and Satanic Crime*, New York: Avon, 1993, p. 77.
8. Mae Brussell, *World Watchers International* broadcast, Monterey, California, December 20, 1980.
9. The two families were close. Scott Hinckley, the brother of John Hinckley, Jr. and a VP at Vanderbilt Energy Corp., was to have been a dinner guest of Neil Bush, the vice president's son, the day after the shooting. Neil, the *Los Angeles Times* reported on March 31, 1981, "said his family knew the Hinckley family because they had made large contributions to [Bush's] campaign."
10. Bresler, pp. 104–5.
11. Synopsis of Bresler text.
12. David and Victoria Sheff, "The Betrayal of John Lennon," *Playboy*, March 1984, p. 188. The Sheffs write: "If some kind of switch was made, it could only have been to make it seem as if some crank had written a letter to Italy in 1981, and with Lennon long dead, had used Chapman's name and the Dakota address as some sort of macabre joke."
13. Bresler, p. 174.
14. Sheffs, p. 183.
15. "Stand by Me: The Elliot Mintz Interview," *Instant Karma*, No. 52, December 1991.
16. Sheffs, p. 178.
17. Mintz, *Instant Karma* interview.
18. Sheff, p. 186.
19. Sheffs, pp.86–190.
20. "Sean Lennon Lives in Fear," AP release, March 11, 1996.
21. Rebecca Mead, "Sean Lennon has a new record—and a theory about his father's murder," *New Yorker*, vol. 74, no. 9, April 2, 1998, p. 45.
22. Fred Fago, "I Read the News Today," *The Social Drama of John Lennon's Death*, Lanham, Maryland: Rowman & Littlefield, 1994, p. x.
23. Fago, p. 120.
24. Quoted in: Albert Goldman, "Rock's Greatest Hitman," *Penthouse*, September 1989. p. 220.
25. Fago, p. 116.
26. Sheffs, p. 186.
27. "A Talk with Jon Wiener," *Instant Karma*, no. 16, June/July 1984. Wiener, an authority on the FBI's case against John Lennon, bases his observations on 26 pounds of FBI and Immigration and Naturalization Service files released under FOIA request and court orders. Wiener has long been embroiled in a battle for release of materials held back for "reasons of national security."
28. Ibid.
29. Sheffs, pp. 187–88.
30. Sheffs, p. 184.
31. Ibid.

CHAPTER TWELVE
What'cha Gonna Do? . . .
The Deaths of Bob Marley and Peter Tosh

I THINK THE CIA SAW BOB MARLEY FOR WHAT HE WAS, A FREEDOM FIGHTER AND A CHAMPION OF THE ANTI-IMPERIALIST STRUGGLE.

BASIL WALTERS, RASTA HISTORIAN, MARCH 1999

MARLEY WAS SO IMPORTANT THAT, WHETHER HE COULD OR NOT, HE WAS PERCEIVED AS BEING ABLE TO SWAY A NATIONAL ELECTION. HE WAS WITHOUT QUESTION THE MOST POPULAR PERSON THAT JAMAICA HAS PRODUCED, AT LEAST SINCE MARCUS GARVEY, AND HE WAS AT THE SAME TIME A VERY FEARFUL FIGURE TO A LOT OF PEOPLE BECAUSE HE COULD CHANGE THINGS IF HE WANTED TO.

ROGER STEFFANS, REGGAE ARCHIVIST

VAMPIRES DON'T COME OUT AND BITE YOUR NECK ANYMORE. THEY CAUSE . . . SOMETHING DESTRUCTIVE TO HAPPEN THAT BLOOD WILL SPILL, AND THOSE INVISIBLE VAMPIRES WILL GET THEIR MEALS.

PETER TOSH

Peter Tosh, born Winston Hubert McIntosh, a preacher's son, on October 9, 1944, transcended his squalid origins to become, like Bob Marley, a widely influential civil rights agitator. And like other black activists before him, Tosh was gunned down. He died on September 11, 1987 at the age of 43. "He was upset with the treatment of his people," wrote biographer John Levy, "It is believed by many that this is the very character trait which led to Tosh's murder." [1]

Witnesses reported that three men took part in the shooting, but only one of them was tried. Dennis "Leppo" Lebban pled innocent but was sentenced after an eleven-minute trial to death row in Jamaica's Spanish Town Prison. Leppo's accomplices remain at large. Mike Robinson, a witness to the shooting, reported that the assailants were "clean cut." They spoke and behaved like "professional hit men," in marked contrast to Leppo, an ex-con from the ghetto with a gritty exterior. Despite the disappearance of the mystery gunmen, Jamaican authorities consider the case closed. [2]

Tosh's interest in music began in the fifth grade with six months of piano lessons. But his musical cathexis came when he happened across a man playing guitar on a stoop. Young Tosh was so enraptured by the sound that he sat half the day watching the man play. When the music stopped, Tosh was "hypnotized." He took the guitar handed him and plucked the tune note for note.[3]

In 1956, Winston and his aunt moved from Savanna-la-Mar to Denham Town in Kingston. His aunt died and he went to live with an uncle in Trench Town—a dreary gauntlet of hovels erected by the Jamaican government (25 or so ruling families) in 1951 after a hurricane scrapped the garbage-dump shanty-towns that sprang up around Kingston, known as the spiritual home of the Rastafarians. It was in this setting that Winston met young Bob Marley and taught him to play guitar. Tosh also met Neville "Bunny Wailer" O'Reilly Livingston in Trench Town, and in 1964–65, Winston changed his name, and the trio, the "Wailin' Wailers," set out to conquer the universe.

"Simmer Down," the first tune recorded at Studio One, immediately throbbed to number one in Jamaica. But the Wailers were drastically underpaid. Each of them earned about three pounds a week, so in 1970 they bailed and signed with famed Jamaican producer Lee "Scratch" Perry. But record producers, "dem pirates and thieves," are notorious for pocketing more than their take. The Wailers recorded three LPs in England for the Trojan label and received precisely nada for these albums or the bootlegs of Tosh's rehearsal sessions marketed by Trojan.

In 1972, the Wailers met Island Records producer Chris Blackwell, and their fortunes turned around. "The group's first collaboration," writes White in *Catch A Fire*, "served as an introduction for many people to reggae music. This album contains many classic reggae tunes, including '400 years' and 'Stop That Train,' both of which featured Peter Tosh on lead vocals. These songs introduced people to the militant, outspoken, candid approach of Peter Tosh, qualities which would remain with him to his grave." These characteristics set Peter apart from his peers. "Unlike most musicians in Jamaica, Peter always let his feelings be known. He cared more about principles and morals than popularity and fame."[4]

His beliefs were completely incorruptible. In 1983, an interviewer asked Tosh if any political groups had sought his endorsement. He acknowledged that he'd been approached, but "they know I don't support politricks and games. Because I have bigger aims, hopes and aspirations. My duty is not to divide them, my duty is to unify the people, 'cause to divide people is to destroy people, and destroy yourself, too."[5]

The band went on to release *Burnin'*, a blunt commentary on political oppression. "Get Up, Stand Up" had Tosh on lead vocal, chanting "stand up for your rights." The album sold briskly, but

Burnin' was the last album to feature Tosh. He left the Wailers after a series of wrangles in the studio with Marley and keen displeasure with producer Chris Blackwell.

In Jamaica, old wounds were opened by a wave of destabilization politics. Stories appeared in the local, regional and international press down-sizing the achievements of the quasi-socialist Jamaican government under Prime Minister Michael Manley. The people should give up faith in themselves and their leader, this was the message. The island was struck by a tidal wave of political violence, sabotage, propaganda, and as Grenada's Prime Minister Maurice Bishop phrased it three years later, the CIA's "pernicious attempts [to] wreck the economy."

PETER TOSH, REGGAE VISIONARY AND CIVIL RIGHTS ACTIVIST, FROM THE FEATURE DOCUMENTARY, **STEPPING RAZOR-RED X.**

"Destabilization," Bishop told the emergent New Jewel Party, "is the name given the most recently developed method of controlling and exploiting the lives and resources of a country and its people by a bigger and more powerful country through bullying, intimidation and violence. In the old days, such countries—the colonialist and imperialist powers—sent in gunboats or marines to directly take over the country by sheer force. Later on mercenaries were often used in place of soldiers, navy, and marines. Today more and more the new weapon and the new menace is destabilization. This method was used against a number of Caribbean and Third World countries in the 1960s, and also against Jamaica and Guyana in the 1970s."[6]

Marley held on to the Wailer name after Tosh's departure, took on new members and wove his lyrics into a revolutionary crucifix to ward off the cloak-and-dagger "vampires" descending upon the island. In June 1976, Jamaican Governor-General Florizel Glasspole placed Jamaica under martial law to quell pre-election violence, which had reached such a pitch that strafing at two Kingston theaters completely perforated the movie screens and they were replaced by whitewashed concrete walls.[7] The People's National Party (PNP) asked the Wailers to play at the Smile Jamaica concert in December. Despite the rising political mayhem, he agreed to perform.

In late November, a death squad slipped beneath the gates at Marley's Hope Road home. As Marley biographer Timothy White tells it, at about 9 PM, "The torpor of the quiet tropical night was interrupted by a queer noise that was not quite like a firecracker." Marley was in the kitchen at the rear of the house eating a grapefruit when he heard bursts of automatic gunfire. Don Taylor, Marley's manager, had been talking to the musician when the bullets cut through the back of his legs. Taylor fell but remained conscious with four bullets in his legs and one buried at the base of his spine. Timothy White's account of the seige on Marley, his wife Rita and their entourage:

> The gunmen were peppering the house with a barrage of rifle and pistol fire, shattering windows and splintering plaster and woodwork on the first floor. Four of the gunmen surrounded the house, while two others guarded the front yard.
>
> Rita was shot by one of the two men in the front yard as she ran out of the house with the five Marley children and a reporter from the *Jamaica Daily News*. The bullet caught her in the head, lifting her off her feet as it burrowed between the scalp and skull.
>
> Meanwhile, a man with an automatic rifle had burst through the back door off the kitchen pantry, pushing past a fleeing Seeco Patterson to aim beyond Don Taylor at Bob Marley. . . . The gunman got off eight shots. One bullet hit a counter, another buried itself in the sagging ceiling, and five tore into Don Taylor. The last creased Marley's breast below his heart and drilled deep inside his arm.[8]

Neville Garrick, a student of Angela Davis and a graduate of the UCLA College of Fine Arts and art director of the *Jamaica Daily News*, took photos of Kingston, Nassau and the Hope Road enclave before and after the shooting. Garrick had film of "suspicious characters" lurking near the house before the assassination attempt. The day of the shooting, he had snapped some photos of Marley standing beside a Volkswagen in mango shade. The strangers had made Marley nervous. He told Garrick that they appeared to be "scouting" the property. In the prints, however, their features were too blurred by shadow to make out. After the concert, he took all of the photographs and prints to Nassau, and when the Wailers and crew prepared to board a flight to London, Garrick discovered that all of the film had been stolen.[9]

"The firepower these guys apparently brought with them was immense," Wailer publicist Jeff Walker recalls. "There were bullet holes everywhere. In the kitchen, the bathroom, the living room, floors, ceilings, doorways and outside."[10]

Marley would sing:

Ambush in the night, all guns aiming at me
Ambush in the night, they opened fire on me
Ambush in the night, protected by His Majesty . . .

The survival of the raggae singer and his entourage appeared to be the work of the Rastafarian god, but on December 5, the Wailers went on despite their wounds to perform one long, defiant anthem at the Smile Jamaica fest, "War."

Until the ignoble and unhappy regimes
That now hold our brothers—
In Angola, in Mozambique, South Africa
In subhuman bondage—
Have been toppled,
Utterly destroyed,
Everywhere is war . . .

Rita Marley had been shot at near point-blank range. She survived and was released from the hospital that afternoon. Rita was still wearing a hospital gown, and had wrapped a scarf around her bandaged head. Roberta Flack flew in for the concert. Flack visited Marley in convalescence before the performance at an armed camp tucked away in the peaks of the Blue Mountains, near Kingston. Only a handful of Marley's most trusted comrades knew of his whereabouts before the festival, but a member of the film crew, or so he claimed—he didn't have a camera—managed to talk his way past macheté-bearing Rastas to enter the encampment: Carl Colby, son of the late CIA director William Colby.[11] And he came bearing a gift, according to a witness at the enclave, a new pair of boots for Bob Marley.[12]

Former Black Panther and cinematographer Lee Lew-Lee (his camera work can be seen in the Oscar-winning documentary, *The*

BOB MARLEY

Panama Deception) was close friends with members of the Wailers, and he believes that Marley's cancer can be traced to the boots Colby gave him before the Smile Jamaica festival: "He put his foot in and said, 'Ow!' A friend got in there—you know how Jamaicans are—he said, 'let's get in here, in the boot, and he pulled a length of copper wire out—it was embedded in the boot."[13] Had the wire been treated chemically with a carcinogenic toxin? The appearance of Colby at Marley's compound was certainly provocative, and so was his subsequent part in the fall of another black cultural icon, O.J. Simpson. (At Simpson's preliminary hearing in 1995, Colby—who happened to live next door to Nicole Simpson when she lived on Gretna Green Way in Brentwood, a mile from her residence on Bundy—and his wife both took the stand to testify for the prosecution that Nicole's ex-husband had badgered and threatened her. Colby's testimony was instrumental in the formal charge of murder filed against Simpson and the nationally-televised fiasco known as the "Trial of the Century."[14])

Ten years after the Hope Road assault, Don Taylor published a memoir, *Marley & Me*, in which he alleges that a "senior CIA agent" had been planted among the crew as part of a plan to "assassinate" Marley.

Lew-Lee recalls: "I didn't think so at the time, but I've always had my suspicions because Marley later broke his toe playing soccer, and when the bone wouldn't mend the doctors found that the toe had cancer. The cancer metastasized throughout his body, but [Marley] believed he could fight this thing." The soccer game took place in Paris. Five months after the boot incident, Marley took to the field with one of the leading teams in the country to break the monotony of the Wailers' *Exodus* tour. His right toe was injured in a tackle. The toenail was detached. It wasn't considered a serious wound at first.

But it would not heal. Marley was limping by July and consulted a physician, who was shocked by the toe's appearance. It was so eaten away that doctors in London advised it be amputated. But Marley's religion forbade it: "Rasta no abide amputation," he insisted. Marley told the physician, "de living God, His Imperial Majesty Haile Selassie I, Ras Tafari, Conquering Lion of the Tribe of Judah . . . He will heal me wit' de meditations of me ganja chalice." No scalpel, he swore, "will crease me flesh. . . . C'yant kill Rasta. Rastamon live out."[15] He flew to Miami and Dr. William Bacon performed a skin graft on the lesion.

But the disease lingered undiagnosed. The cancer spread throughout his body.

Isaac Ferguson, a friend and devotee, observed the slow death of Bob Marley first-hand. In the five years separating the soccer injury from cancer diagnosis, Marley remained immersed in music, "ignoring the advice of doctors and close associates that he stop and obtain a thorough medical examination." He refused to give up recording and touring long enough to consult a doctor. "He would have to quit the stage and it would take years to recoup the momentum. This was his time and he seized upon it. Whenever he went into the studio to record, he did enough for two albums. Marley would drink his fish tea, eat his rice-and-peas stew, roll himself about six spliffs and go to work. With incredible energy and determination, he kept strumming his guitar, maybe 12 hours, sometimes till day-break." [16] Reggae artist Jimmy Cliff observed after Marley's death: "What I know now is that Bob finished all he had to do on this earth." Marley was aware by 1977 that he was dying and set out to compress a lifetime of music into the few years remaining.

Invisible Vampires

I AM NOT A POLITICIAN BUT I SUFFER THE CONSEQUENCES. **PETER TOSH**

In 1975, Secretary of State Henry Kissinger, on a diplomatic junket to the island, assured Jamaican Prime Minister Michael Manley in a private meeting that there was "no attempt now underway involving covert actions against the Jamaican government." [17] But in the real world something of a Caribbean pogrom was underway, overseen by the CIA. [18] At the time Kissinger croaked his denials to Manley, a destabilization push was already underway. The emphasis at this stage was on psychological operations, but in the election year of 1976 a series of covert interventions, employing arson, bombing, and assassination as required, completely disrupted Manley's democratic socialist rule. [19]

An arsenal of automatic weapons somehow found their way to Jamaica. The CIA's thugs, directed by a growing coven of pin-striped officers reporting to the American embassy in Kingston, quietly organized secret police cadrés to stoke political violence. Huge consignments of guns and advanced communications gear were smuggled onto the island. One such shipment was intercepted by Manley's security patrols—a caché of 500 man-eating submachine guns. [20]

The firearms were shipped to the island from Miami by the Jamaica Freedom League, a right-wing paramilitary faction with roots in the CIA, financed largely by drugs. Peter Whittington, the group's second in command, was convicted of drug trafficking in Dade County. The funds were laundered by the League at Miami's Bank of Perrine, the key American subsidiary of Castle Bank, then the CIA's financial base in Latin America. The bank was owned and operated by Paul Helliwell, bagman for the Bay of Pigs invasion, accused even by the conservative *Wall Street Journal* of involvement in the global narcotics trade.

A paramilitary force was mustered to quell the Rastafarian backlash.

Tosh's "duppies" (ghosts) quelled dissent by borrowing the chemical warfare tactics of the 1960s. In a year's time, Marley saw the Rastafarian resistance disintegrate because a ruthless, highly-organized cocaine-heroin syndicate arose, apparently, from the Jamaican sand. The sudden abundance of hard narcotics in Jamaica wounded the Rastafarian movement with the burning spear of addiction.

Tosh and Marley both promoted ganja as an alternative, a Rastafarian sacrament, a statement of independence and cohesion against the brutal strategems of colonial rule. This was the path of political resistance joyously followed by herbman Tosh, who ran through two pounds of reefer a week.[21] He not only smoked Guiness Record-breaking volumes of marijuana—Tosh rhapsodized about his spliffs, demanded the "shit-stem" legalize it.

Like his old partner Marley, Tosh's chosen weapon in the Rasta revolution was free expression, and they were crucified for it. For the first time in Jamaican politics, public figures openly denounced the governing elite. Peter Tosh, in particular, split from his peers in the local music scene by serving up impassioned political "livalogues" at his public performances. While Bob Marley saw the wisdom in softening his political statements ("The War is Over"), and Bunny Wailer slipped into a snug harbor of seclusiveness, Tosh pushed on alone, the cursing, joint-smoking, speechifying black militant until his death six years after the passing of Marley. Tosh "don' wan' peace," he shouted to Jamaican concert-goers in September, 1978, and he wasn't given any. The Rastafarian told interviewer Steven Davis, co-author of *Reggae International* (Rogner & Bernhard GMBH, 1982), about one of his scrapes with Jamaican police:

> I was waiting for a rehearsal outside Aquarius Studio on Half Way Tree [a main Kingston thoroughfare], waiting for two of my musicians, and I had a little piece of roach in my hand. A guy come up to me in plain clothes and grab the roach out of my hand. So I say him, wha' happen? He didn't say nothing, so I grab the roach back from

him and he start to punch me up. I say again, wha' happen, and he say I must go dung so ["downtown" in police jargon]. I say, dung so? Which way you call dung so? That's when I realized this was a police attitude, so I opened the roach and blew out the contents. Well, him didn't like that and start to grab at me aggressively now—my waist, my shoulder, grabbing me and tearing off my clothes and things. Then other police come and put their guns in my face and try brute force on me. . . . Now eight-to-ten guys gang my head with batons and weapons of destruction. They close the door, chase away the people and gang my head with batons for an hour and a half until my hand break trying to fend off the blows. I run to the window and they beat me back with blows. I run to the door and they beat me back with blows. Later I found out these guys' intentions was to kill me, right? What I had to do was play dead by just lying low. Passive resistance.

In the *Red X Tapes*, Tosh elaborated on the night he spent at the local police station house. Ten police officers bludgeoned him for two hours with their batons. He received serious head wounds and was scarred for life by the beating.[22]

It was one of many beatings endured by Tosh, but they resulted in the opposite of the intended effect. The beatings made him stronger. This was no child of Moses, but Malcolm X with roped hair and a spliff dangling from his defiant lip. Tosh's music smoldered with vengeful ferocity. He stepped up the anti-government pronouncements. Tosh had a guitar custom-built in the shape of an M-16 rifle and explained to his minions, "this guitar is firing shots at all them devil disciples." Music was his own spear in the struggle "against apartheid, nuclear war and those 'gang-jah' criminals."[23]

Jamaican secret police and the CIA tailed Peter Tosh through it all. He chose to call his autobiographical boxed set *The Red X Tapes*, because, he said, government documents about him always had a red "X" marked on them.

The suppression of Rastafarian protest escalated in the late 1970s and grotesque human rights abuses were commonplace. Some nine months after the near-death experience of Peter Tosh, three leaders of the Jamaican Labor Party were murdered execution-style. The taxi they'd flagged down was stopped in Denham Town. The officers ordered the three out of the car, searched it and them. The suspects stood with their hands up. Without provocation, the commanding officer ordered the police to "KILL!" After the murders, a police motorcade circled the Ministry of Security with horns blaring. The din was nearly loud enough to drown out the derisive laughter of the police.[24]

The political climate in the Caribbean sweltered with the escalation of American covert operations well into the next decade. Radio Free Grenada's final broadcast (American bombers took out the station) was Bob Marley's "War." Eugenia Charles, the ultra-conservative prime minister of Dominica, admitted that the strategists behind the Grenada invasion "weren't worried about military intervention coming out of Grenada—we were worried about the spread of its ideas." [25]

In September 1980, Bob Marley suffered a stroke while jogging in Central Park. He was released by a physician the following day and recuperated in his room at New York's Essex Hotel. Rita Marley flew in from Pittsburgh and choked when she saw him. Her fears rose into uncontrollable sobs, "Wha' has happened to you?"

"Doctor say brain tumor black me out," Marley told her. [26]

Isaac Fergusson caught the dying rebel's performance at Madison Square Garden a few days before, and realized then that something was terribly wrong, even as Marley gripped his guitar "like a machine gun" and "threw his ropelike hair about," a "whirlwind around his small black face. The crack of a drum exploded into bass, into organ." Midway into the set, the Wailers stood back and Marley performed solo, "These songs of freedom is all I ever had . . ." Why, Fergusson wondered, was he singing this alone? Why the past tense?

"Emancipate yourself from mental slavery . . ."

Fergusson noticed that Marley "was always rubbing his forehead and grimacing while performing." A Rastafarian devotee of Marley's offered this explanation: Hidden lasers fixed to spotlights above the stage "burned out his brain." The following weekend, Fergusson stopped to visit Rita Marley and Judy Mowatt. He asked about Bob's condition. "We don't know for sure," Rita told him, "the doctors say he has a tumor in his brain." In a silent moment, Fergusson realized that Marley was dying. [27]

A Holistic Nazi

The singer was convinced at last to seek medical treatment. He was admitted to the Sloan-Kettering Cancer Center in Manhattan. Tests revealed that the cancer had spread to Marley's brain, lungs, and liver. He received a few radiation treatments but checked out when the New York papers bruited that he was seriously ill. Marley consulted physicians in Miami, briefly returned to Sloan-Kettering, then Jamaica where he met with Dr. Carl "Pee Wee" Fraser, recommended to him by fellow Rastafarians. Dr. Fraser advised that Marley talk to

Dr. Josef Issels, a "holistic comprehensive immunotherapist" then practicing at the Ringberg Clinic in Rottach-Egern, a small Bavarian village located at the southern end of Tegernsee Lake. Marley traveled to Bavaria and checked into the clinic.

Dr. Issels met him, looked him over and allowed, without naming sources, "I hear that you're one of the most dangerous black men in the world."[28]

The portrait offered by publicity releases from the Issels Foundation is imposing enough: Dr. Issels, born in 1907, founded the first hospital (financed by the estate of Karl Gischler, a Dutch shipping magnate[29]) in Europe for comprehensive immunotherapy of cancer in 1951. "He was the Medical Director and Director of Research."

All well and good . . . until it is considered that by this time, Dr. Issels was 44 years old. Certainly, his medical career did not begin in 1951. Why the unexplained gap in his bona-fidés? During WWII, it seems, Dr. Issels could be found plying his "research" skills in Poland, at the Auschwitz concentration camp, working aside Dr. Joseph Mengele, no less, according to several of the Wailers who have investigated the German "alternative" practitioner's past. Bob Marley, the "dangerous" racial enemy of fascists everywhere, had placed his life in the hands of a Nazi doctor, Mengele's protegé, an accomplice of the "Angel of Death" in horrific medical atrocities committed against racial "subhumans."

Lew-Lee recalls that Marley rejected conventional cancer treatments, "wanted to do anything but turn to Western medicine. This may have been a mistake, maybe not. Dr. Issels said that he could cure Bob. And they cut Bob's dreadlocks off. And he was getting all of this crazy, crazy medical treatment in Bavaria. I know this because Ray von Evans, who played in Marley's group, we were very close friends, [told me] Bob was receiving these medical treatments, and Ray would come by every two or three months, 1979–80, and told me: "Yeah, mon,they're killing Bob. They are KILLING Bob." I said, "What do you mean 'they are killing Bob?'" "No, no, mon," he said. "Dis Dr. Issels, he's a Nazi!" We found out later that Dr. Issels was a Nazi doctor. And he had worked with Dr. Mengele."[30]

Dr. Issels would then be one of scores of Nazi practitioners to escape the attention of the Nuremberg Tribunal. Michael Kater, a professor of history at York University in Canada, found that physicians of the Hitler period were steeped in Nazi racial doctrines at medical school, and that many of them continued to practice undisturbed by war crime tribunals: "It was in a conventional medical culture infiltrated from one side by a science alienated from humanity and from another by charlantry that young physicians in the Third Reich were raised to learn and prepare for practice, with many pre-destined to practice after 1945."[31]

Dr. Joseph Issels first offered his alternative cancer therapies in a nazified atmosphere of ruthlessness and quackery. In the 1930s, chronic cancer patients consulted Dr. Issels and received his experi-mental "combination therapy," a regimen of diet, homeopathic reme-dies, vitamins, exercise, and detoxification, among other holistic approaches. (Today his clinic offers training in cancer immunization vaccines, UV blood irradiation, oxygen and ozone therapy, "biolog-ical dentistry" [tooth extraction], immunity elicitation by mixed bac-terial vaccine, blood heating, and so on.[32])

The medical establishment, particularly in the UK, has long rallied against some of Issel's therapies. Gordon Thomas, a former BBC producer, reported in a televised documentary that Dr. Issels was arrested in September, 1960. The police warrant alleged, "the accused claims to treat . . . cancer. . . . In fact [he] has neither reliable diagnostic methods nor a method to treat cancer successfully. It is contended [that] he is aware of the complete ineffectiveness of the so-called . . . tumor treatment." The warrant noted that Issels was a flight risk, that "he had prepared for all contingencies by depositing huge amounts in foreign banks."[33]

Marley, unaware of his physician's past, was placed on a regimen of exercise, vaccines (some illegal), ozone injections, vitamin and trace minerals, and other treatments. In time, Dr. Issels also intro-duced torture. Long needles were plunged through Marley's stomach to the spine. The patient-victim was told that this was part of his "treatment." The torture continued until Marley foundered on the threshold of death.[34]

Cedella Booker, his mother, visited him three times in the course of these "treatments." She found Dr. Issels to be an "arrogant wretch" with the "gruff manners of a bully," who subjected her dying son to a bloodless brand of "hocus-pocus" medicine. Mrs. Booker: "I myself witnessed Issels' rough treatment of Nesta [Marley]. One time I went with Nesta to the clinic, and we settled down in a treatment room. Issels came in and announced to Nesta, 'I'm going to give you a needle.'" Dr. Issels "plunged the needle straight into Nesta's navel right down to the syringe. [Marley] grunted and winced. He could only lie there helplessly, writhing on the table, trying his best to hide his pain. 'Jesus Christ,' I heard myself mumbling." Issels ridiculed the patient for grimacing, yanked out the needle and strolled casually out of the room. Marley was left groaning with pain. "I went and stood at his side and held his hand."[35]

"With every visit," she recalls, "I found him smaller, frailer, thinner. As the months of dying dragged past, the suffering was etched all over his face. He would fall into fits of shaking, when he would lose all control and shiver from head to toe like a coconut leaf in a breeze. His eyes would turn in his head, rolling in their sockets until even the white jelly was quivering." [36]

Marley's torment was aggravated by forced starvation. "For a whole week sometimes," Booker laments, her son "would be allowed no nourishment other than what he got intravenously. Constantly hungry, even starving, he wasted away to a skeleton. To watch my first-born shrivel up to skin and bone ripped at my mother's heart." Marley weighed 82 pounds on the day of his death. [37] The starvation diet must have devastated his immune system and rushed his demise. It also caused him intense pain. "It would drag on so, for one long painful month after the other, and every day would be a knife that death stabbed and twisted anew in an already open, bleeding wound." The agony "wrapped him up like a crushing snake." [38] Starvation left Marley with a knotted intestine, and Dr. Issels was forced to operate the clear the obstruction.

Death finally claimed Marley on May 11, 1980. In Jamaica, the 20th was declared a national day of mourning, and Marley's wake at the National Arena was attended by some 30,000 mourners.

Peter Tosh was not put off his guns by the death of Bob Marley. "Message music," he told interviewer Roger Steffans in 1980, "is the only music that have heartbeat." [39] After a disappointing collaboration with Mick Jagger, Tosh released *Mama Africa* in 1983, and "Not Gonna Give It Up," an appeal for continued resistance to Africa's apartheid policy. "Where You Gonna Run?" addressed the self-serving delusions of political indifference.

Peter Tosh found the bloodshed and hypocrisy of death squad justice in the third world unbearable. He was so obsessed with hidden evil and the upswell of violence in Jamaica that they visited him in his sleep. He had "visions" of "destruction [and] millions of people inside of [a] pit going down. And I . . . say, 'Blood Bath, where so much people come from?' And looking in the pit, mon, it the biggest pit . . . but the way the people was crying, it was awful." [40]

By 1987, the year of Tosh's murder, Jamaican musicians were censored by shell-casing politics. The island's *Daily Gleaner* reported that Winston "Yellowman" Foster, stopped at a police roadblock and frisked for drugs, resisted detainment. One of the officers hissed, "You want to go like Tosh?" [41]

And when Tosh went there was nothing random about it. Witnesses and friends insist that he was a political hit. They are convinced that Tosh was killed for his statements on human rights, black liberation and the legalization of marijuana.

The knock came on the evening of September 19, 1987. Tosh was throwing a small party at his home, and Mike Robinson, a local radio personality, answered the door. Leppo Leppan, an ex-convict and old friend of Tosh's from the Wailers' Trench Town days, strolled in. Behind him two strangers—described by witnesses as "clean-cut," "professional hit-men," definitely "not local"—produced pistols and insisted on talking to Tosh. The intruders followed Robinson into the living room and ordered everyone to lie on the floor, face down. Leppo demanded money. Tosh explained he had little cash on hand. One of the men searched the house and found a macheté. He threatened to decapitate Tosh. Shots were fired. Peter Tosh and two others, Doc Brown and "Free I" Dixon, were dead.

Shortly thereafter, the aftermath of Jimi Hendrix's death was revisited—Tosh's New York apartment was entered and burgled. The city of New York seized a number of 10-inch master tapes, and these were stashed away in a warehouse by NYC Public Administrator Ethel Griffin and remained there for years.[42]

Tosh's killers remain at large. Wayne Johnson, producer of the *Red X Tapes*, cites an unnamed official of the Jamaican government who divulged to him that one of the gunmen was a police officer. The Jamaican government conducted a cursory investigation, ignoring critical leads, and quickly declared the case closed with Leppan's conviction. The hurried, token investigation led many Jamaicans to suspect that the government had concealed the factual underpinnings of the case.

Tosh's murder has been followed by the violent deaths of other black activist musicians in Jamaica and elsewhere, among them:

1987 **Major Worries**, musician, shot to death (Jamaica).
1988 **Tenor Saw**, musician, shot to death (US).
1990 **Nitty Gritty**, musician, shot to death (US).
1992 **Pan Head**, musician, shot to death (Jamaica).
     Dirksman, musician, shot to death (Jamaica).
1994 **Garnett Silk**, musician, died in an arson attack on his family home (Jamaica).
1995 **Carl "Briggy C" Marsden**, musician, shot dead in London.
     Ken Sarowiwa, musician, hanged by the Nigerian government.
1996 **Jason Wharton**, musician, shot dead outside London nightclub while sitting in a car (UK).
2000 **Dani Spencer**, vocalist, drowned off the Jamaican coast February 27.

NOTES

1. John Levy, "The Life of Saint Peter," *The Dread Library*, April 22, 1998, http://debate.uvm.edu/dreadlibrary/jlevy.html.
2. Eric Williams, "Who Killed Peter Tosh?" *High Times*, no. 221, January, 1994, p. 18.
3. Timothy White, "In the Path of the Steppin' Razor," www.boomshaka.com/tosh/razor.html. Other biographical details garnered from Hank Holmes and Roger Steffens. "Reasoning With Tosh," *Reggae Times*, 1980, and John Walker, "Tough Tosh," *Trouser Press*, December, 1983.
4. Timothy White, *Catch a Fire: The Life of Bob Marley*, New York: Henry Holt, 1992.
5. David P. Szatmary, *Rockin' in Time: A Social History of Rock and Roll*, New Jersey: Prentice-Hall, 1987, pp. 164–65.
6. Maurice Bishop's address to Grenada's New Jewel Movement, March 13, 1979.
7. White, p. 285.
8. White, pp. 288–29.
9. White, p. 337.
10. Roger Steffans, interviewer, "The Night They Shot Bob Marley—The Untold Story," *The Raggae & African Beat*, June, 1985, p. 20.
11. White, p. 291.
12. Author interview with Lee Lew-Lee, Los Angeles, October 30, 1997.
13. Lew-Lee interview.
14. On February 3, 1995, the *Los Angeles Times* reported: One of those witnesses offered new details about arguments between O.J. Simpson and his ex-wife. Catherine Boe testified that Nicole Simpson would not let her ex-husband into her house on one occasion. . . .

    Prosecutors had hoped to show that Simpson was stalking his wife during the early months of 1992, and asked Boe and her husband, Carl Colby, about an evening when they called police after spying [sic] a suspicious man outside. That man turned out to be Simpson. . . .

    During his testimony, Colby said he called police in part because he found it odd that a person of Simpson's "description" was in the neighborhood at that hour. As he said that, a black alternate juror rolled his eyes toward the ceiling, and another alternate, also black, chuckled to herself.

    "What the prosecution described as O.J. stalking Nicole might be interpreted by some African-American jurors as a classic example of white middle class people overreacting to the presence of an unknown black man in their neighborhood at night," said UCLA law professor Peter Arenella.
15. White, pp. 3–4.
16. Isaac Ferguson, "So Much Things to Say," in Chris Potash, ed., *Reggae, Rasta, Revolution: Jamaican Music from Ska to Dub*, New York: Schirmer, 1997, pp. 56–57.
17. Ernest Volkman and John Cummings, "Murder as Usual," *Penthouse*, December 1977, p. 114.
18. Ellen Ray and Bill Schaap, "Massive Destabilization in Jamaica," *Covert Action Information Bulletin*, no. 10, August-September 1980, pp. 13, 16.
19. William Blum, *The CIA: A Forgotten History*, London: Zed Books, 1986, p. 301.
20. Jerry Meldon, "The CIA's Dope-Smuggling 'Freedom Fighters,'" VET-

ERANS OF THE CIA'S DRUG WARS, Profile: Luis Posada Carriles,"
High Times, December 18, 1998. The inevitable CIA-trained Cuban exiles
beached in Jamaica, among them Luis Posada Cariles, an ex-secret police
official under Cuban dictator Batista, currently a full-fledged agent of the
CIA. Meldon, chairman of the Department of Chemical Engineering at
Tufts University in Medford, MA, writes of the drug-smuggling
"freedom fighter" and his role in the Bay of Pigs:

A top-secret element of the invasion plan was "Operation 40," whose
personnel included Posada Cariles, future Watergate burglar Felipe de
Diego, and sundry Mafia hitmen. Its objective was to secure the island
by eliminating both local politicians and members of the invasion force
deemed insufficiently in favor of bringing back Batista as dictator.

Operation 40 remained intact following the Bay of Pigs fiasco, in
which 114 brigadistas died, and was deployed later on in sporadic raids
on Cuba. An Operation 40 task force led in 1967 by Carriles' CIA classmate Felix Rodriguez (later to find immortality as "Max Gomez," running
guns to the dope-trading Contras in Nicaragua and then testifying about
it in 1987 before the Senate Iran-Contra investigators) supervised
Bolivian police in the capture and murder of Che Guevara.

Operation 40 had to be officially disbanded in 1970 after one of their
planes crashed in southern California with kilos of heroin and cocaine
aboard. But this did not interfere with business, even though later the
same year federal narcs busted 150 suspects in "the largest roundup of
major drug traffickers in the history of federal law enforcement."
President Nixon's Attorney General, John Mitchell, celebrated the
destruction of "a nationwide ring of wholesalers handling about 30
percent of all heroin sales and 70 to 80 percent of all cocaine sales in the
United States." Mitchell did not mention all the Operation 70 heroes
who had been netted in this grand operation.

The *Jamaica Daily News* openly identified the intruders: "Knowing a
coup is going to be tried, sighting all the signs and publishing them, pin-
pointing even the week and month—does not prevent it from being
tried. Neither does knowing about CIA involvement head it off." The
meddling of the American government "is beyond doubt" considering
"the plotters' contact with the US embassy [and] the pattern of destabilization which only the CIA could coordinate." It was the Chilé coup
revisited. "There are obvious economic advantages [in] keeping cordial
relations with the US. But not to tell a people when war has been
launched against them. . . . It cannot be too early to begin to build a
[national], indeed revolutionary unity."

21. Williams, p. 18.
22. Williams, p. 19.
23. Roger Steffens, *Peter Tosh Biography*, Honorary Citizen Box Set, Sony
    Music Entertainment, 1997.
24. White, p. 301.
25. Dave Marsh, ed.,"Number One with a Bullet," *Rock & Roll Confidential
    Report: Inside the Real World of Rock & Roll*, New York: Pantheon, 1985, pp.
    141–42. Radio Free Grenada was succeeded by the U.S.-sponsored
    Spice Island Radio, operated by the DoD's Psychological Operations
    Section. A 12-man team of Navy journalists blew in from Norfolk,
    Virginia, recruited a few local announcers, and Spice Island Radio was
    born. Dave Marsh, veteran editor of *Creem, Crawdaddy, Village Voice* and

Rolling Stone, reports: Their first broadcast called on Grenadians to lay down their arms. The head of the Navy team, Lt. Richard Ezzel, told Reuters, "We wanted to save lives," (This plea might have been more effective if directed at American GIs). Ezzel went on to say, "When we first came down we were told to play nothing but reggae and calypso music; later we found out that people did not want to hear reggae but wanted to hear more rock and roll and country music." Ezzel said his conclusions were based on extensive tours of the island by his announcers . . . While we find it hard to swallow Ezzel's assertions about reggae (a reggae song called "Capitalism Gone Mad" was number one in Grenada at the time of the invasion), recent visitors to the island have told RRC that Spice Island's mix of Quiet Riot, Hall and Oates, the Beatles, Asia, calypso and reggae is very popular. Unfortunately, there is little reason to believe that PsyOps is serious about their stated goal of bringing democracy to the Caribbean. The aforementioned Ms. Charles, who flew to Washington right after the invasion to mug for the cameras with Ronald Reagan, has been having opponents of her regime shot as she tried to pass legislation that would punish alleged anti-state conspirators with death by hanging. In Barbados, Prime Minister and US ally Tom Adams seeks to expel the respected journalist Ricky Singh for his opposition to the invasion. US cries of "Democracy for Grenada" ring hollow in light of continued support for brutal dictatorships in Haiti and the Dominican Republic. ("Remember 1965? The kids are all grown up now but the death squads are still alive.") Lt. Ezzel says that his men will stay on long after any US pullout, "until the Grenadian government can take over the job." When you consider that the US has occupied Puerto Rico since 1898, it looks like Spice Island Radio may be number one in its market for a long time to come.

26. White, p. 309.
27. Fergusson, p. 57.
28. Cedella Booker and Anthony Winkler, *Bob Marley: An Intimate Portrait by his Mother*, New York: Viking, 1996, p. 191.
29. "Josef M. Issels, MD," Issels Foundation release, Future Medicine Publishing, Inc., November 7, 1997.
30. Lew-Lee interview, October 30, 1997.
31. Michael H. Kater, *Doctors Under Hitler*, Chapel Hill: University of North Carolina Press, 1989, p. 235.
32. Issels Foundation November 7, 1997 release.
33. Gary Null and Leonard Steinman, "Suppression of Alternative Cancer Therapies: Dr. Joseph Issels," *Penthouse*, August, 1980, p. 186. The article canonizes the late Dr. Issels with lavish praise founded largely on the hostility of the medical establishment toward the German practitioner. The authors glance over Issel's activities during the war years. Gary Null, co-author, continues to consider him to be alternative medicine's answer to Lee Salk, and endorsed the clinic in a winter 1999 fundraising appearance on KCET, the PBS affiliate in Los Angeles, in books and elsewhere.

The medical community, Dr. Issels complained at the time of his arrest, had launched a "conspiracy" to force him out of business. In 1954, he was not allowed to speak at a medical conference in Sao Paulo, Brazil. A couple of years later, he argued, a "conspiracy" of twelve physicians met privately at Hinterzarten in the Black Forest to plan "an end to the charlatan Issels." In 1960, the doctor was arrested, charged with fraud and manslaughter. The verdict was guilty. Issels appealed, his attorney ushering before the court a parade of whole-body experts and patients supposedly cured by him. He was acquitted in 1964, survived the "conspiracy" and reopened his clinic . . . but there remained sinister cathars within the medical community who disapproved of his methods. The American Cancer Society blacklisted Joseph Issels. And in the early 1970s, a commission of cancer specialists assembled to determine whether his treatments had merit. The commission visited the clinic and concluded in the final report that, though "excellently run," all of the evidence collected "suggests that Dr. Issels' main treatment regimen has no effect on tumor growth. He aims to put each patient in the best possible condition to combat the disease, which is admirable, but there is no evidence from our examination and their notes that it makes a significant contribution to their [patients'] survival. We searched for every possible indication of tumor regression not due to cytotoxic drugs and found none that was convincing."

34. Bob Marley's mother to Lew-Lee.
35. Booker and Winkler, pp. 189–91.
36. Ibid, p. 179.
37. Roger Steffans, taped interview, January 16, 2000.
38. Booker and Winkler, pp. 180–83, 187.
39. Roger Steffans, "Reasoning with Peter Tosh," *Reggae Times*, 1980.
40. Levy.
41. Randall Grass, "The Stone that the Builder Refused," *Down Beat*, January, 1986.
42. Williams, p. 20.

CHAPTER THIRTEEN
Gang War: Sons of CHAOS vs. Thugs
A Tupac Shakur and Notorious B.I.G.
Assassination Digest

YOU KNOW THAT COP WHO PULLS YOU OVER, WHO DIDN'T REALLY HAVE TO GIVE YOU A TICKET BUT HE GAVE YOU ONE ANYWAY? WE'RE GONNA MULTIPLY HIM 100 TIMES, AND NOW YOU HAVE THE CHIEF OF POLICE. MULTIPLY HIM ABOUT 100 TIMES, AND YOU'VE GOT AN FBI AGENT. MULTIPLY HIM APPROXIMATELY 1,000 TIMES AND YOU'VE GOT A CIA AGENT. MULTIPLY THIS AGENT ANOTHER 10,000, AND YOU'VE GOT THE HEAD OF THE CIA. ICE T, THE ICE OPINION: WHO GIVES A FUCK?, NEW YORK: ST. MARTIN'S, 1994.

A fog machine in the police establishment conceals the killers of rap artist Tupac Shakur, gunned down at a stop light in Las Vegas on September 7, 1996. The assailants are dim shrouds in a toxic cloud of disinformation. Police officials in Las Vegas and Compton have hinted alternately that the rapper was shot by a death squad under the direction of Marion "Suge" Knight, founder of Death Row Records—implausible because the thug impresario was himself wounded in the attack—or the late Orlando Anderson, a 22-year old Pac fan widely reputed to be a "gang-banger"—an honor student, in fact, not a gangsta. Although Anderson has been publicly identified by evidence leaked to the corporate media, all who knew Anderson maintain he was "not at all violent."[1] It will be evident that a police stonewall, subsequent killings, a strategy of disinformation, the ignoring of witnesses, and the presence of undercover agents from Los Angeles and New York at the subsequent murder of rapper Notorious B.I.G. suggest conversely that both rappers were murdered by hit squads under the sanction of federal officials.

Cathy Scott, a reporter for the *Las Vegas Sun*, penetrated the secretive handling of the Tupac case by authorities, and reported:

> No one followed the mortuary van carrying Tupac Shakur's body from the hospital to the morgue. The van drove three blocks without being noticed. An autopsy was done the evening of [Friday] Sept. 13, 1996, almost immediately following his death, according to authorities. While the autopsy report is not deemed by Nevada state law to be

public information, the coroner's report is available to the public. However, after I bought a copy for $5, an office employee later said it had been given to me in error, and that they would not be releasing it to anyone because of the ongoing homicide investigation. To my knowledge, I am the only reporter to have a copy of that report.

Coroners found that Tupac had no illegal drugs in his blood when shot, but he had been heavily sedated at University Medical Center. He had been shot in his right hand, hip and chest just under the right arm. A trauma center surgeon removed a bullet from his pelvic area. "Tupac's injuries included a gunshot wound to his right chest with a 'massive hemothorax' and a wound to the thigh with 'the bullet palpable within the abdomen.'" The diagnosis was a gunshot wound to the chest and abdomen, and post-operative bleeding.[2]

The murder "investigation" has been side-tracked at every turn by detectives in Compton and Las Vegas, who have consistently managed to avoid gathering leads. Key witnesses to Tupac's murder died in a timely fashion. Others were shunned by homicide detectives.

Yafeu Fula, the eyewitness, was unable to provide a description of the trigger-man. He was murdered himself two months after Shakur was pronounced dead. On November 14, 1996, the wires reported, "Witness to Tupac's Murder Killed":

> One of Tupac Shakur's backup rappers who witnessed the fatal shooting of the hip-hop star was gunned down in a New Jersey housing project this weekend. So far, police are saying that the slaying of 19-year old Yafeu Fula has no connection with Tupac's death.
> But Fula's death will further stymie the slow-moving murder investigation. "It's another dead end for us," said Las Vegas police Sgt. Kevin Manning, the lead investigator.
> Fula, a member of Shakur's backing group Outlaw Immortalz, was riding with bodyguards in the car behind Shakur when the rapper was shot by unknown assailants returning from the Tyson-Bruce fight September 7 in Las Vegas. . . .
> Strangely enough, Fula was also murdered the night of a Mike Tyson fight. Evander Holyfield defeated Mike Tyson just hours before Fula was killed.
> Meanwhile, Shakur's driving companion and Death Row Records head Marion "Suge" Knight is sitting in a Los Angeles courtroom today accused of drug-related probation violations. . . . Later this month, federal prosecutors will contend he used marijuana in violation of a 1994 firearms trafficking conviction in Las Vegas.
> Think the Tupac killing will ever be solved?[3]

Other witnesses, dismissed by police as "uncooperative," complained to reporters that no attempt had been made to solicit their testimony. Two of Tupac Shakur's entourage informed authorities that they saw who murdered him but were never asked to identify suspects. These witnesses—Malcolm Greenridge, one of Shakur's back-up performers, and Frank Alexander, a bodyguard—were also driving behind the rapper when the assailants opened fire. But Greenridge and Alexander were never contacted by homicide investigators about the killing. Metro Police Sergeant Kevin Manning countered with an attempt to discredit them. They "gave us taped statements on the night of the shooting that are totally inconsistent" with their public statements, he said. Manning also assured reporters that investigators had finally contacted one witness and intended to contact the other—several months after witnesses had complained to the press of police inaction.

Greenridge and Alexander were clear about the killing. "I saw four black males in a white Cadillac as it rolled by our car just before Tupac got shot," he recalls. "I couldn't see which of those four people pulled the trigger, but I saw the gun come from the back seat out through the driver's front window, and I saw the driver. I did see all four faces for a few split seconds before the shooting, though, and I told the police that. I can't promise you I could identify them, but nobody has ever even asked me to try."

Frank Alexander asked: "Could I identify the killer of my friend Tupac Shakur if the police showed me photos or a lineup of suspects? Possibly so. The thing is that the Las Vegas Metro Police never even tried to show me a photo of the shooter. Nor did they call me at any time for a line-up or to ask me anything concerning the shooting and death of Tupac." Both witnesses stated that they did not pursue

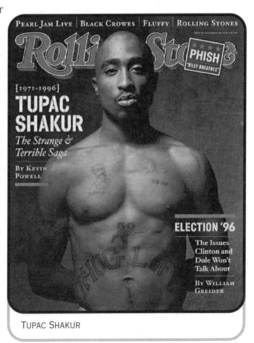

TUPAC SHAKUR

the issue with Las Vegas police because they distrusted them. Just after the shooting, "the police shoved guns in our faces and threatened us," Greenridge said. "They made us lay face down in the middle of the street. Even after they realized we were telling the truth, they never apologized." Greenridge told reporters, "If you ask me, I don't think they really care who killed Tupac. [He] was just another black man that had a strong opinion—and now he's out of the way."

Six months after the Las Vegas assault, the "investigation" was still ostensibly bogged down in police apathy. The *Sun's* Cathy Scott reported in March:

> When a producer from *Unsolved Mysteries* called last year and asked me to go on camera, my first response was, "Don't you have anyone else you can interview?" For six months, Metro homicide detectives have investigated Shakur's murder. They didn't want to be interviewed for the *Unsolved* piece, claiming the publicity "won't help them solve the crime."
>
> Tupac and Biggie each performed for record labels that were the targets of federal investigations. The nights they were killed, each was with their record label producers (Tupac was with Marion "Suge" Knight, owner of Death Row Records on the West Coast, and Biggie was with Puffy Combs, owner of Bad Boy Entertainment on the East Coast). Are the killings connected? That's one of three questions narrator Robert Stack poses on *Unsolved Mysteries*.
>
> "Today, disturbing questions haunt the investigation," Stack says. "Why were Tupac's trusted bodyguards unarmed? Why did the killer seem to target only Shakur? In the midst of the jam-packed Las Vegas Strip, how did the gunman know where Tupac would be?"

In the information vacuum of the "dead-end" investigation, rumors spread like a continental brush fire. Sergeant Manning claimed that more than half of the tips following the March 14 *Unsolved Mysteries* segment on Shakur were theories that the rapper is still alive. "I was at the autopsy," Manning reported. "His mother was at the hospital when he died. The doctors, the nurses were there, the people from the mortuary and the coroner's office were involved. For him not to be dead, you would have to have a conspiracy on line with JFK being assassinated by the Central Intelligence Agency." One tipster claimed Shakur's close friend, Marion "Suge" Knight, killed the rapper. More than 300 tips were received, but only one appeared promising, claimed Manning: "There was only one that piqued our interest to the point that it appeared the individual probably has at least some information or knowledge about the case, But they didn't leave a name or phone number."[4]

Richard Fischbein, an attorney for the Shakur estate, complained that Las Vegas police were not really interested in finding the gunmen. "I've called and pushed and prodded them," he said, "and these guys aren't doing anything. So that leaves us with the mother forced into a position of having to deal with this situation on her own, and that's an outrage. I have my own theory, and that is that they're trying to create the Disneyland of the Far West in Las Vegas and the last thing in the world that they want is a story about black-gang drive-by shootings taking place in their town. So this is not something they're going to bring to a big trial that will be covered by the national press."[5]

Afeni Shakur observed tersely, "It was clear to me from day one that the Las Vegas police never had any interest in solving the case of my son's murder." Yet the Associated Press reported five months after the slaying: "Three Los Angeles men are suspects in the drive-by shooting of rap star Tupac Shakur, but police say uncooperative witnesses have stymied their investigation."[6] Witnesses unanimously deny this statement and maintain that it was police who were "uncooperative."

In the Spring of 1997, a stink arose over the concealment of the trigger-man's identity by Las Vegas police: "MTV News reported on Tuesday that it had obtained a 29-page document prepared by police in Compton, California, which was attached to a motion filed in court by attorneys for Death Row Records chief Suge Knight. This document reveals that only days after the shooting in Las Vegas of rapper Tupac Shakur last September, cops already had the name of the man gang informants say pulled the trigger."

Sergeant Manning acknowledged to reporters that detectives had "no suspects" in the case—nevertheless, Orlando Anderson had not been "ruled out." The sergeant wasn't accusing anyone . . . exactly. "It may be a play on words a little bit," he explained, "but that's just the way we do business."[7]

Official "word play" stoked the fog machine obscuring the identities of the killers, recalling the smears of political activists in the COINTELPRO/CHAOS period. Compton police prepared an affidavit in October citing unnamed "informants" falsely placing Anderson in gang activity. He was arrested during a sweep of the city and questioned about another, unrelated case, the murder of Edward Webb, but no charges were filed. Detectives from Las Vegas arrived and grilled him about the Shakur killing but were unable to establish a connection. There was also no evidence that he had shot and killed

Webb. Deputy District Attorney Janet Moore released Anderson but refused to explain her decision to reporters.[8]

While detained for questioning, Anderson was publicly condemned by police, described falsely as a street thug and a murderer. It was hinted at press conferences that Compton police had apprehended the killer of Tupac Shakur. But "if Orlando was indeed a gang-banger," *Details* reported, "he certainly wasn't a run-of-the-mill one. 'He wasn't that type of person at all,' says Tyrise Tooles, a friend and former classmate of Orlando's at Dominguez High School in Compton. 'He was a real friendly person.'" The accused killer of Shakur also attended William Howard Taft High in the Valley, a school of advanced students. He was immersed in family life, had never been convicted of a crime, did not indulge in drugs, even marijuana or tobacco, loved sports, planned on running his own recording studio—not exactly the profile of a gangsta Crip, as police alleged.[9]

On March 21, Anderson spoke to reporters from CNN: "I want to let everybody know . . . I didn't do it," he said. "I been thinking that maybe I'm like a scapegoat or something."

His lawyer, Edi M.O. Faal, was on hand for the interview, and added, "This young man is almost acting like a prisoner now. He is very careful where he goes, he is very careful when he goes out." Anderson denied publicly that he was a member of the Crips, and there is no indication that he ran with the gang, but police in his hometown of Compton defamed him anyway.[10] The bogus charges didn't help Anderson's reputation in Compton, particularly with the Crips. After his release, he confided to his lawyer, "You know, I don't think I'm going to have a long life." The comment was prophetic— Orlando Anderson was shot and killed by a Corner Pocket Crip in a street confrontation on May 29, 1998.

The Tupac Shakur GeoCities Web Site suggests that the famed rapper was a political target, the latest in a series of covert operations waged against his family:

> The tale of Tupac Shakur, who lived so fast and died so young, is at once more tender and more tragic than that of the woman-hating thug we saw in stories about him. Quiet as it was kept by the media and by Tupac himself, the effusively talented singer/writer/actor was the heir apparent of a family of black revolutionaries, most of whom wound up jailed, exiled or dead during the 1970s and 1980s. His ties to the remarkable Shakur family must have been a weighty psychic burden for the rap artist. The individual members of the extended clan commanded almost mythic respect from radicals of the black power

period, especially in New York. This defining part of Tupac's background, incredibly, has been generally glossed over by the music and social critics trying to make sense of the contradictions that permeated his life. Given the radical diehard commitment of those relatives, it is no wonder that Tupac believed police agents were trailing him, like hunters after their prey. What was truly amazing was the grace with which, as an actor and rapper, he tied together feelings of love with the righteous anger that was a family legacy.

Tupac Amaru Shakur was born in 1971 to Afeni Shakur, a Black Panther, who carried the rapper-to-be in her womb while she was in jail, accused in a bomb plot. The Manhattan District Attorney tried to link 21 Panthers to the alleged plot, but the prosecutor's office found itself red-faced when a jury quickly rejected the charges. It is now believed the defendants were victims of an FBI-led attempt to neutralize Panther Party members across the country.

Afeni never revealed publicly who Tupac's father was. But one thing she did acknowledge: that the father was not Afeni's husband, Lumumba Shakur, who was the lead defendant in the Panther case. Exhausted from the trial and angry at the romantic betrayal by Afeni, Lumumba left his wife and her newborn son; but Afeni quickly moved in with Lumumba's adopted brother, Mutulu, who would become Tupac's stepfather and spiritual counselor for the rest of the younger man's life. Those who knew the family describe Mutulu Shakur as the most influential male figure in Tupac's life, the man who taught him to stand up for himself and never to back down from a fight. But Mutulu, later to be known as Dr. Shakur, because of his training in acupuncture, was eventually to be taken from Tupac. In 1986, he was arrested as the reputed mastermind of the 1981 Brinks robbery, in which two Nayack, New York policemen and a Brinks guard were killed. To this day, Dr. Shakur denies that he had anything to do with the holdup, but he was nonetheless convicted and is now doing 60 years.

In an interview two years ago at the federal prison in Lewisburg, Pennsylvania, where he was being held at the time, Dr. Shakur would not say if he saw Tupac during the years he was on the run from the Brinks charges. But it must have been painful for adolescent Tupac to know agents were scouring black neighborhoods all over the country looking for his stepfather. During this time, Afeni and Tupac moved from Harlem to Baltimore. In an added trauma for Tupac, Lumumba Shakur, who remained on good terms with the family, was found dead in Louisiana several days before Mutulu was arrested. Mutulu says he suspects Lumumba was murdered by someone (perhaps a police informant) who learned of Mutulu's whereabouts and decided to kill two birds with one stone, taking the two brothers out of circulation.

By this time, at age 15, Tupac must have been thoroughly convinced that to be a Shakur was to confront the possibility of death at an early age. He was learning such lessons almost before he could walk. In 1973, when Tupac was a toddler, his uncle, Zayd Shakur, was traveling on the New Jersey Turnpike with his companion, Assata Shakur, when they were stopped by a trooper. In a shoot-out that followed, Zayd and Trooper Werner Foerster lay dead. Assata, once known as Jo Anne Chesimard, was wounded and later charged and convicted in the killing of the trooper. Taking the legend of the Shakurs to new heights, Assata escaped from prison in 1979 and fled to Cuba, where she is living now under a grant of asylum from the government of Fidel Castro. Assata, dubbed the "soul" of the Black Liberation Army, is arguably the most famous member of Tupac's extended family. Even as he climbed the ladder of stardom and fought publicized battles with the law—including the sex assault case and an allegation that he wounded a police officer in Georgia—Tupac stayed in close contact with his stepfather Mutulu, talking with him by phone and seeking advice from him. Mutulu (born Jeral Wayne Williams) maintains he was having an impact on the young man, guiding him from street instincts and post-adolescent confusion, into a more coherent use of his energies.

Mutulu praised the tender songs that Tupac would write, the ones with positive messages about family life and responsibility, like "Brenda's Got a Baby." Together, the step-father and -son team drew up a "Code of Thug Life," which was a list of rules discouraging random violence among gansta rappers. All of this was done away from the glare of media attention, and perhaps there was good reason why Tupac did not want to publicize his relationship with Mutulu. He was already taking enough heat from local police around the country. Why aggravate the situation by further provoking federal agents who might have been monitoring Mutulu and his revolutionary associates? After all, federal authorities were known to be still interested in cap-turing Assata, who was close to Mutulu. Assata says she escaped from jail in 1979 because she had learned of a plan to have white prisoners assassinate her. Federal authorities said Mutulu was part of the team that broke Assata out of prison. It is perhaps difficult for some to remember the passion that Assata and her associates inspired in the law enforcement community. After I first wrote about Assata in 1987, I did a phone interview with FBI official Ken Walton, who was promi-nent in the effort to capture her after her jail break. He told me in measured, angry words that he "or somebody like me" will one day capture Assata and bring her back to the States.

Esysni Tyehimba, Tupac's personal manager, has long been a friend of the Shakur family. Tyehimba recalls that they dealt extensively with COINTELPRO issues. "We worked around a lot of political prisoners and . . . the black liberation movement over the years in different locations. This [shaped Tupac into] the person that he was." Tyehimba's family operated the Center for Black Survival. "We had a youth group called the New Afrikan Panthers, and [Tupac] became the chairperson of that organization." The very first song Tupac recorded was "Panther Power." Karen Lee, a publicist and friend of the Shakur family, recalls early attempts by authorities to discredit the rap singer when he was coming to terms with his growing popularity. "Tupac couldn't understand why it was front-page news when he was arrested that time in Atlanta" for shooting a pair of white, off-duty cops on October 31, 1993. Lee told reporters in the rap press that when the charges were dropped, "and one police officer involved was found guilty [of firing at Shakur and making false statements], it was a story on, like, page 85 that nobody knew anything about."[11]

Tupac was booked on a rape charge the following year. During the trial in November 1997, he was robbed on the street and shot five times. Tupac checked out of the hospital the same day and appeared in court the next. He was sentenced on February 5, 1995 to four-and-a-half years at Rikers Island Prison in New York, but was released when Knight posted a $1.4-million bond eight months later. Charles Fuller, the band's road manager and a codefendent in the sexual assault case, maintains that they'd been set up by the legal system. "Right before we got sentenced," he recalls, "Tupac said that he felt like an injustice was being done to us."[12]

The agony of the rap industry was exacerbated on March 9, 1997 by the killing of 24-year-old Brooklyn rap artist Christopher Wallace, otherwise known as Notorious B.I.G., in Los Angeles. On March 10, MTV News reported:

The 24-year old Brooklyn rapper, whose real name was Christopher Wallace, had attended the annual Soul Train music awards and was sitting in his GMC Suburban after leaving a post-ceremony party

NOTORIOUS B.I.G.

thrown by *Vibe* magazine at Los Angeles' Petersen Automotive Museum. Police say an unidentified gunman riddled the vehicle with bullets, and Wallace was then rushed to Cedars Sinai, where he was pronounced dead. The killing of B.I.G. was the second in the last six months, the first coming with the shooting death of Tupac Shakur in Las Vegas last September. . . . Despite the fact that the shooting occurred outside a party that reportedly boasted 1,000 guests, police told reporters they have few leads in the case. . . .

Biggie Smalls was a central figure in the alleged ongoing feud between the East coast and West coast rap camps, and particularly between Bad Boy Entertainment and Suge Knight's Death Row Records. Despite the fact that Bad Boy head Sean "Puffy" Combs and Death Row rapper Snoop Doggy Dogg made a very public statement recently announcing that there is no feud, Smalls' death led many to speculate that the shooting could have been related to the perceived ill-will between east coast and west coast rappers. However, sources close to Bad Boy and Death Row quickly dismissed the speculation in a *Los Angeles Times* report. "This was a professional hit," an unidentified source told reporters for the newspaper.

Law enforcement officials and the media speculated that the shooting was the culmination of a supposed East Coast-West Coast rivalry. But Phyllis Pollack, a publicist with Def Press in Los Angeles offered that the "feud" was but a publicity stunt. "It's unfair to speculate that the deaths were the result of a coastal feud," she insisted. "Sure, there's been this competition, but that's been since day one, We don't have artists on the West Coast saying, 'Let's kill off all of those East Coast rappers so we can sell more records on the East Coast.'" Jesse Washington, managing editor of *Vibe* magazine, noted there was some enmity between the rappers, but cautioned against writing off the murder as a result of it. "It's too early to attribute this to a coastal rivalry, Tupac revenge or anything else because there [are] just so many different possibilities and aspects to this whole situation," he said. "The saddest thing about all of this is they have literally generated tens of millions of dollars in sales of records, magazine sales and ratings," he said. "I mean, these were two popular artists."[13]

Once again, there were no suspects and police were reportedly stymied. But Mutulu Shakur lived with political assassinations his entire adult life, and looked elsewhere for the identities of the culprits in a letter to the Wallace family under the heading, "The Shakur Family Extends Our Sympathies to Ms. Wallace, Sister Faith, and Brother Biggie's Son and Daughter."

To Biggie's Family:

We believe the loss of Biggie and Tupac will have a tremendous impact on our younger generation. When all the facts are received and analyzed, it will show through all the negative and false accusations. . . . Brother Biggie acted in a principled way toward our son and his public actions were principled by their very nature which was true to the life game in which he lived. Our family has not come to any final conclusion as to who killed our son, Tupac. Nor why he was killed. His murder and the death of Yafeu "Kadafi" Fula, son of Yaasmyn Fula and P.O.W. Sekou Odinga, a month after Tupac, and the senseless murder of Javana Thomas, the daughter of Freedom Fighter Innie Thomas and the late B.L.A commander John Thomas, has our family and extended family in constant grief as well as searching for the truth in all matters. . . .

We are continuing our investigation as to determining the truth. . . . We do know that Brother Biggie was a part of an industry that has been under attack from the highest form of government officials. They have targeted Tupac, Sister Souljah, Ice T, Ice Cube, and Snoop Dogg to just name a few. The object of this attack reportedly was the lyrics' contents and the connection to crime. "If" this was the only case, why would devil worshipers (music and artist) not be hounded out also? Since they openly worship the devil in a so-called God-fearing country. (Their music and profane religion outright denounces the government while preaching mayhem, destruction and even death to their parents, government and even nonbelievers in their philosophical satanism). Yes, we must take responsibility for our own actions.

We must acknowledge that we have powers to shape minds and souls. Tupac, Biggie and Yafeu all could bring us closer to the real deal or turn us in upon ourselves. That power is not easy to comprehend when your only goal is to "come up." The struggle of saving and speaking has been a tremendous task for most if not all leaders. But this government, and those who have profited from the music culture of Black people, really know "power" and how to utilize it both internally and externally. Their goal has been long range and very specific to their economical survival and political agenda. Whereas our loved ones, our rappers, wanted to explain their pain and identity from where they came, and describe their present life and at times asked us to hope for a better tomorrow, if all things were fair. If our family's (SHAKUR's) lack of response to rumors and allegations contributed to any confusion as to what principle we stand on, let it be known and clear!! We do not believe in COINCIDENCES. We believe history has demonstrated that the murders of Black people (young and old) who can have a profound impact, those who refuse to "bow down," even if they themselves are not clear on the reasons why, have and will be targeted by the government at its highest level. These murders have historically proven over time to have the hand of government secret agents or the stimulation by the government for negative response, and was initiated by these agents working on behalf of the government and their secret agendas.

We mourn Brother Biggie and Tupac with the rest of the Black Nation because they (our son, brother, father and leader in their own rights) have clearly been victims of a set of circumstances . . . implemented outside of their control [or] ability to influence. I disagree with the method of discussing issues of our internal contradictions in the entertainment media. Tupac in his *Makaveli* record clearly changed his wrongful view of who shot him [in 1994] and who was heading it in New York, and why?

That's not to say that we know the *Makaveli* allegations [are] correct, only that any "fan" of Tupac's would surely have known that Tupac revised his wrongful [stance] against Biggie's involvement concerning his shooting in New York. And he wanted his "fans" to know it. It is common knowledge that Brother Biggie was under surveillance by the FBI or other government agents. And his every movement was reportedly being watched concerning a parole or possible parole violation. How come those agents did not protect him, or at least apprehend or pursue the people who did the shooting (and the same must be said for my son Tupac)? The tactics by law enforcement agencies in the past ha ve been to arrest these high profile artists on gun violations. Leaving them in a "Catch 22" situation to violate parole by defending themselves. Or leaving themselves defenseless, making them easy prey for a would-be assassin and stick-up kid. Surely, the FBI was at the party. . . .

What we must understand is that our warriors are needed when it has been proven beyond contradiction that the CIA were principal importers of Crack Cocaine and Cocaine period into the hood, initiating the newly created drug laws that were blatantly racially motivated to set into motion tactics of genocide to destroy and lock away our brothers and sisters for the rest of their lives.

They have also created conditions that breed the worst in us. Look at how long the struggle in South Africa was extended because of the fighting of (African on African) Zulas against A.N.C and P.A.A.C. Rap music and the Hip-Hop nation is a movement unclear of its final objectives, but a movement nevertheless, with potentials this government already fully understands and is prepared to destroy. If we look back in our history on the Black Nationalist Movement, the assassination of Bunchy Carter and John Huggins, two great Panthers on the West Coast, by the members of US organizations run by Mr. Ron Karanga.

After years of my investigation as a member of the National Task Force for COINTELPRO Litigation Research, in connection with Geronimo Ji Jagas' [Pratt] trial, [I am aware that] the motivation and participation in the murders by the FBI has been proven beyond a doubt. The murder-assassination of Robert Webb, a West Coast Panther functioning out of New York, killed on 125th St. and 7th Ave., sparked a vengeful killing of another great Panther, Sam Napier. The assassination of Robert Webb was revealed to be FBI motivated as well as their direct participation in his assassination which in design was to split the East Coast and West Coast connection. At that time, many of us functioned out of our emotions and ignorance and played into it. These types of specified killings helped to destroy our movement, accomplishing the governments' goals. Don't go for it!!! Learn from our past mistakes. Act at all times by rationale and reasoning. We do not want the death of Tupac or Biggie to be used as a base for internal fractional side contradictions. Nor for Biggie and Tupac to be used to fuel further strife, dissension and destruction internally by the Federal/Mass Media governing the situation. In the name of Biggie and Tupac, stop playing yourselves, and start putting resources into the real struggle.

Show love to your warriors, pay attention to the game that's being played on/against us. SEARCH FOR TRUTH!!! Don't look at who shot Biggie and Tupac, but WHY they were shot. Don't be fooled by the media that (seldom if ever had a kind word for rappers) has never shown real concern for [our] welfare. STOP FAKING TUFF . . . BE TUFF!!!

To all the Thugs, Live by the code, protect yourselves at ALL times. Failure to do so could cost us all.

SINCERELY,

DR. MUTULU SHAKUR, STIFF RESISTANCE [14]

Mutulu Shakur's deduction that secret police assigned to the surveillance of Biggy Small must have witnessed the murder proved correct. Unfortunately, none of the undercover agents from Los Angeles and New York who saw the killing stepped forward to provide investigators with a description of the gunmen—a violation of law regardless of their failure to intercede in the killing or pursue gunmen. As the *Las Vegas Sun* reported in April: "At least one police officer and possibly as many as six acted as security guards for The Notorious B.I.G. and may have witnessed his slaying. . . . However, none came forward to say they were there, including the one off-duty officer who was in a car directly behind the rapper." Damion Butler, Small's road manager: "If they were there all that time . . . it just seems impossible to me that they didn't see the incident. Where did they go?" It so happened that plainclothes police officers from New York were in the area, according to spokesmen, during the shooting as part of "a federal investigation of the Rap industry." But the Justice Department and police in Los Angeles and New York have all refused to comment on the presence of undercover officers at the murder scene.[15]

On February 5, MTV News reported that the Las Vegas Police Department was skeptical an arrest could be made unless more witnesses stepped forward—yet all of the undercover officers at the murder site participated in a conspiracy of silence. They would doubtless have offered to give depositions and attend line-ups if the killers had been gang-bangers. Mutulu Shakur's conviction that secret police killed his stepson and Notorious B.I.G. proves increasingly feasible.

Any civilian witness would have quite possibly been prosecuted for withholding evidence in an ongoing homicide investigation, but only one of the officers who witnessed the killing and stonewalled was disciplined. In August, an off-duty cop moonlighting as a bodyguard for Smalls the night of the murder, was threatened with a 24-day suspension. Inglewood Police Chief Alex Perez told the press that the unnamed officer's violations "ranged, on the low end, from failure to obtain a permit to work off-duty, ranging all the way to conduct unbecoming an officer." Furthermore, it emerged that the police officer hired to work the rapper's security detail had "a criminal record."[16]

The blue wall of silence encircles a leading suspect in the Smalls case, David A. Mack, a former LAPD officer since convicted of bank robbery and currently serving a 14-year sentence. Police files contain a note that an eyewitness had placed Mack at the murder scene. Another reports that Mack hired an old friend to shoot Smalls. Amir Muhammad, alias Harry Billups, the old friend, had been a classmate of Mack's at the University of Oregon. He disappeared after visiting Mack in prison on December 26, 1977, and police are still searching for him.[17]

Periodically, LAPD officials hint that Death Row's Suge Knight may have had a hand in the killings of Notorious B.I.G. Robin Yanes, Knight's attorney, emphatically denies police claims of a connection to Mack: "A year ago it came and they're recycling it to cover their butts. Suge doesn't know Mack."[18] The same tactics used to shift suspicion from undercover agents to Orlando Anderson in the Shakur case have been hauled out to connect Knight to the "retaliatory" hit on Smalls. In April 1999, it was widely reported that Knight was "under investigation." Search warrants were handed around at the record label's headquarters and other locations, and a purple Chevrolet Impala owned by the company was impounded. But there were no arrests, and no charges have been filed. Police spokesmen refused to comment on why Knight was considered a "suspect." "He was in custody at the time, so he didn't pull the trigger," Lieutenant Al Michelena, speaking for the

LAPD's robbery-homicide unit, told reporters. "We are investigating the possibility of him being implicated in this. We would certainly consider him a possible suspect." More police "word play"? Michelena refused to discuss a possible motive and all documents related to the search warrants were sealed. The purple Chevy was owned by Death Row, but hadn't been registered for about two years and was believed to have not been used during this period, Michelena explained. To date, no evidence has surfaced linking Knight to the shooting of Biggie Smalls, he has not been prosecuted, yet police spokesmen continue to imply that he is a "suspect." [19]

At present, the murders of Tupac Shakur, Biggie Small—also Yaefu Fula, Rolling 60 Crip Jelly Johnson, Jake Robles, Randy "Stretch" Walker and Genius-Car-Wash-Owner Bruce—remain "unsolved."

NOTES
1. William Shaw, "Wrong Man, Wrong Place, Wrong Time?" *Details*, September 1999, p. 193.
2. Cathy Scott, "Behind the Scenes of 'Unsolved' Shakur Mystery," *Las Vegas Sun*, March 14, 1997.
3. "Witness to Tupac Murder Killed," E! Online News Service, November 14, 1996.
4. Anonymous, "Callers say Shakur's death just a bad rap," *Las Vegas Review-Journal*, March 22, 1997.
5. Neil Strauss, "Change of Story in Shakur Case," *Las Vegas Sun*, March 18, 1998, courtesy of the *New York Times*.
6. AP Release, "Cops Eye Three in Shakur Murder," *Nevada Business Journal*, February 4, 1997.
7. Shaw, p. 197.
8. Shaw, p. 196.
9. Shaw, p. 194.
10. Anonymous, "Orlando Anderson Speaks About Tupac Murder," *MTV News Gallery*. The segment originally aired on March 21, 1997.
11. Friends and family of Tupac Shakur, "Back 2 the Essence," *Vibe* magazine special commemorative issue, October 1999, pp. 103–107.
12. *Vibe* interview, p. 107.
13. AP release, "Is the 'Rap War' for Real?" March 10, 1997.
14. Mutulu Shakur letter, Fortune City Tupac Shakur website.
15. AP release, "Police Saw Rapper Shooting," *Las Vegas Sun*, April 23, 1997.
16. Michael Goldberg, ed., "Notorious B.I.G. Security Guard Suspended— Off-duty cop who worked for Biggie the night he was murdered had criminal record," *Music News of the World*, Aug 2, 1997.
17. Matt Lait and Scott Glover, "Ex-LAPD Officer is Suspect in Rapper's Slaying, Records Show," *Los Angeles Times*, December 9, 1999, p. A-1.
18. Ibid., p. A-43.
19. AP release, "Knight Investigated in B.I.G. Murder," *Las Vegas Sun*, April 21, 1999.

CHAPTER FOURTEEN

Dancing on the Jetty:
The Death of Michael Hutchence, et al

POP EATS IT YOUNG, THAT'S FOR SURE **MICHAEL HUTCHENCE ON KURT COBAIN**

On November 22, 1997, the day Michael Hutchence was found tethered by the neck to a door fixture at the Ritz-Carlton Hotel in Sydney, Australia, Reuters placed his death in context: "If Michael Hutchence's death is eventually ruled a suicide, the INXS vocalist would join a long list of rockers who have taken their own lives. . . . Joy Division singer Ian Curtis built a career on songs filled with angst, paranoia and death. After making inspired hits such as 'She's Lost Control,' 'Transmission' and 'Love Will Tear Us Apart,' he hanged himself in his Manchester, England home in 1980. Richard Manuel, pianist and vocalist with the Band, hanged himself in a Florida hotel room a month shy of his 43rd birthday in March 1986. Little had gone right for him since the group broke up in 1976, and a subsequent reunion—without main man Robbie Robertson—further depressed him. . . . Psychological problems may have played a part in the 1979 death of soul-pop singer Donny Hathaway, who fell to his death from a 15th floor hotel room in New York City. Hathaway, who was 34, best known for his duets with Roberta Flack. . . ."

The mortality rate among rock musicians—who, as a group receive more than a share of capital, sexual gratification, and public adoration—is extremely high. Depression is often cited as the prelude to death among these pitiful creatures. Of course. Michael Hutchence was despondent over a custody battle and destroyed himself. Case clos . . . .

But hold the phone, if you please. Kym Wilson, a friend of the vocalist's, spent some five hours with him the morning he died. She was the last person to see him alive and reported, "He was concerned about the custody hearing but I wouldn't say he was depressed. His attitude was that he believed he was right and that he and Paula should get custody of the children and if they didn't have luck this time, they would keep fighting on. I never for one instant think he thought that would be the end." Hutchence had spoken "with such excitement of his future—I had really never seen him with so much to look forward to."[1]

God hides in the details, so before rushing this case file to the "Day the Music Died" morgue, one last check for Him in the flotsam of details related to a very peculiar death is in order. There was no inquest. Friends of Hutchence told investigators that the "happy/depressed" rock singer was "involved in kinky sex over the years," and though it's fairly certain that he was not the first rock musician to indulge in "kinky sex," authorities explored auto-eroticism as the cause of death.

The salacious indictment originated with Australian police, appeared in the *New York Post*, took on a life of its own, gathered momentum on the newswires, sprinted across the airwaves and barreled through the world media machine. On December 24, police spokesmen announced that they were anxious to quash this ugly rumor. Argumentative "paranoids" might ask why this particular bit of speculation was fed to the press in the first place. The "mainstream" media ran with it—and both passed the buck to the tabloid press, as *E! News Online* reported: "Authorities have not officially ruled Hutchence's case a suicide, although that's where they've indicated they're leaning, in spite of tabloid reports that the 37-year old singer accidentally hung himself while practicing an oxygen-deprivation masturbation game."

Two weeks after his death, INXS members called a press conference to complain about a cover story on their late lead vocalist entitled "Auto-Eroticism—the Sex that Kills" in *New Weekly* magazine. The article played on the conjecture that Hutchence did not commit suicide but hung himself accidentally. The stills, lewd S&M bondage scenes, were shot by fashion photographer Helmut Newton two weeks before Hutchence died. The magazine's cover featured a photo of Hutchence chained, a ravishing tart, barely clad in leather, arching over him. Another portrayed the tart wearing a saddle, with Hutchence the domineering equestrian. Surviving INXSers announced that they were considering legal action. A spokesman for the band found the article "incredibly insensitive."[2] It was a smear reminiscent of Albert Goldman's postmortem demolition jobs.

All around, it was a damned peculiar death. Senior Constable Mark Hargreaves of the New South Wales Police media unit, asked by reporters why Hutchence was naked when he hung himself, replied: "It was early in the morning, he could have just gotten out of bed. It's hard to determine if he did it on purpose or by accident."[3]

He didn't leave a suicide note behind.[4]

The night of his death, Hutchence had dinner with his father and stepmother at a local Indian restaurant. They laughed throughout the meal. His father expressed concern about Michael's personal problems, but was reassured, "Dad, I'm fine."

The INXS vocalist "was an unlikely candidate for suicide," noted Glenn Baker, an Australian pop music historian. "He was the consummate rock star. He took on the role of a star so comfortably. He floated above the pressures. Why he would choose this moment to throw in the towel I think will always remain a mystery." Ian "Molly" Meldrum, a television celebrity in Australia and close friend, said he last saw the singer in Los Angeles eight weeks before. Meldrum told reporters: "He seemed so happy and at peace, and even said to me, 'I've never been happier in my life.'" [5]

Zinta Reindel and Tamara Brachmanis, guests at the Ritz during Hutchence's last stay there, talked to him the night before his "suicide," and recalled, "He looked like he was a bit high on something . . . but he was happy." Why not? He was branching out into a thespian career in a Quentin Tarantino production and working on a solo album. His daughter was to be christened soon. Why abandon her without so much as a note?

Significant details were excluded from most press accounts. Corporate outlets reported: "SYDNEY, Australia—Michael Hutchence, the lead singer for the rock band INXS, was found dead Saturday in a Sydney hotel . . . shortly after midday. The INXS front man was in Australia preparing for the band's 20th anniversary tour. His body was discovered by a maid when she went to make up the room. Prescription pills were found scattered over the floor of his suite and there were bottles of alcohol on a sideboard." [6]

Pills, mostly antibiotics, Prozac, booze and a hotel room in a state of squalor—a death scene completely consistent with suicide. Hutchence died of asphyxiation. His body was still warm when he was found suspended from a door, the leather belt looped around his neck.

Music critic David Fricke, writing in *Rolling Stone*, supplemented the standard metro daily obituary: "His body bore the marks of a severe beating (a broken hand, a split lip, lacerations)." [7]

MICHAEL HUTCHENCE

Yet Australian police found "no evidence" of foul play. Derek Hand, the new South Wales coroner, stated without reservation: "The standard required to conclude that his death was a suicide has been reached."[10] But the coroner's report did not address the protruding contradictions. Did Hutchence break his own hand? Did he bludgeon himself until his lip bled, then beat himself into a pulp, and by doing so break bones in his hand? Then how, with one good hand and the other in excruciating, throbbing pain, did he manage to loop the belt through the door brace and around his neck securely enough to hang? The coroner didn't address the lingering questions, but was so confident of his verdict that he advised against an investigation: "Nothing will be gained by holding a formal inquest," he concluded. A homicide probe would consume unwarranted "time and expense."

Case clos . . . but, please, one more small peek at the record.

The "suicide" verdict may have been self-evident to a trained medical examiner, but it wasn't universally accepted. Paula Yates appeared on Australian television in March, 1998 to declare publicly that she sought legal advice to contest the finding. She said that Hutchence considered suicide the most cowardly act in the world. "I will be making it abundantly clear that because of information that I and only I could know about, I cannot accept the verdict. And I won't have my child grow up thinking that her father left her, not knowing the way he loved her." She acknowledged that Hutchence may have been depressed, but Hutchence's infant daughter was his passion, his "reason to live."

"In no way do I accept the coroner's verdict of suicide."[9]

The Devils Outside

Whatever Paula and only Paula knew, it's certain that the name Michael Hutchence appeared on more than one enemies list.

Hutchence was a political activist. His will designated Amnesty International and Greenpeace as the benefactors of the lion's share of his assets. And like many popular musicians on the left, the authorities harassed and set him up for a fall. In a July 1998 interview that appeared in a fan newsletter, Colin Diamond, Hutchence's attorney and former executor of his estate, was asked about the vocalist's September 1996 opium bust and his defense that the narcotic was planted by police.

"Perhaps you should try and figure it out for yourself!" Diamond snapped. "Michael and Paula were out of the country and during that time only a few people had any real access to the place: Bob Geldof,

Anita Debney, the nanny who used to work for Bob for twelve or so years, and a woman called Gerry Agar, who had developed a grudge against both Paula and Michael. The police were called days after the nanny claimed she'd found two Smarty packets with opium in them. Geldof immediately had a new custody application before the courts, 'in light of recent events.' The local police and prosecutors had the media on their case. There was enormous pressure on them, but even they had to admit something was a bit fishy. [The court] dropped all charges, remember, and Michael was issued with a certificate of non-prosecution by the Crown."

When asked if Hutchence "got off" fairly, Diamond snapped again: "Got off, GOT OFF?? I think the question should be who tried to get him on. You figure it out!"[11] The barrister turned on his interrogator again when asked about the late singer's complicated finances, the "missing millions" reported by the Australian press:

> **Q:** You've copped a bit of a hiding in the press as some sort of financial Svengali to Michael, with suggestions that, with regards to his estate, all is not as it should be. You've refused point-blank to speak to the media before this, so let me ask you directly: Where's the money?
> **Diamond:** None of your business. That's the point; it's private. Don't you guys get it? It's PRIVATE.

The word "private" is not to be found in the dictionary used by most daily news reporters—seven months later Australia's *Courier-Mail* found the "missing millions," and a horribly intriguing "Mafia Tie To Rock Star's Lost Riches."

It was reported that Hutchence "was involved in property dealings with a company allegedly connected to the Mafia. Bruno Romeo Sr., an alleged high-ranking member of the *L'Onorata Societa*, or Calabrian mafia, and his family are current and former directors of a company which sold a Gold Coast bowling alley for $2.25 million to a trustee company linked to the former INXS front man. A police intelligence report alleged Romeo was a key member of Italian organized crime groups." The National Crime Authority, in search of cocaine, descended upon the bowling alley in 1995. "Company records indicate Harbrick Pty. Ltd., whose former directors include Bruno 'The Fox' Romeo, a convicted drug dealer, also borrowed $270,000 as part of the deal." Colin Diamond "signed the earlier loan documents."

Lawyers and accountants of Mafia-owned Harbrick were hauled to court by Hutchence's mother, Patricia Glassop, and stepsister, Tina Hutchence, in a bid to recoup millions of dollars in assets. Harbrick

Ltd. was the nexus in an intricate web of companies, some of them based offshore. The purpose of the lawsuit was to force Harbrick to declare an estimated $25 million in assets not included in the Hutchence estate.

"The bowling alley at 378 Marine Pde., Labrador is one of five multi-million dollar properties worldwide which Mrs. Glassop and Ms. Hutchence claim should have been included in the singer's estate and divided according to his will," the newspaper reported. "The NCA . . . targeted a person associated with Harbrick." This would be Bruno Romeo, Sr., 69, "jailed for 10 years in 1994 over his role as the ringleader of an $8 million cannabis-growing operation on remote pastoral leases in Western Australia." Bruno was a director of Harbrick, a family-owned operation, "from 1988 to 1990. His son, Bruno Lee Romeo, 42, who was jailed for eight and a half years in Western Australia in 1987 for conspiring to cultivate a 1.5 hectare cannabis crop, is still a director of the Queensland-registered firm. The other director is Romeo Sr.'s son-in-law, Guiseppe 'Joe' Sergi, 42 . . . sentenced to five years jail after being convicted over a marijuana crop in 1982." [12]

Court documents revealed that the representatives of Harbrick in the loan agreement also worked for a baroque score of offshore companies that helped themselves to the finances of Michael Hutchence. *The Sydney Morning Herald* reported on May 29, 1998, "both sides have been told in writing that Hutchence had nothing to do with the investments."

His mother and sister charged before the bench that the £16 million in dispute had been siphoned off by Colin Diamond. Australian tax inspectors said that the vanishing funds meant that his widow and daughter might not receive a cent of the inheritance. Outraged, the family filed suit in the Queensland Supreme Court against Colin Diamond and Andrew Paul, Hutchence's Hong Kong-based tax consultant. Companies in Australia, the United Kingdom, France and the British Virgin Islands controlled the singer's income.

In fact, the Hutchence clan complained that the pop singer had relinquished most of his assets, including luxury automobiles and property in the south of France, Australia and London. His immense wealth had completely vanished into a black grotto of investments and trust accounts, and most, perhaps all of these firms were managed through discretionary trusts administered by Colin Diamond and Andrew Paul. Hutchence himself was penniless the day he allegedly looped a belt around his neck and found oblivion.

Many of Hutchence's most cherished possessions "were not actually owned by him," noted the *London Telegraph* in April 1999, "but were controlled by companies—themselves under the control of others. Beneficiaries have been told that only Mr Hutchence's personal effects will be distributed to them." [13]

The *Sydney Morning Herald* reported on March 8, 1998 that Hutchence "died almost penniless. But up to $30 million worth of property, cars, shares, bank accounts and income streams from his music and publishing—believed to have belonged to Hutchence—is held by obscure trusts in tax havens stretching from Hong Kong to the British Virgin Islands." Closed hearings on the will were requested by Andrew Paul, who had the temerity to ask that legal expenses in the pending litigation be underwritten by the estate. "The looming court battle has been variously reported as a 'squabble over the estate' or 'the family contesting the will.'" complained the *Herald*, "but this is not so. All members of the estranged family have agreed that Hutchence's will . . . was fair. What is disputed is the claim by his executors that there is nothing in the Hutchence estate to distribute." [14] Too much funny business, and still no investigation of the singer's death. Reporter Vince Lovegrove, reports *New Idea Magazine*, "was the last person to interview the rock star, and has hinted at a conspiracy to cover up what really happened." [15]

The financial ties to the Calabrian Mafia raise the specter of Michael Hutchence's close friend, Gianni Versacé, the celebrated fashion designer gunned down on the front steps of Casa Casuarina, his palatial South Beach home, by a serial killer on July 15, 1997, only five months before the INXS vocalist was found dead. Versacé, in fact, was raised in the south of Italy, a locale dominated by the Calabrian Mafia. The *Telegraph* reports that Versacé "would become inflamed with rage at suggestions that he had links with the Mafia." [16] But another *Telegraph* story notes, "There have long been reports that Versacé, whose family comes from Calabria in southern Italy, had been financially involved with the Mafia" (and so was Hutchence, without his knowledge. "It had been rumoured that he borrowed mob money to expand his business, and had been paying 'protection money.'" [17]

In Europe, the press ran rampant with allegations of Versacé's Mafia connections. Newspapers in Italy and Ireland offered stories on the designer and the Mob. The Russian Information Agency ran a feature on the topic.

Then there was the dead mourning dove found lying beside Versacé's body. The dove was rumored to be a "hit man's calling card," but police denied there was any connection to the Mafia. Seems one of the .40 caliber bullets that struck Hutchence's friend in the head ricocheted off the front gate of his house, a police spokesman explained, sending a lead fragment hurtling skyward. The fragment struck a dove sailing overhead in the eye, killing it instantly. The dove (the reincarnation of John Connally?) plummeted to the gutter, bounced and dropped beside Versacés dead body.[19]

But the conclusion of a private detective formerly employed by the fashion designer was sharply at odds with the official verdict. Frank Monté, an Australian P.I.—and former recruiter of mercenaries for the African campaigns of the 1960s—told radio shock jock Howard Stern and other interviewers that he was convinced "both Versacé and Cunanan were murdered by the Mob." He said that he'd been hired by the designer to investigate the killing of a friend's lover, and was recruited again to follow up on reports that employees of his own company had been laundering mob money. The private eye held that Versacé was gunned down because he intended to turn evidence of the laundering operation over to Italian police. Andrew Cunanan, Monté insisted, was a patsy kidnapped and "suicided" to provide the cover story. The investigator was so confident of the Mafia connection that he publicly advised Cunanan, after Versacé's murder, to turn himself in or he would be next.

Ten days after the slaying of Versacé, Monté told reporters: "Nothing that has happened since then has changed my mind."

He could not shake off certain unresolved discrepancies. Cunanon is reported to have stolen a .40 caliber pistol and used it to shoot Versacé twice in the head and subsequently turned it on himself. Cunanon was so badly disfigured by one blast that police were unable to identify him at first—but the same gun left two small, pristine holes in Versacé's skull. The private investigator was skeptical that the stolen gun could have produced drastically dissimilar wounds, and complained that FBI ballistic tests had been "fudged."[13]

The funeral of Gianni Versacé in Milan Cathedral was attended by Diana Spencer, the Princess of Wales, a month before her own death in a Parisian tunnel. As it happened, another social butterfly and friend of Michael Hutchence with organized crime connections was Dodi Fayed. Dodi's uncle was arms dealer Adnan Khashoggi of Iran-Contra fame. Mohamed al-Fayed, Dodi's father, is "one of the richest men in Britain," notes the *St. Louis Tribune.* "The source of al-Fayed's wealth always has been somewhat murky. Born poor in Alexandria, Egypt, he acquired a university education and married Samira Kashoggi, sister of the fabulously wealthy Saudi Arabian arms dealer. His brother-in-law gave al-Fayed his start in business by putting him in charge of his furniture-importing interests in Saudi

Arabia."[20] He is said to have sicced Donna Rice on Gary Hart to sabotage his bid for the Oval Office. Dodi and his uncle introduced Marla Maples to Donald Trump. Denise Brown, a gadfly in organized crime circles with a black book of mobbed up boyfriends, dated Dodi. Al Fayed and Adnan Khashoggi were closely associated with the Sultan of Brunei, who has been accused by an American beauty queen of presiding over a white slaver's harem.

Dodi Fayed and Diana Spencer were killed in a car crash on August 31, 1997, four months before Michael Hutchence died.

Intelligence officials withhold files on the accident and have steadfastly refused to declassify them. In November, 1998, in response to a Freedom of Information Act request filed by the proprietors of the *APBNews* website, the National Security Agency confirmed that it had on file "39 NSA-originated and NSA-controlled documents" concerning the crash, but "refused to release them." The NSA insisted that the files were "top secret," and their release, it seems, could bring about "exceptionally grave damage to the national security." Press accounts of the secret files moved Al Fayed to undertake a series of lawsuits in Baltimore and Washington district courts for their release. His demand included any intelligence that might be cabbaged away in CIA, DIA and NSA files. Each agency was sued separately in February 1999, and to date Fayed and the media have been denied any classified files pertaining to deaths of his son and the estranged princess.[21]

The Deep Politics of Pop music

Roger Bunn, director of the Music Industry Human Rights Association (MIHRA) in the UK, lives in the eye of the corporate music beast, and had his own perspective on the death of the core member of INXS. These letters from Bunn were circulated to rock musicians, journalists and researchers in late November, 1997.[22]

MIHRA

Talking Sense about Hutchence, News Reports
The Really Really Spoilt? The flight is over?

Paula Yates threw champagne over a Thai airport official who was asking her to reboard the plane. Paula, out of her box on champers and prescription drugs and in company with her lawyer and child was smuggled out of her hotel to view the body of the recently deceased. There is to be an airline report on the incident.

Pride of the Welsh, Tom Jones, has suggested that the band will "be devastated" and Michael Hutchence "was a nice guy".

So that's it, huh? Death due to hanging?

Sorta unusual that . . . even for the music industry. Those wonderful featured artists. Really light up the sky every now and then. Maybe we should consider making the poor darlings an endangered species?

Think about this the next time you buy your next conglomerate primitive/folk music. Every time you buy, every time you watch a movie using well known material, you add strength to the cartel monopolies because nobody else is allowed (by their governments' l ack of legislation and their ineffective inquiries and "monopolies boards." And that, now he had "reached his peak," MH is probably worth far more to his conglomerate dead than alive.

I spoke to a close friend tonight. He suggested that Paula was so outta her head that Sir Bob had every legitimate right to keep an eye on his kids. My friend was not a fan of "herself." In fact in the past he had always avoided an introduction.

However, apart from being a less than mediocre music journalist employed by the Cartel and lousy singer (for the Boomtown Rats), Sir Bob is still being condemned by the industry's creative "cognicenti" of using the kudos and money he obtained by reinventing and promoting himself with "LIVE AID" to gain his title.

He blamed Paula for just about everything to do with the situation that lead to the strange death of a man who was probably one of the "sub-normal featured artists" used by the industry to maintain it's monopoly over 95 percent of the western world market.

MIHRA first came into contact with Micheal after he had contacted Central TV's, (now Carlton TV) John Pilger and David Munro in relation to "Death of a Nation," their doc about the genocide in East Timor. He was after all ashamed of his nation's appeasement policies on Indonesia. But like the rest of these elite musical figures, Michael was isolated and uncontactable in person and so the proposed "INXS benefit concert for ET" never took place.

Then MH became a waste of MIHRA 's and British Coalition for East Timor's time. In fact, to do such a concert would have laid the band open to a court case by a well known UK promoter who was looking to sue INXS as soon as they performed, as they had reneged upon a previous contract to appear in London.

"The sexiest man alive," Michael was brash and brutal. He punched the paparazzi who had locked on to the affair he was having with Paula Yates, herself well used to controversy during her long (for showbiz) marriage to "Bob" the TV tycoon.

The police are now seeking a man in his forties with a weird haircut and beard, a taste for kudos and titles.

Pop saint Sir Robert Geldof of "LIVE AID" (or something even more patronizing) should call his lawyer immediately, just in case.

"And where were you between the hours of . . . Sir Robert?" Are INXS fans now thinking of building another long living $ Shrine to yet another isolated god of the paparazzi?

MH was 37 years old and although INXS was not selling conglomerate product as much as over their previous five year span, they had gone back to Austalia to plan yet another tour.

Featured artists are sometimes Very Strange, sometimes very unprofessional "creators" indeed. The Stones are a much iconed and imperfect example of the "kick back at society" role model syndrome that now exists, not to enlighten society but simply to make even more money. Similar to the overpowering ethic of the six conglomerates.

The Music Publisher's Association rules the world of music and the six conglomerate recording companies with their old friends MTV and Rupert Murdoch in close association, they really really don't care a damn about governments or legislation because the industry turns over $120-billion a year. They can afford to be and are very generous to both sides of any argument or national election.

Music is the third richest industry on the planet. To do this they have to seek "talent" and provide the public with a marketing false god syndrome so that it can consistently buy its products. But unlike sport (if one gets the right invitations), the talent of an athlete will stand a chance of reaching the commercial surface. Whereas this may be a difficult struggle for some athletes, in the music industry there is no such thing as true competition.

Who judges what is good an what it not, the audience? The Artist and Recording Manager from the record company down for a fleeting visit to catch the band playing live? This person is probably readying himself to fly for the weekend to Mex with a couple of groupies and a few ounces of coke on one of his clients' accounts.

"Double indemnity" is a very tough clause indeed. Into this world comes children on the make and the genuinely talented.

When an artist's "usefulness" to a conglomerate is over, things can get a little "sticky." Lawyers tend to proliferate and costs rise. Michael Hutchence may have been "trouble" to deal with.

In recent years artists have begun and won more battles in the courts than over the whole of the previous four decades. Artists, that are said to be "difficult to work with," are winning and are becoming "the norm." Sometimes, if I were a tycoon with a problem, maybe I would think to myself, "I wish that little faker were dead, then I could become his career".

Was Michael more trouble than he was worth? Tom Jones doesn't think so. Tom says that "Michael was a sensible guy."

BIG and influential Bob Geldof

Bob Geldof . . . journalist (ha!), he worked for "Melody Maker," one of the papers OWNED by the six member Cartel. . . .

Bob and Midge Ure (a nice guy and ex-neighbour of ours) who played in Ultravox started LIVE AID the concert that went around the world and raised, millions and KUDOS and MONEY for the Third World and the conglomerates as the guys got tons and tons of news exposure when their careers were seriously faltering. Suddenly Brave Bob was on every TV in the land, day after day.

So the Show/Music biz doyens got together and did the first big Wembley Concert, they did not consider putting something together like MIHRA outta this massive bundle of cash, they were the EXCLUSIVE FEATURED ARTISTS and were the "untouchables." The promoter of LIVE AID, Harvey Goldsmith, also arranged the Concert (some say on behalf of the UK and US Govts) for the Kurds after Desert Storm.

Kids in a Serious Playground . . .

So Midge and Bob got back into the world headlines saying, "I want to stay in the background, outta the headlines" huh? Of course Amnesty and the NGOs were very pleased with LIVE AID, and the chaps all went off on a happy tour around Africa showing their "solidarity" with all the natives. So AFTER all the dosh had been made and the limos paid for and the HARVEY GOLDSMITH (recently honored) Promotion Agency got their good works publicized, the money started to get dispersed.

Some LIVE AID money bought a ship full of SPOILT GRAIN from an Indian businessman to go to SOMALIA or somewhere. As the docks were on strike, the grain ship stayed in dock, the ship eventually left dock when strike finish, the ship arrived, Lo and Behold the grain was discovered to be SPOILT, inedible, it cost LIVE AID millions, that's just one example, there may be others, we do not know them, maybe one could begin to ask more loudly?

But where did it ALL go? Certainly some of the KURDISH GROUPS wanted it to buy arms to stop Saddam H from exterminating their right to live where they choose and do the work that George Bush and John Major, without the support of the 29 member coalition, couldn't, or refused to do.

Which was to take out Saddam H. To the displeasure of Paul Simon and some of the other artists appearing, the UK/US Govt bought bread for the Kurds instead of bullets. So under John Major, Sir Bob became a TV TYCOON. Sir Bob owns the production company that does the BIG BREAKFAST SHOW for young people 5 days a week. "Big Bob" they call him at the office. And it seems like TV power is now his most favourite "toy". . . .

Again under PM Major Sir Bob gained his title, Sir Bob of something as one of the showbiz awards from the "Krown." Sir Bob doesn't bother too much with being a "singer" anymore. Midge is now living in Cal . . . He probably can be contacted through his Cartel (RCA) contract but we would rather not.

Right now Geldof now lives at his mansion in Kent and his house at 129. We have the address on file somewhere because when we started MIHRA we wrote to the TOP HUNDRED PRS EARNERS IN THE UK. One of the hundred we wrote to was Sir Bob. Only one responded. Bob Geldof, the man of "vision" was Not that singular person.

In fact the person who did write, really didn't write at all. And so that's why MIHRA returned the tiny cheque from Mark Knopfler to his manager ED BICKNELL. Head of AURA, the organization that represents the UK Featured Artists in their indecently hasty chase for the multi-millions of Euro royalties about to hit the UK after Brussels started ruling on the lack of econ-system in the UK music industry and the "policies" of the UK Musician's Union

But you are not going to hear us saying that the death of Michael Hutchence on the 21st November 1997 was a hit by the mob. . . .

Buddy Holly would only be the first.

MIHRA's sources also says that Cath, ex-girlfriend of Jimi Hendrix, has exhausted herself trying to reopen an inquiry into his death and as she is married to his doctor, has now given up. As it was through this contact that Jimi became a star in the UK and later the world, I suggest we take this as "gospel."

NOTES

1. Mike Gee, *The Final Days of Michael Hutchence*, London: Omnibus, 1998, p. 152.
2. "INXS fury at photos of bondage," *South China Morning Post*, December 11 1997.
3. Gil Kaufman, "Police Say INXS Singer Left No Suicide Note," *Music News of the World*, December 5, 1997.
4. Ibid.
5. Geoffrey Lee Martin, "Hutchence seemed so happy, say friends," *London Telegraph*, Issue 914, November 24, 1997.
6. Gee, p. 150.
7. Ibid.
8. David Fricke, "The Devil Inside," *Rolling Stone*, January 22, 1998, p. 17.
9. Derek W. Hand, *Inquest into the Death of Michael Kelland Hutchence*, February 6, 1998.
10. "Yates in Legal Move to Fight Suicide Verdict," *London Telegraph*, March 30, 1998.
11. Diamond interview transcribed by Leah Sungenis, as *INXS newsletter*, July 1998. In May 1998, six weeks after the suit was filed by Hutchence's family against Diamond and co-executor Andrew Morrison Paul, the Australian attorney told the Queensland Supreme Court that he wanted to be released from any legal responsibility for administering the estate.

    The diversion of Hutchence's income makes hash of Diamond's boasts of a bosom relationship with the late singer, and in fact the *Morning Herald* reported on May 29, 1998 that Colin Diamond, "who has been described as one of Hutchence's closest friends, did not attend the funeral or the scattering of his ashes."
12. Paul Whittaker and Rory Callinan, "Mafia Tie To Rock Star's Lost Riches," *The Courier-Mail*, February 13, 1999.
13. Mark Chipperfield, "Hutchence family fights for 'missing' fortune," *Sunday Telegraph*, April 19 ,1998.
14. Ian Verrender, "Fight begins for control of Hutchence assets," *Sydney Morning Herald*, March, 8, 1998.
15. Leigh Reinhold, "Angry Kim—I didn't kill Michael—A year later, Kym Wilson is still haunted by Michael Hutchence's death," *New Idea Magazine*, Always INSX website.
16. Caroline Davies, "Boy Raised Among the Brothels Who Became a Fashion Star," *London Telegraph*, July 16, 1997.
17. James Langton, "Did Mafia silence Versacé to hide financial scandal?" *Sunday Telegraph*, July 27, 1997.
18. "FBI Hunt Gay Serial Killer After Versacé Shot Dead," *London Telegraph*, July 16, 1997.
19. Bruce Taylor Seeman, "A murder theory takes wing: `Dead bird clue' fosters speculation," *Miami Herald*, July 27, 1997.
20. Anonymous, "Dodi's Royal Romance Was Coup for Father," *Salt Lake Tribune*, September 3, 1997.
21. Tami Sheheri, "Al-Fayed Demands Spy Agency's Diana Files," APBNews.com, April 19, 1999.
22. Open correspondences from Roger Bunn, MIHRA, November 24 and 30, 1997.

MUERTE!
DEATH IN MEXICAN POPULAR CULTURE
Edited by Harvey Stafford

Mexico is a country obsessed with blood
and gore. The biggest selling magazines,
Alarma! and *Peligro!*, week after week
promote the most extreme examples of
death they can find. Why does Mexican culture, a strange amalgam of
Catholicism and Santeria, go so far with bloody sensationalism?

The photographs within *Muerte!* were largely snapped by the biggest photographers from Mexican tabloids, and are printed in this book for the first time.
Muerte! also includes text from Diego Rivera, Eduardo Matos Moctezuma,
Jorge Alberto Manrique, Alberto Hijar and Victor Fosada explaining Mexican
death-consciousness.

Editor Harvey Stafford's own stunning paintings, inspired by Mexican tabloid
photography, are also included, along with Stafford's saga about confronting
Mexico's tabloids in person.

10 × 8 ✦ 208 pgs ✦ ISBN 0-922915-59-8 ✦ $24.95

To order from: Feral House
2554 Lincoln Blvd. #1059 Venice, CA 90291

Individuals: Send check or money order. For shipping, add $3.50 for first item, $1.50
each additional item. For credit card orders: call 800 967-7885. Orders to Canada for
shipping, add $4 for first item, $2 each additional item. Other countries: for surface rate,
add $5 for first item, $4 each additional item. For airmail, add $11 first item, $9 each
additional item. Non-U.S. originated orders must include check or international money
order for U.S. funds drawn on a U.S. bank. Foreign credit card orders: fax completed order
form to 213 689-4728.

Book Trade: Feral House titles are distributed to the book trade through Publishers Group
West 800 788-3123. Titles are also available through Last Gasp 415 824-6636, Ingram,
Baker and Taylor and other regional and specialty distributors. Foreign Distribution
Canada: Publishers Group West Canada, Marginal Distribution 705 745-2326. United
Kingdom and Europe: Turnaround, London 181 829-3000. Austrailia: Tower Distribution
02 9975-5566.